WALLEYE WARRIORS

An Effective Alliance against Racism and for the Earth

RICK WHALEY
WITH WALTER BRESETTE

Foreword by
WINONA LaDUKE

New Society Publishers
Philadelphia, PA   Gabriola Island, BC

Walleye Warriors: An Effective Alliance against Racism and for the Earth.
Copyright © 1994 Rick Whaley and Walter Bresette. All rights reserved.
Inquiries regarding requests to reprint all or part of this book should be addressed to:
New Society Publishers, 4527 Springfield Avenue, Philadelphia, PA 19143.

Excerpts from *History of the Ojibway People* by William W. Warren (Saint Paul, MN:
Minnesota Historical Society Press, reprint ed., 1984) reprinted with permission.
Excerpts from *Chippewa Treaty Rights: The Reserved Rights of Wisconsin's Chippewa
Indians in Historical Perspective* by Ronald N. Satz (Madison, WI: Wisconsin
Academy of Sciences, Arts, and Letters, 1991) reprinted with permission.
Excerpts from *Native American Issues* published by the Friends National Committee
on National Legislation reprinted with permission.
Photos from the Wausau Daily Herald and Milwaukee Sentinel reprinted with
permission.
Excerpts from *A Sand County Almanac* by Aldo Leopold (New York: Oxford
University Press, 1949) reprinted with permission.
Excerpts from "When the Stone Begins to Turn" by Jackson Browne (©1989 Swallow
Turn Music) reprinted with permission.
Cartoons by Joseph Heller reprinted with permission.
The Chippewa Moon Series, illustration and design by Walter Bresette (© 1988
Sunshine Studios, PO Box 1350, Bayfield, WI 54814), reprinted with permission.

Cover art by Paul Calhoun   Cover design by Parallel Design
Book production supervised by Jenna Dixon   Typeset by ProProduction
Proofread by Jolene Robinson   Index by Mary Griffenhagen Neumann
Printed in the United States of America on partially recycled paper with soy ink by
Capital City Press of Montpelier, Vermont.

To order directly from the publisher, add $2.50 to the price for the first copy, 75¢ for
each additional copy. Send check or money order to:

In the United States   *In Canada*
New Society Publishers   New Society Publishers/New Catalyst
4527 Springfield Avenue   PO Box 189
Philadelphia, PA 19143   Gabriola Island, BC V0R 1X0

ISBN USA 0-86571-256-5 Hardcover   ISBN CAN 1-55092-204-1 Hardcover
ISBN USA 0-86571-257-3 Paperback   ISBN CAN 1-55092-205-X Paperback

New Society Publishers is a project of the New Society Educational Foundation, a nonprofit, tax-exempt, public foundation in the United States, and of the Catalyst
Education Society, a nonprofit society in Canada. Opinions expressed in this book do
not necessarily represent positions of the New Society Educational Foundation, nor the
Catalyst Education Society.

Contents

    Walter Bresette

    Ancient prophecies bring the Anishinabe *(Chippewa) to Wisconsin . . . A woodland identity . . . Nineteenth-century treaties left the Chippewa off-reservation harvesting rights . . . Spearfishers test their suppressed rights by spearfishing in Wisconsin, 1974 . . . The* Voigt *decision upholds the Indian right to spearfish*

    Walter Bresette

    Background: American Indian sovereignty rights from 1600 to 1954 . . . Washington state backlash . . . Wisconsin backlash: Court decisions fuel a swirl of anti-Indian publicity and public outcry, 1983–1987 . . . The beginning of crisis: Anti-spearing groups protest at Butternut Lake's boat landing and declare victory, 1987

     White Backlash Today   129

     Rick Whaley

     *The parallels to the Deep South; the legacy of the civil rights
     movement . . . Nightriders: An eyewitness report from Sarah
     Backus . . . The rise of the New Right: The rhetoric of "equal
     rights vs. special rights" . . . "African-American Roots": A speech
     by Walter Bresette . . . Deep South, Deep North: Similarities
     and differences*

Part IV   THE CULMINATION OF YEARS OF BATTLES: 1990   155

7   Small Miracles and Heavy Hitters: The Third Year of Spearing
     and Witnessing, 1990   156

     Rick Whaley

     *Wisconsin proposes to buyout Lac du Flambeau's treaty rights . . .
     Grassroots support blossoms for the spearers and the Witness . . .
     Fires of Prejudice . . . Spearing and strategy: The spearfishing
     season begins . . . Successes of the Witness*

8   Interwoven Issues: Indian Treaty Rights and the Mining Threat   180

     Rick Whaley

     *A brief history of mining in Wisconsin . . . Pro-mining
     politician James Klausner's ascendency to power . . . Wisconsin's
     mines: Resource colonization by multinational companies . . .
     Indian treaty rights as a potentially powerful tool against
     mining interests . . . Envisioning a sustainable economics*

Part V   A SOLIDARITY SUCCESS STORY   201

9   Healing, Not Winning: The Fourth Year of Spearing and
     Witnessing, 1991   202

     Rick Whaley

     *Healing despite continued racism by anti-treaty forces . . .
     Timber rights . . . Sand Lake: The protestors' last stand . . . The
     fisheries . . . The Witness presence is helpful and valued . . . A
     peaceful end to the spearing season . . . Reconciliation as respect
     for cultural differences and finding common ground*

Illustrations

Wisconsin Names and Organizations

Wisconsin Chippewa Reservations

Bad River
Lac du Flambeau (LdF)
Lac Courte Oreilles (LCO)

Mole Lake or Sokaogon
Red Cliff
St. Croix

Intertribal Organizations

Great Lakes Indian Fish and Wildlife Commission (GLIFWC): Chippewa intertribal agency created after *Voigt* decision to manage harvestable resources and do public outreach/education on fisheries, treaties, environmental issues. James Schlender, director.

Great Lakes Intertribal Council. Joe Bresette, director.

Voigt Intertribal Task Force. Created after *Voigt* decision to coordinate political reponse to and implementation of off-reservation harvesting. Made up of representatives from various Chippewa tribes. (Tom Maulson was 1990 chair.)

Wisconsin Indian Resource Council. (University of Wisconsin–Stevens Point, Stan Webster, former director.)

Grassroots Chippewa Organizations

Anishinabe Niijii. Mining watchdog group centered at LCO.

Anishinabe Akeeng. White Earth, Minnesota.

Bad River Spearing Coordinators (c/o Carl Rose).

Ojibwe People for Justice (c/o Ester Nahgahnub and Jim Northrup, Sawyer, MN).

Pembina Anishinabe (c/o Terrance Nelson, Manitoba, Canada).

Red Cliff Spearing Association (c/o Andrew Gokee).
St. Croix Spearing Coordinators (c/o Ed Bearheart).
Wa-Swa-Gon Treaty Association. Led by Tom Maulson, Lac du Flambeau.
WOJB Radio, at LCO.

Support Groups for Chippewa Treaty Rights

American Civil Liberties Union (ACLU): handled lawsuit against STA–W on behalf of *Wa-Swa-Gon* and LdF tribal government.
Citizens for Treaty Rights (CTR): hosted 1988 Witness.
Green groups: Lake Superior Greens, Milwaukee Greens, St. Croix Valley Greens, Upper Great Lakes Green Network, Wisconsin Greens, *Green Net* newspaper.
Honor Our Neighbors Origins and Rights (HONOR): key mainstream religious organization supporting Native rights.
Midwest Treaty Network (MTN), organized in 1989, includes Madison Treaty Rights Support Group and many Wisconsin support groups, and the Twin Cities Witness for Non-Violence and Indian Treaty Rights Committee (Chicago); MTN now coordinates spring boat landing Witness.
Orenda: first off-reservation support group (Birnamwood, central Wisconsin).
Witness for Non-Violence: Milwaukee group 1988–1992. Also refers more generally to the peace presence and documenting process at spring boat landings in northern Wisconsin where spearfishing occurs.

Wisconsin Anti-Treaty Protest Organizations

Equal Rights for Everyone (ERFE), 1984–1987, headed by Paul Mullaly.
Protect Americans' Rights and Resources (PARR), started in 1985, Larry Peterson, president.
Stop Treaty Abuse–Wisconsin (STA–W), started in 1987, Dean Crist and Al Soik, leaders.
Wisconsin Alliance for Rights and Resources (WARR), 1984–1987: precursor to PARR led by Larry Peterson.

Official Wisconsin Organizations Aligned Against Chippewa Treaties

Wisconsin Department of Natural Resources (WDNR), headed by Buzz Besadny; Division of Enforcement officers: George Meyer and Ralph Christensen.
Governor Tommy Thompson (Republican) and Secretary James Klauser, Department of Administration.
Wisconsin Counties Association (WCA), Mark Rogacki, executive director.

Acknowledgments

We would like to thank the following people and organizations:

Special thanks to our families for their strength and support through all the years of witnessing, and for putting up with the demands of writing this book;

And to our editors at New Society Publishers, Marie Bloom who started this project, and Barbara Hirshkowitz and Yvonne Keller who made it a reality;

Eddie Benton-Banai, Merle Wolford, George Amour, and Marilyn Benton for their help and their teaching;

The *Wa-Swa-Gon* Treaty Association and all the spearfishers and their families for their courage and success, and for their stories;

The many supporters of *Anishinabe* rights for their years of work and for their stories;

The foundations who contributed to this book and to the Witness program at critical times: Wisconsin Community Fund, Project Resist (Boston), CS Fund (California), A. J. Muste Institute (New York), ACLU–Wisconsin, and the Peace Education Project of the Mobilization for Survival (Milwaukee);

Al Gedicks for his research and activism on mining in Wisconsin, especially his extensive contribution to chapter 8 in this book;

All the photographers, especially Paul Calhoun, Amoose, and Dale Kakkak for their contribution to this book;

The recording artists: Bobby Bullet, Jackson Browne, and Steven Van Zandt for the use of their lyrics;

The cartoonists: Mike Konopacki, Joseph Heller, Stuart Carlson, John Potter, Kirk Anderson, and Bill Sanders for their support;

Zoltán Grossman for the excellent maps he did for this book, and for his advice and extensive review of the text;

Rick Jungers, Rob Danielson, and our friends at MATA (Milwaukee community-access cable TV) and Marla Donato at Earth Network (Chicago) for their videos, which helped on background and stories for the book;

Bob Simeone and Ron Ackley for their advice and background on

Wisconsin forestry, and Tom Quinn for the same on Wisconsin farming;

Rudolph Ryser for his research on the national anti-Indian movement; Professor Ron Satz for his detailed work on the history of Chippewa treaties; Great Lakes Indian Fish and Wildlife Commission (GLIFWC) for maps, photos, and background information;

Walt Kelly, Kevin Whaley, Brian Pierson, Waring Fincke, and Lew Gurwitz for legal review;

Zoltán Grossman, Cathy Debevec, and Carol Edgerton of Madison Treaty Rights Support Group for other research and review and support, and also to Sharon Metz, Karen Harvey, Margo Adair, and Dyoni Thompkins for the same;

Dori Gerger and Dorothy Fowler for transcribing interviews; and

The Midwest Treaty Network for carrying on the work of the Witness and other cultural solidarity work.

To all the organizations and individuals who made such valuable contributions to our cause and to this book, the authors give our heartfelt thanks.

Foreword

Winona LaDuke

> *Gitchi Manitoo. O dah pin wah ow ah saymah omah sha mah moo (y) ahn. O oo mushkeekeee omah gi giteegahning. Dahgah o gah wee doo kak gon gay mo (m) ood. Megwetch.*
>
> *Great Spirit. Please accept my offering of tobacco in return for the medicine I am taking from your garden. May it help the person who will use it. Thank you.*

This is a prayer offered by a person from the White Earth reservation in northern Minnesota while harvesting medicinal plants. This is a prayer recognizing the relationship of the harvester to the land, and to the medicines that she is harvesting; and this is a thanksgiving, an offering to reciprocate for the medicine. This is the way we live. Thankfully.

This book is a story of the struggle of *Anishinabe* (Chippewa) people to continue a way of life. This struggle is central to our cultural survival, our spiritual survival, and absolutely central to the conflict between industrial society and Native peoples on this land. These *dibajimoininiwug* (storytellers) are carefully retelling the stories of the *Anishinabe* and sharing the voices of the women and men in the context of this struggle. I would like to place it all in a larger *dibajimoin* (story), that of the present struggle over land and resources on Turtle Island.

Let me begin with something about the *Anishinabe* from our territory. I am *Anishinabikwe*, from the *Makwa Dodaem* (Bear Clan), of the Mississippi band—a little further west than Lac du Flambeau. I only know a little, but from what I know, I understand that our traditional society, our traditional view says that natural law is preeminent. Natural law is superior to the laws of

WINONA LADUKE is director of the White Earth Land Recovery Project and president of the Indigenous Women's Network.

nations, of states, of conservation officers, and of cities. In fact, it is superior to the laws of all humans. And we are all accountable to this natural law.

The *Anishinabe* people, like other indigenous or land-based peoples, have tried to live in accordance with this law. We have set up our own codes of behavior and ways of living, characterized by the term *mino-bimaatisiiwin*—translated as "the good life" or, alternatively, as "continuous rebirth." Through this strict code of ethics and behavior, enforced by the social strength of intact, long-lived communities, we have been able to live sustainably on our land for thousands of years. Quite frankly, the example of the *Anishinabe* people, and other indigenous peoples, is the only continuous example of living sustainably on this land, on Turtle Island. We hope there will be more.

This is in stark contrast to another way of living—that of industrial society, or, as some put it, "settler society." I will argue that the United States and, to a great extent, many Americans continue to live with the value system of a "settler society," a society in which a "frontier" remains integral to its world view. This causes a conflict between that settler society and the land upon which those individuals have come to live.

Simply stated, many of the values of the United States conflict with the natural world, with natural law. For instance, a perception of "man's mastery of nature" dominates the value system of most Americans. This perception includes concepts such as "wild" versus "tamed" or "wilderness" and "primitive" versus "civilized." Another very deep-set perception is that man has some god-ordained right to "conquer" this America. Those concepts are central to the legacy of the quincentennial and the present state of relations between Native and settler in North America.

This legacy has been manifested in most relations between the *Anishinabe*—"the people"—and this United States. Beginning in 1781 and ending in 1929, the U.S., Canadian, British, and French governments signed over forty treaties with the *Anishinabe* people—treaties regarding our aboriginal territory. These treaties are an interpretation of our legal rights in relationship to the United States and to British common law, and for the most part are a grant of rights and land use from the *Anishinabe* people to the United States, with some reserved rights remaining. These treaties are only a part of the agreements between the *Anishinabe* and the United States, Great Britain, France, and Canada that cover our land.

Our aboriginal territory encompasses the southern part of four Canadian provinces and the northern part of five U.S. states. We today continue to live within this territory, with an estimated population of around 250,000 members of our Nation—the single largest first nation in North America. We are still alive; we are still here. Despite it all.

In the 370 treaties between the United States and Indian nations, over two billion acres of land changed hands with less than 140 million acres remaining in Indian hands in 1868. Between 1815 and 1860, the period of greatest "westward expansion," some 260 treaties were signed. These treaties embodied some 720 land seizures from 1784 to 1894. The United States did not "claim" its land holdings by conquest, but by agreement. That is how the United States claims to have "purchased" some 95 percent of its public domain for an alleged $800 million. This series of agreements has been characterized as the largest real estate transaction in history. The treaties and agreements signed between the *Anishinabe* and the various settler governments have been signed mostly for the economic benefit of the United States. To fulfill a notion of "progress," of "manifest destiny." They fulfill an industrial demand that has changed with each generation.

There was once a twenty-five hundred-pound rock of pure copper resting on what is known as the Keweenaw Peninsula. This rock, called the Ontonagon boulder, rested for thousands of years on the shore of Lake Superior. By 1800, this boulder had been sighted by European explorers, and the United States (still located on the eastern seaboard) ordered a mineral inventory of the region and a study of Indian title to it. By 1869, four treaties had been signed between the United States and Indian people in the region, guaranteeing U.S. prospecting, mineral, and settlement rights in the territory. The Keweenaw mineral deposits, accompanied by the Mesabi Iron Range, were to provide the resource foundation for many major mining companies. As early as 1849, 100 percent of all copper production came from the Keweenaw Peninsula "ceded by the Anishinabe" in 1842. Between 1845 and 1860, over one hundred copper companies were incorporated in Minnesota, Wisconsin, and Michigan territories. By 1890, the Great Lakes region led the world in copper production and, beginning that same year—for almost the next fifty years—the Mesabi Iron Range was to be the source of almost three fourths of all U.S. iron ore production. Basically, the expropriation of *Anishinabe* resources, or the access to them, provided the foundation for much of the wealth now present in the United States.

Reservations and reserved treaty rights are what remain of our original hold-ings—small islands of land within a vast continent of non-Indian land holdings. Those territories, however, remain to be the essence of our lives, our culture, and our future. In providing for future generations in our treaties, the *Chi-Anishinabe* (the ancestors) understood that the lakes, trees, fish, wild rice beds, and deer would remain our sustenance. And they are today. On most *Anishinabe* reservations in our territory, the land-based economies remain strong and remain a centerpiece of our culture, our way of life, and our survival.

In a study done on the White Earth reservation in Minnesota, the significance of the land-based economy and way of life was apparent. (Percentages may vary on the other Chippewa reservations in Minnesota and Wisconsin, but these figures are representative of the importance of this subsistence economy.) While unemployment was listed by the Department of Labor at approximately 75 percent, most people were "employed" in a land-based economy. Over 75 percent harvest one or more deer annually, 65 percent harvest ducks, geese, or small game, 35 percent harvest twenty-five or more fish annually, 45 percent harvest wild rice (for own use, and for sale of excess), and berries or medicines. Seventy-two percent had gardens, 58 percent had been sugarbushing (maple syrup making), and over 45 percent produced handcrafts for their own use and for sale. Overall, in many Native communities the traditional land-based economy, and in fact this way of life, remains a centerpiece of the community.

This way of life and the values associated with it (*mino-bimaatisiiwin*) are at the center of the conflict between settler society and native society and come into play in the conflict over spearfishing in northern Wisconsin. For generations the federal government, churches, and educational institutions have sought to undermine this economy and this way of life. The Bureau of Indian Affairs in the late 1800s would encourage the transition from "Indian activities" to "wage work" and assess the progress made by the Indian agent in "civilizing the Indians." Churches would many times reinforce the colonial values of the Indian agent, arguing that land-based economies were "primitive" and that those participating in these economies were "lazy." Educational institutions, particularly boarding schools, disrupted the traditional economy by withdrawing the young people from the community, hoping to indoctrinate them into a different way of thinking. But . . .

We are still here. We are alive. We will survive—from resistance to the James Bay hydroelectric projects in Canada, to protecting treaty and cultural rights in northern Wisconsin, to ensuring the rights and health and full political participation of indigenous women throughout the Western hemisphere. And while Native communities face the onslaught of mining companies seeking uranium, coal, oil, natural gas, and forests, we will still be here. And our cultural practices—from the spearing of fish to the harvest of wild rice—remain. These land-based economies, this way of life, is still the only way of life in North America demonstrated to be sustainable.

The past five hundred years has indicated that "civilization," "progress," "development," and "wealth" are for the most part exacted at a very high price: the extinction in the past 150 years of more species than since the Ice Age; and the extinction of two thousand Indigenous nations of people in the western hemisphere alone. This *dibajimoin* is about our way of life, our lives, and our struggle to sustain it all. It is also about this United States—and the struggle of values and ways of living central to all of our survival. This is about us all.

> We do not have thousands upon thousands of dollars. We do not have great mansions of beauty. We do not have priceless objects of art. We do not live the life of ease, nor do we live in luxury. We do not own the land upon which we live. We do not have the basic things of life which we are told are necessary to better ourselves. . . . But today, I want to tell you that we do not need these things.

What we do need, however, is what we already have. What we do need has been provided to us by the Great Spirit. . . . We need to realize who we are and what we stand for. And we need to begin to resist the temptation to be just like the white man. . . . We are the keepers of that which the Great Spirit has given to us, that is our language, our culture, our drum societies, our religion, and most important of all, our traditional way of life.

—Egiwaateshkang, George Aubid, Sr., 1989
Past War Chief of the Mississippi Band, *Anishinabe*

To the memory of my parents, Blanche and Henry Bresette
To the memory of my mother, Patricia Whaley

GITCHI MONIDO GISISS
(The Great Spirit Moon)

Introduction

Walt Bresette

AN OBSCURE COURT RULING in early 1983 in favor of the Lake Superior Chippewa, a Woodland Native nation in the upper Great Lakes, turned into a violent struggle against Chippewa people and their exercise of off-reservation harvesting rights. This treaty rights battle garnered national and international attention, with the media focusing on the racism and conflict of sports versus subsistence fishing. This is this story behind that media story that began January 25, 1983. Beyond these headlines and symptoms of the problem, we offer a perspective on the social, political, economic, and environmental earthquake that hit Wisconsin in the 1980s. It is a story of various groups responding, sometimes violently, to the court ruling and of new people responding to that violence. It is a tale of fear, political denial, and the attempted looting of Chippewa rights and northern Wisconsin resources. It is a tale of vile and violent racism and of official plundering of law, with a near-"old West" mentality overtaking Wisconsin. And it is a tale that speaks to other violence, other struggles, other similar forces, where people and earth are victimized.

But it is also a tale of ancient voices resonating from the past through the rootedness of today's Native people. It is a tale of nonviolent warriors punching at the social and political membranes, making room for the future. It is a tale of European-American allies and Native and African-American legacies of the

1

struggle and vision. It is a tale of journey and empowerment for Chippewa and their supporters. Witnesses tell tales of nonviolent resistance of Gandhian proportions: "I was at Selma and I was at Marquette Park, but Trout Lake was the worst," said one boat landing veteran with Clergy and Laity Concerned, "but the Chippewa did not react [to the violence]."

This book presents eyewitness accounts from two of the participants in that struggle. Both of us have our family roots in northern Wisconsin. We both are searching for the social, ecological, and economic visions for our time and place here. We came together, I from my rural reservation organizing and my co-writer from his Milwaukee urban organizing, to try and stem the tide of social backlash against Chippewa rights. Our story covers the worst years of boat landing disturbances (1987–1991), and analyzes the social, political, and economic forces that swirled around this controversy. The authors hope that supporters of nonviolent activism and those who believe that antiracist struggles are inseparable from Earth struggles, will find value in the lessons of our modest but valuable success story in Wisconsin. We also hope that it is a good memento for the hundreds, even thousands, of people who journeyed to the landings to witness or who supported Chippewa rights in other ways during these years. This struggle was a chance for all to intervene in history before the lynchings (i.e., political murders) began, and we were successful.

We set off to co-write this book. Because of family demands, ill health, and my speaking engagements (not to mention court appearances), I have left most of the writing and final putting together of the book to my friend and organizing cohort, Rick Whaley. The early chapters, 1, 2, and 4, represent my writing and thinking and the various discussions I've had with Rick and other audiences. The other chapters cover the Witness organizing, the annual boat landing dramas, the political intrigue swirling around us, and the lessons we've uncovered along the way. Our closing chapter offers our combined analysis of what happened, where multi-racial and Green organizing stands today, and where urban-rural connections can continue to be made.

While the boat landing drama centers around Lac du Flambeau, where the spearers are called walleye warriors, we offer our admiration and thanks to all the *Anishinabe* (*Anishinabeg*) spearers and their families who suffered through these times and stood their ground for our rights and cultural history. We offer our heartfelt gratitude to those supporters who helped make a nonviolent resolution a reality in Wisconsin. We hope our story offers hope for what can be in the next five hundred years.

One note about terminology. *Anishinabe*, "the original people," is our name for our people. *Chippewa* is the French name (see story in chapter 1) for the *Anishinabe*. Because many of us call ourselves Chippewa today and because our struggle is called "Chippewa treaty rights" by the courts, the press, and the solidarity movement, "Chippewa" is the main handle we use in the book. We have used the current public (and historians' academic) terms for other Native nations as well, e.g., Sauk and Fox, Oneida, etc. We have used the terms *indigenous, Native American* and *Indian* interchangeably as is often done in our movement organizing and education. For those who have strong feelings for or against the use of some of these terms, we ask your forbearance.

This tale of tales tries to put perspective and context to this small battleground in 1980s Wisconsin. In order to understand its significance, the historical context must be understood. In September of 1989, I attended the Arctic to Amazonia Conference in Massachusetts. The conference brought together indigenous people who were all under various threats to their lands, resources, or rights. From British Columbia to New Zealand to the Amazon, Native peoples told tales of expropriation of land, culture, and resources, and of threats to their very existence. This has been the story of the last five hundred years for indigenous cultures in the North and South Americas. On a smaller scale, this is exactly what happened in northern Wisconsin. One of the main forces at work here, we were to discover, was the attempted development of a minerals resource colony. As multinational interests are being squeezed out of the Third World, many are coming back home. And home is often rural America: farms, small villages and towns, forests, animals, and Indians. So, our tale grew from one of a band of Woodland People trying to survive to a tale of the fight for the continuance of rural culture.

This is a story of cultures coming together not only in the political struggle against racism and resource colonization, but also the coming together of visions of many cultures. We talk about one little sliver of one little tribe in one little tiny chunk of the earth. But it's really the same story told in many places, all saying the same thing. What does the Hopi prophecy say? One day there will exist a house of mica (glass) where all the world leaders will gather and the Hopi should tell these leaders they are destroying the land and life on earth. What do the Inuits of Canada and the aboriginal people of New Zealand say about the intertwining of place and culture? What did Sigurd Olson say about western culture's severing of spiritual roots and the divorcement from nature? Was Thoreau correct about the value of simple living and its ecological correctness? Are Meridel LeSueur's words about the power of women to heal themselves and to fight the earth murderers still important? All of these voices now are coming together collectively, creating a multicultural choir, all saying the same thing: save the earth to save yourselves.

In this five hundreth year of resistance and dignity, please join us in this retelling of a solidarity success story—the boat landing Witness in Wisconsin —and in the challenges of the struggles ahead.

[1992]

PART I

The History Behind Indian Spearfishing Rights

(The Sucker Spawning Moon)

*The Anishinabe were given two gifts
by the Creator: the ability to dream and
the gift of tobacco.*
—Joe Rose, Bad River Chippewa

A Brief History of the *Anishinabe*

Walt Bresette

WHEN TWO BROTHERS FROM one Chippewa village in northern Wisconsin acted to assert their rights, they unwittingly led the others of us on a journey of identity and of historical place. However, their act of sovereignty in 1974 was not isolated. They were expressing a renewed sense of Chippewa identity traceable to a legacy that emerges out of the mist of human history. In order to understand the significance of the acts of these two Chippewa brothers, we must meet their ancestors and the paths from which they came.

The Tribble brothers are from the Lac Courte Oreilles (LCO) Reservation in the northern part of what is now called Wisconsin—one of the fifty states that make up the United States of America. LCO is one of the small areas (about 70,000 acres) that remains of the once vast territory of a people called the Chippewa *(Ojibwe)*. The Chippewa once controlled lands from Niagara Falls to the northern Great Plains and on both sides of the upper Great Lakes. In Wisconsin alone there were almost 20 million acres of Chippewa territory.

Today six Chippewa villages in northern Wisconsin make up this part of the story. In addition to LCO, they include Red Cliff and Bad River reservations, across the bay from each other on the southwestern shores of Lake Superior, both within sight of Madeline Island. Inland, near the Michigan border in northeastern Wisconsin, sits the Sokaogon or Mole Lake Chippewa Reservation. Fifty miles west of Mole Lake and about one hundred miles inland is the Lac du Flambeau (LdF) Reservation. To their west about one hundred miles is

LCO, and sixty miles southwest of LCO is the St. Croix Chippewa, not a contiguous reservation but scattered parcels of land in northwest Wisconsin.

These six villages are part of the group called the Lake Superior Chippewa, a band of the Chippewa that signed treaties with the United States throughout the nineteenth century. This band is comprised of additional villages in Michigan's Upper Peninsula and in the northern portion of Minnesota. These different villages, whose leaders signed the respective treaties, today inherit the band-wide identity of Lake Superior Chippewa. However, since those earlier days, especially since statehood, village autonomy and state (Wisconsin) identity have undermined the political value of the Lake Superior Band as a whole.

With land reservations in three states, the Lake Superior Band is only one part of the nation we call *Anishinabe*. Four other distinct bands exist in the United States, but that is only half of us. The rest are in Canada, under various forms of tribal autonomy yet under Canadian federal or provincial controls in Ontario, Manitoba, Saskatchewan, and Quebec. While we were once the largest group in North America, we now comprise only about 250,000 (in the United States and Canada). But even our small numbers are further diminished by separation between states, provinces, and countries.

Like other indigenous people, our name for ourselves is different than what we are called. *Anishinabe,* which roughly translates to *spontaneous beings* or *original people,* is how we name ourselves. However, we are most commonly known as the Chippewa. *Chippewa* is an anglicized term stemming from the earlier colonial and treaty era and has ambiguous origins. A common explanation is that the more subtle term *otchipway* described the footwear favored by the *Anishinabe*. It meant "to pucker" and was known to mean "people with puckered moccasins." It's now a common term even used by the *Anishinabe,* although with variations. In Minnesota, the preferred spelling is *Ojibwe;* other spellings include *Chippeway* and *Ojibway.*

One can imagine those early treaty sessions, all conducted in English, as a foreshadowing of later processing of other non-English-speaking immigrants at Ellis Island. "Who are you?" the treaty secretary would ask. *"Gitch gummi inniniwug,"* our delegates would respond, meaning "The people of the Great Lakes." Not understanding, he would ask others. "Who are these people?"

"They are *otchipway;* people with puckered moccasins." He spelled it *Chippewa* and in all subsequent official documents we've remained *Chippewa.*

Despite the colonial taking of our homeland through warfare or coerced treaties, small patches of lands remain, usually called "reservations." However, larger land areas within the former homeland remain under partial jurisdiction of our tribal governments. These land areas for the Lake Superior Chippewa and some other tribes are called "ceded territory," or lands that were sold in treaties. With the Lake Superior Chippewa, a return to recognition of this partial jurisdiction resulted from the Tribble brothers' actions in testing off-reservation harvesting rights in 1974. The federal court upheld the hunting, fishing, and gathering rights reserved in our cession treaties. The court said that, since the treaties were signed, there has been no intervening action that gave the state jurisdiction over the Chippewa. Because the courts are set up by district, this case dealt only with the Wisconsin villages of the Lake Superior Chippewa. But the legal and political ramifications have touched all the *Anishinabe* and forced us to revive the concept of unity among the bands.

Origins and Culture of the *Anishinabe*

"We are *Anishinabe*," the elders remind us. We are not Chippewa, not *Ojibwe*, but *the original people,* we are *spontaneous beings* created by the Great Spirit. The elders tell how Creator used a *Megis* (sea) shell to breathe life into the Original Man. Like the *griots* found by the late Alex Haley in his classic story, *Roots,* our elders remember.

"The Great Spirit had a vision and in it he saw how the earth was created," says Eugene Begay, an elder from LCO:

> First came what we now call the inanimate life—the soils for growth and the water and air for life. Then the vegetation—the place where all our medicines come from. And then, the animals—our teachers. Finally, came the people.
>
> Each creation is dependent on the other. The people, the last creation, are the weakest and most dependent. Yet, it is us pitiful people who are destroying all the other creations. We have forgotten both the vision and where we fit in our relationships. Once we destroy the other creations, we destroy ourselves.[1]

Many stories, many lessons come from the tales our elders remember. *Anishinabe* speak of two creations: the first that ended in a massive, cleansing flood; and the second that emerged from the flood survivors, aided by *Weneboojoo*, the great trickster-uncle. He held special privilege and powers and through his exploits we have learned the meanings of life.

According to William Warren in his *History of the Ojibwe People,* the *Anishinabe* migrated to the upper Midwest in the early 1400s.[2] Other stories agree generally on the dates but say we returned here after a lengthy migration out east and then back. Not contested by other scholars, these conclusions are reiterated by Edward Benton-Banai, a contemporary Chippewa educator and *Midewiwin* member from the Lac Courte Oreilles Reservation. Benton-Banai has written a traditional history of the *Anishinabe* entitled *The Mishomis Book*.[3] Seven prophets came to the *Anishinabe* when they lived by the Great Salt Water to the east. Each prophet gave a prophecy known as a Fire. The early Fire prophecies guided the way along the St. Lawrence Seaway and through the Great Lakes (as they later became known). The Fire prophecies also marked the decline and rebirth of traditional, spiritual ways. While details and dates may vary, all agree that the *Anishinabe* have been here for many centuries and came following many centuries of migration.

Anishinabe Seven Fires Prophecy

The first prophet said to the people, "In the time of the First Fire, the *Anishinabe* will rise up and follow the Sacred Shell of the *Midewiwin* Lodge. The *Midewiwin* Lodge will serve as a rallying point for the people and its traditional ways will be the source of much strength. The Sacred *Megis* will lead the way to the chosen ground for the *Anishinabe*. You are to look for a turtle-shaped island that is linked to the purification of the Earth. You will find such an island at the beginning and end of your journey. There will be seven stopping places along the way. You will know that the chosen ground has been reached when you come to a land where food grows on water. If you do not move, you will be destroyed."

The second prophet told the people, "You will know the Second Fire because at this time the nation will be camped by a large body of water. In this time the direction of the Sacred Shell will be lost. The *Midewiwin* will diminish in strength. A boy will be born to point the way back to the traditional ways. He will show the direction to the stepping stones to the future of the *Anishinabe* people."

The third prophet said to the people, "In the Third Fire, the *Anishinabe* will find the path to their chosen ground, a land in the West to which they must move their families. This will be the land where food grows on water."

—Edward Benton-Banai, *The Mishomis Book*

Warren's view is worth reporting because he was bilingual and experienced traditional culture in the mid-1800s, learning the stories and finally writing them down in the years 1851–1853. Warren (1825–1853) was Chippewa–European-American (known then derogatorily as a "half-breed") and had been educated in eastern schools and was later a legislator in Minnesota Territory. Warren's primary sources were tribal elders and members of the *Midewiwin* (Grand Medicine Society), a religious institution of the *Anishinabe*. Looked upon favorably by the tribal elders, he visited often and asked questions of them incessantly. Below is the migration story as told to Warren in the 1840s by elders on Madeline Island, the former religious center of the Lake Superior Chippewa:

While our forefathers were living on the great salt water toward the rising sun, the great *Megis* (sea-shell) showed itself above the surface of the great water, and the rays of the sun for a long period were reflected from its glossy back. It gave warmth and light to the *An-ish-in-aub-ag* (red race). All at once it sank into the deep, and for a time our ancestors were not blessed with its light. It rose to the surface and appeared again on the great river which drains the waters of the Great Lakes, and again for a long time it gave life to our forefathers.

Warren called the migration story an allegory, citing the elders of the tribe who said that the story represented the fluctuations of the Grand Medicine Society. The shell represented the practice of the religion and began when the *Anishinabe* first faced hardship on the eastern seaboard, "many strings of lives ago." The elders continued:

The Great Spirit, at the intercession of [*Weneboojoo*], the great common uncle of the *An-ish-in-aub-ag*, granted them this rite wherewith life is restored and pro-longed. Our forefathers moved from the shores of the great water, and proceeded westward. The *Me-da-we* lodge was pulled down and it was not again erected, till our forefathers again took a stand on the shores of the great river near where *Me-ne-aung* (Montreal) now stands.

The elders told Warren that this pattern was repeated many times. Each time that the religion foundered, the *Megis* resurfaced and the *Anishinabe* would migrate west and establish a new village. The *Megis* was seen again at Sault Ste. Marie in Michigan:

It remained for a long time, but once more, and for the last time, it di-sappeared, and the *An-ish-in-aub-ag* was left in darkness and misery, till it floated and once more showed its bright back at Mo-ning-wun-a-kaun-ing [Madeline Island], where it has ever since reflected back the rays of the sun, and blessed our ancestors with life, light, and wisdom. . . . For the last time the *Me-da-we* lodge was erected on the Island of La Pointe [Madeline Island], and here, long before the pale face appeared among them, it was practiced in its purest and most original form. Many of our fathers lived the full term of life granted to mankind by the Great Spirit, and the forms of many old people were mingled with each rising generation. This, my grandson, is the meaning of the words you did not understand; they have been repeated to us by our fathers for many generations.[4]

Madeline Island became the center from which the *Anishinabe* branched out into autonomous, independent villages in Wisconsin and northern Minnesota.[5]

A Woodland Identity

The traditional way was renewed again, honoring the upper Great Lakes land the *Anishinabe* had come to. The freshwater lakes and streams and bountiful forests were home to other beings whose spirits and gifts were interwoven into the fabric of *Anishinabe* politics and culture. The Chippewa clan system, the framework for governing the autonomous villages, was a reflection of the forest beings:

The Crane and Loon clans were chieftans, those people with natural leadership abilities;

The Fish or Water clan people were the intellectuals, philosophers, mediators;

Bear clan provided the protectors, policing the borders of the village to keep out intruders. They also became expert at knowing which herbs and medicines could be harvested and used;

Martin clan was the warrior clan;

Deer clan were the gentlest people, the poets;

From the Bird clan came the spiritual leaders of the people.[6]

Each clan had its own social and political function in providing leadership and balance to the community. Representatives from each clan had their own special place in the *Midewiwin* Lodge.

The other beings, plants and animals, that shared this bioregion not only provided signs for cultural living, they were means of survival. But they were only taken in moderation and the tobacco offering was laid on the earth to thank this life for giving the *Anishinabe* life. The spring harvest of game, especially fish speared in the lake shallows, was plentiful and no species was ever wiped out. The tradition of extinguishing species was reserved for the European settlers who annihilated, among other species, the passenger pigeon in Wisconsin.

Along with fish, deer were especially important and rewarded good hunters and their villages. The venison and the seasoned hides were crucial to survival in the harsh northern winters. In spring, a hunter could bring some large animal he had killed and give it to the parents of the woman he was courting as proof of his prowess and ability to provide for their daughter.[7] Buckskin was used for drums, clothes, and bedding. A human hand-shaped piece of buckskin was an emblem of one's word, or a call to war if painted red.[8]

Each family had its share of the sugar bush; the maple sap ran in late winter. Summer brought the berries—June berries, blueberries, strawberries, chokecherries, raspberries, and cranberries. A first fruits offering was made to *manido* (Spirit) and to the graves of ancestors. Wild rice, the food that grew on water, triggered the southern migration of many birds and was harvested by the Chippewa in the late autumn. Medicinal plants were gathered from the streams and woodlands.

The forests also gave the *Anishinabe* the materials for their wigwam homes and for transportation—birch bark canoes and, for winter, toboggans and snowshoes. Birch bark was also used for basket making or for writing down songs, messages, and even sacred teachings. Spearfishing torches were sticks with birch bark rolled tightly at the end, dipped in pitch, and lit for this nighttime spring harvest. The bright colors of woodland flowers and of the northern sunsets still inspire the colors of *Anishinabe* finger weavings today.

A naming ceremony for a child was begun by asking a medicine person for a name from the spirit world. A dreamcatcher might also be hung for a young one to catch her bad dreams and burn them off in the morning sun. In death, a person joined the Dance of Ghosts (the Northern Lights), journeying to be with those on the other side. This way of living, before the Europeans came, embodied a relationship to the land that was spiritual and practical, successful and sustainable.

These abbreviated glimpses of the origins and culture of the Chippewa underlie the more recent recorded history and even the actions of modern villagers. For many Chippewa, especially traditional elders, the events of today are weighed in this much larger context. Last year's court decision and this year's new dance barely register against the backdrop of millennium of time and experience.

The Treaty Era, 1825–1854

The fur traders and pale faces and black coats and longknives and timber barons who are part of past history for most citizens are still being interpreted and incorporated into the *Anishinabe* experience. What they did is still with us. The United States has great libraries but poor memories; the *Anishinabe* the reverse.

Once the United States established physical supremacy, the process of solving other barriers to expansion began. Many treaties with the Indians followed. For the Lake Superior Chippewa there are four treaties with the United States that need to be understood in terms of today's claims. The first was the 1825 Prairie du Chien Treaty of "peace and friendship." The purpose of the treaty was to establish borders between Native territories. The United States attempted to "stabilize" the region between tribes then competing for diminishing hunting and beaver-trapping territory. Native people in the Midwest were in the way of expanding U.S. populations and markets in need of resources and land.

Lake Superior Chippewa delegates, including leaders from Madeline Island, traveled to the Prairie du Chien talks, joining others who claimed title to the upper Midwest. This gathering continued the earlier Thomas Jefferson policy (president 1801–1809), which included getting land through "cessions" in exchange for debt to white traders, and also played into the removal policies of Andrew Jackson (president 1829–1837). The long-standing U.S. policy of removal was to affect Native nations in Wisconsin throughout its territorial and state history.[9]

Lake Superior Chippewa delegates at the 1825 negotiations claimed as their territory northern Wisconsin, the western portion of Michigan's Upper Peninsula and the northeastern portion of Minnesota, including all the islands in

Lake Superior. In signing the Prairie du Chien treaty, the United States acknowledged this ownership. Shortly thereafter, the region was mapped according to tribal territories. In retrospect, it was the necessary first step in disenfranchising Native people of their homelands. The treaties of 1837, 1842, and 1854 between the United States and the Lake Superior Chippewa are called "cession" treaties and could only happen after the upper Midwest was defined by Native interests via the Prairie du Chien 1825 treaty. When the Lake Superior Chippewa delineated their territory, the United States was able to hone in on the Chippewa lands to accomplish the expansion and resource aquisition policies in the region.

University of Wisconsin–Eau Claire Professor Ronald Satz, in a detailed review of the negotiations behind these treaties, notes that the 1837 treaty was designed to secure timber rights to an estimated 9 to 10 million acres of Chippewa forests. Territorial governor and superintendent of Indian affairs Henry Dodge negotiated with Chippewa delegates from Minnesota and some from inland Wisconsin over territory primarily in northern Wisconsin. Dodge felt there was a threat of war from whites if lumbering was not allowed on these lands. The United States not only desired the timber wealth and the chance to extend trade with the Chippewa, but sought to diminish British influence in the area as well. Dodge's persistence in getting the timber, vagueness about the representation and rights of Chippewa remaining in Wisconsin, and some behind-the-scenes bribery helped secure the land cession for $630,000 in annuities and provisions to the Chippewa, plus $100,000 to mixed bloods and $70,000 to settle Chippewa debts with fur and other traders.[10] Article 5 of the 1837 treaty did specify that the Chippewa had the right to hunt, fish, and gather on the lands they had ceded.

The 1842 treaty was designed to secure the Chippewa's copper-rich regions along the shores of Lake Superior and on Isle Royale. Copper deposits were known to the Chippewa who had mined them for centuries for arrowheads, utensils, and body ornaments. After the 1837 treaty, lumberjacks and traders soon realized greater wealth could be gained from the mineral deposits on Chippewa lands. T. Hartley Crawford, commissioner of Indian affairs in three administrations (Martin Van Buren, William Harrison, and John Tyler, the three presidents who followed Andrew Jackson), rejected a proposal for a Chippewa–U.S. joint venture in mining.[11] Instead, he pushed for full U.S. control of the area. Robert Stuart, acting superintendent of Indian affairs in Michigan, negotiated for the United States in the 1842 treaty with the Chippewa at La Pointe, Madeline Island.

Stuart claimed the Chippewa had already given up rights to minerals and that the United States would do them a favor and pay them well for their land and copper. Besides, he told them, the U.S. government would eventually take their land anyway. Learning from previous negotiations (and knowing they could not win a war with the United States), Chippewa negotiators

The Fourth Fire Prophecy told of the coming of the Light-skinned Race. "You will know the future of our people by what face the Light-skinned Race wears. If they come wearing the face of brotherhood, then there will come a time of wonderful changes for generations to come. They will bring new knowledge and articles that can be joined with the knowledge of this country. In this way two nations will join to make a mighty nation. This new nation will be joined by two more nations so that the four will form the mightiest nation of all. You will know the face of brotherhood if the Light-skinned Race comes carrying no weapons, if they come bearing only their knowledge and a handshake.

"Beware if the Light-skinned Race comes wearing the face of *ni-boo-win'* (death). . . . Their hearts may be filled with greed for riches of this land. If they are indeed your brothers, let them prove it."

The fifth prophet said, "In the time of the Fifth Fire there will come a time of great struggle that will grip the lives of all Native people. At the waning of this Fire there will come among the people one who holds a promise of great joy and salvation. If the people accept this promise of a new way and abandon the old teachings, then the struggle of the Fifth Fire will be with the people for many generations. The promise will be a false promise. All those who accept this promise will cause the near destruction of the people."

—Edward Benton-Banai, *The Mishomis Book*

gained assurances from Stuart that they would not have to leave as long as they lived peaceably with whites. However, the treaty was written to say any such removal would be at the pleasure of the U.S. president. The terms of the 1842 treaty stipulated continued hunting rights and "the usual privileges of occupancy" as well as payments of $31,200 a year for twenty-five years to the Mississippi and Lake Superior Chippewa, and money for "mixed bloods" and debts to traders. La Pointe Subagent Alfred Brunson later complained to Wisconsin territorial and U.S. officials that the Chippewa had been treated unjustly in receiving seven cents an acre for millions of acres rich in copper, fish, and timber. At Stuart's request, Crawford and the U.S. War Department dismissed Brunson from his duties as La Pointe subagent with the Chippewa.[12] All totalled, the United States gained from the 1837 and 1842 treaties an estimated 100 billion board feet of timber, 150 billion tons of iron ore, 13.5 billion pounds of copper, 19 million acres of land, and fish, fowl, and game numbering in the billions.[13]

The Chippewa became caught in the intrigue of Minnesota territory and Wisconsin (a state since 1848) politics and the change of administration in

Washington, D.C. when, in 1850, President Zachary Taylor ordered them removed from Wisconsin west across the Mississippi River. The reasons given for this move by federal and Minnesota territory officials were to prevent "injurious contact" between whites and Chippewa, to get the Indians away from (white) whiskey sellers, and to congregate the Chippewa in the West to promote civilizing them. The 1850 Removal Order shocked and outraged the Chippewa, especially those who had signed the 1842 treaty. Chief Buffalo of La Pointe sent messengers to all the Chippewa villages to see if any had broken the peace with whites. They found no reason that might have caused the pleasure of the president to turn against them so they began to plan a response. They were joined by European-Americans who rallied in their support against the Removal Order:

> A vigorous lobbying campaign of the Wisconsin legislature, various missionary groups, regional newspapers, and many local whites aided the Wisconsin Chippewas in their resistance to the Removal Order. . . . Cyrus Mendenhall, an eyewitness to the 1842 treaty parley and mining entrepreneur associated with the Methodist Episcopal Mission Society, rallied ministers, physicians, local officials, merchants, mine foremen, lumbermen, and other influential citizens between Sault Ste. Marie and La Pointe for support for the Chippewas . . . Northern Wisconsin mine owners and whites who employed the Chippewas as fishers, sailors, guides, and hunters raised what Minnesota Governor Ramsey called "almost insuperable" obstacles to their removal.[14]

Minnesota Territory Governor Ramsey and La Pointe subagent John Watrous continued to conspire to lure the Chippewa to northern Minnesota.[15] They moved the location of the 1850 annuity payments and promised services due the Chippewa from La Pointe to Sandy Lake in Minnesota, three to five hundred miles away from various Chippewa villages in Wisconsin. They urged Chippewa to bring their families, but failed to provide adequately for them. While Ramsey bragged that the removal plan was now working, Congress failed to appropriate the annuity funds in time. Winter set in, food supplies ran short, infectious diseases spread, and by winter's end 630 Chippewa had died, at Sandy Lake or en route home to Wisconsin. After the Sandy Lake death march, Indian Affairs Commissioner Luke Lea suspended the Removal Order in 1851 pending further review. Support continued to build in Wisconsin for allowing the Chippewa to stay, but by spring 1852 Chief Buffalo had grown impatient with U.S. politics.

Chief Buffalo was over ninety years old when he led, by canoe and train, a delegation from Madeline Island to Washington, D.C., in 1852 to try and overturn the Removal Order. Along the way, the delegation petitioned European-Americans in support of the Chippewa cause. When they arrived in Washington, they drew up a document to give President Millard Fillmore. They reminded the

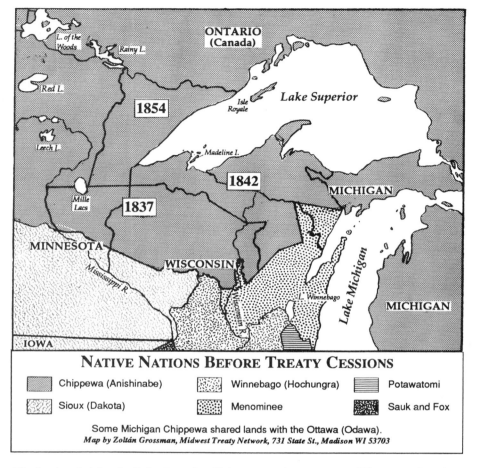

NATIVE NATIONS BEFORE TREATY CESSIONS

Chippewa (Anishinabe)	Winnebago (Hochungra)	Potawatomi
Sioux (Dakota)	Menominee	Sauk and Fox

Some Michigan Chippewa shared lands with the Ottawa (Odawa).
Map by Zoltán Grossman, Midwest Treaty Network, 731 State St., Madison WI 53703

The land ceded by the Lake Superior Chippewa under pressure of European-American settlements and threat of war, in 1837, 1842, and 1854. Now parts of northern Wisconsin, Minnesota, and Michigan. (*Anishinabe* peoples still live in Canadian provinces of Ontario, Manitoba, and Saskatchewan, and Quebec, but these areas are not, of course, territories ceded to the United States or covered in these U.S. treaties.) This is the land "where food grows on water" that the Chippewa came to in the late 1300s.

Ceded Territory is an Environmental Zone: The great ancient pine forests of Wisconsin, Michigan, and Minnesota; the place and spirits of Woodland Culture. Headwaters of the Mississippi River, plus six major Wisconsin rivers, and home of the Upper Great Lakes—Lake Michigan and Lake Superior. The bountiful lakes and streams and dense forests under which lay fertile soil, valuable minerals, and granite bedrock.

Ceded Territory is an Economic Zone built on the wealth of forests, farms, and minerals. Now an economically depressed area dependent on tourism, dairy farms, timber and woodworking industries, paper mills, and scattered university centers. The authors argue that Ceded Territory should be a **Toxic-free Zone and a model Economic Development Zone** for renewable energy technologies, sustainable agriculture, and tourism, in-scale and respectful of place and cultures.

The prophet of the Sixth Fire said, "In the time of the Sixth Fire it will be evident that the promise of the Fifth Fire came in a false way. Those deceived by this promise will take their children away from the teachings of the elders. Grandsons and granddaughters will turn against the elders. In this way the elders will lose their reason for living . . . a new sickness will come among the people. The balance of many people will be disturbed. The cup of life will almost be spilled. The cup of life will almost become the cup of grief."

—Edward Benton-Banai, *The Mishomis Book*

president of the promises made at the 1842 treaty negotiations. They detailed the grievances of the Sandy Lake incident, the many lives lost and the fact that they were shortchanged on the annuity payment and given rotten food. With persistence and some luck, they managed to get an audience with Fillmore, who was more sympathetic to the situation of American Indians than his predecessors had been. He agreed to rescind the Removal Order, make restitution for annuity short pay, and said future annuities would be paid again at La Pointe.[16]

In the 1854 Treaty with the Chippewa, the United States secured the mineral-rich Minnesota northern shore of Lake Superior, but not until the Chippewa insisted upon permanent reservations in Wisconsin: Bad River, Red Cliff, Lac Courte Oreilles, and Lac du Flambeau. Thus forced to choose reservations as their only option for staying in Wisconsin, the Chippewa chose places where the resources didn't move, i.e., where the best wild rice beds and maple groves were. They didn't worry about the resources that did move like deer or muskrat, or where the best fishing was, because they reserved rights to harvest off-reservation.[17]

The treaty era ended in 1854, and with it almost all the rights to the land and subsistence well-being the Chippewa had known. The treaties codified what little was left of sovereignty and homeland, and then were almost forgotten. The woodland way of life would be contained and subject to assault by the coming era of missionaries, boarding schools, popular prejudice against Indians, and overt state disenfranshisement of Chippewa political and cultural rights. The woodland spirits and identity receded.

The *Voigt* Decision

While the sale of Chippewa territory was hardly a deal benefiting both parties, the results were very much like a real estate transaction. In fact when late-twentieth century courts affirmed the treaty rights on this former homeland, they characterized the treaties as deeds to property. When the surface of the territory was sold in 1837, 1842, and 1854, in effect an easement was placed on the sale that reserved, in perpetuity, the right to hunt, fish, and gather.

The court records show how the Lake Superior Chippewa clearly intended to reserve these rights. It is less clear why they so readily consented to the sale to begin with. Benjamin Armstrong, in *Early Life Among the Indians* (published in 1892 by Thomas Wentworth), argued that even the actual sale should be in contention. Armstrong said that the earlier treaties were understood to sell the United States only the minerals and timber, and only that crop of timber, "not the roots," as Chippewa Chief Flat Mouth remembered in 1864. Armstrong was a noted interpreter for Chief Buffalo, the aging principal chief of the Lake Superior Chippewa who resided throughout his life on Madeline Island. It was Armstrong's writings that we used extensively in the 1972 Wisconsin Supreme Court ruling (the *Gurnoe* decision) affirming Chippewa fishing rights on Lake Superior. These rights were reserved in the 1854 treaty.

However, the argument over the actual sale of the land in the 1837 and 1842 treaties was never raised in the major 1970s and 1980s decisions on the Tribble brothers' case that so affect Chippewa rights today. In winter 1974, the Tribble brothers, Fred and Mike, notified Wisconsin Department of Natural Resources (WDNR) wardens of their intent to spear off-reservation. They crossed the imaginary reservation line on frozen Chief Lake near Lac Courte Oreilles, cut a hole in the ice and speared a fish. WDNR wardens arrived shortly thereafter and arrested them. The Tribble brothers contested Wisconsin's authority to arrest them, as the state had done to generations of Chippewa off-reservation hunters and fishers since the early 1900s. They based their challenge on the nineteenth-century treaties and the specifically reserved rights of the Chippewa. The LCO tribal government joined the case against the head of Wisconsin's DNR, Lester Voigt, and the case was heard before U.S. District (Western Wisconsin) Judge James Doyle. The Chippewa argued that the reserved off-reservation harvesting rights were indeed property rights and, like any other heir to property, today's Chippewa were the political successors to these transactions and the legal heirs. They further argued that these rights were never extinguished nor had there been any subsequent federal action that explicitly gave to the state of Wisconsin any jurisdictional authority over these Chippewa rights.

In 1978, Judge Doyle ruled against the Chippewa saying that, once reservations were established after the 1854 treaty, off-reservation gathering rights were extinguished. LCO appealed and in 1983 the U.S. Court of Appeals for the Seventh Circuit reversed Doyle's ruling, saying that the treaties had standing in law. The usufructuary (property) rights of the Chippewa to hunt, fish, and gather on public lands off the reservation were affirmed. This would become known as the *Voigt* decision (which Voigt and Wisconsin lost) or *LCO I*. The U.S. Supreme Court refused to hear Wisconsin's appeal, thus upholding the appeals court ruling. Doyle was then instructed to clarify the extent of these rights in northern Wisconsin.

Although frail from two bouts with cancer, Judge Doyle was alert and very much in control of the vast amount of documents and complex arguments being raised. The six-day trial began on December 9, 1985. Prior to the arguments that detailed the resources, methods of harvest, and areas where the harvesting rights could be used, Doyle asked that the parties describe the atmosphere of the time in which the treaties were signed. Dr. Charles Cleland, a University of Michigan ethnohistorian, was the only expert witness called for the week-long trial. He also was used to rebut the state's argument that, since the region was eventually settled, all rights reserved in the treaties were automatically abrogated.

Of note here is this atmosphere asked for by Judge Doyle: a snapshot of history that would enable the judge to make a better decision. What the judge heard was great history about the Chippewa during the first half of the 1800s. Unfortunately, this history was largely unknown, and is still elided in most school texts in Wisconsin. Eventually, the judge ruled with every argument raised by the Chippewa in this phase of the trial.

One of the significant shifts noted by Cleland in his testimony was how the fur trade forced the Chippewa to shift from a reciprocal to a market economy. Until the explosive demand for furs by European markets, most Native people maintained self-sustaining economies. In order to fill the fur orders, traders needed to procure more furs. The Chippewa, as the primary suppliers in the area, had no concept of market economies, which demanded excess production. Under the reciprocal economy, the Chippewa traded only what was needed for consumption and any excess was used in barter for goods not locally produced.

Nonetheless, the shift occurred. Cleland called it chemical warfare, noting that alcohol was used deliberately to weaken the spirit of the Chippewa, creating not only a dependency on the chemical but a dependency on the currency (excess furs) in order to maintain access to alcohol and tools introduced by the fur traders. Once alcohol was introduced to an area, the shift to a market economy accelerated.

Ironically, the Chippewa now used the results of these earlier policies to argue their rights to resources and methods of harvest. While the state of Wisconsin tried to paint the Chippewa as unfortunate victims of manifest destiny, Cleland successfully argued that once the shift occurred the Chippewa were very much aware that they were now in a sophisticated economy. And once that was established, the Chippewa's rights to property, rather than just the lifestyle of the nineteenth century, was accepted by Doyle.

In many ways, variations of this argument continue to surface by those opposed to Chippewa rights. While today's Chippewa villages, people, and lifestyle have indeed changed considerably, the courts have said change alone does not constitute the loss of property or rights. The treaties, instead of fixing the Chippewa like a snapshot in a particular era, in fact, preserve the opportunity to grow and change. Rather than prescribe a fixed lifestyle, they protect the right to remain dynamic. And, like other land transactions, like deeds, they record the event and agreements within.

Judge Doyle ruled in favor of the Chippewa in 1985 and the state appealed to the U.S. Court of Appeals, Seventh Circuit, which, in *LCO II*, upheld this Doyle ruling, reaffirming the Chippewa's usufructuary rights on off-reservation lands. In 1987, Doyle's decision, known as *LCO III*, completed the first phase of the *Voigt* litigation when Doyle delineated the Chippewa's right to: 1) harvest fish, game, and plants off-reservation on public lands (and on private lands if proven necessary to provide a modest living); 2) use both traditional and modern methods in the hunting and gathering; and 3) barter or sell the harvest. Doyle affirmed the state of Wisconsin's right to make restrictions on the harvest if they were needed to "conserve a particular resource." What remained to be clarified in the next phases of *Voigt* were who would regulate the harvest, the meaning of "modest standard of living," the extent of fishing and timber rights, and what back damages were due the Chippewa for the many decades of denial of the off-reservation harvest.

The seventh prophet that came to the people long ago was said to be different from the other prophets. He was young and had a strange light in his eyes. He said, "In the time of the Seventh Fire a *Osh-ki-bi-ma-di-zeeg* (New People) will emerge. They will retrace their steps to find what was left by the trail. Their steps will take them to the elders who they will ask to guide them on their journey."
—Edward Benton-Banai, *The Mishomis Book*

Doyle's decisions reaffirmed ceded territory as a legal concept. The Chippewa and the whole state of Wisconsin would begin to learn what ceded territory could mean as a political and economic reality in the late 1980s and 1990s. What was still lost was ceded territory as a cultural concept, and this would begin to be restored as the *Anishinabe* today reclaimed our history and culture while we built grassroots activism with our neighbors and allies in northern Wisconsin.

In conclusion, I would like to emphasize a few key issues that the rest of this story attempts to detail. The first is that the Chippewa, like other people native to this continent, have not only a unique legacy but, in today's legal reality, an internationally recognized status that can be used to protect the environment, for everyone and all beings.

Secondly, treaty rights within the territories that were ceded are the best potential environmental protection device that currently exists. If the Chippewa model succeeds, Native rights will be the last bastion of environmental and economic stability on the continent. In chapter 8, we will discuss the concept of ceded territory as a tool for environmental and economic stabilization.

Thirdly, the sovereign rights of the Chippewa are like those rights that everyone had but has in various ways given up. Chippewa sovereignty will last and be an effective tool only if the Chippewa representatives act like sovereigns. This sovereignty demands self-knowledge and self-confidence. If the Chippewa, in exchange for short-term economic prizes, forget history or stop listening to the stories of the elders, we will once more fall into darkness as though the *Megis* Shell has once more vanished. These recent actions and victories are indeed reminiscent of times long, long ago.

Notes

1. Eugene Begay workshop training for U.S. Forest Service, April 1991, Lac du Flambeau Reservation, Wisconsin.

2. William W. Warren, *History of the Ojibwe People* (St. Paul: Minnesota Historical Society Press, 1885, 1984 reprint edition.

3. Edward Benton-Banai, *The Mishomis Book: The Voice of Ojibway* (St. Paul: Red School House (643 Virginia St., St. Paul, MN, 55103, 1988. Prophecies reprinted with permission).

4. Warren, *History*, pp. 79–80.

5. By the early 1800s, the main settlements were Leech Lake, Red Lake, and Sandy Lake in Minnesota, Lac Courte Oreilles and Lac du Flambeau in Wisconsin, and the Snake River and Yellow River villages near the St. Croix River on the Minnesota-Wisconsin border. Harold Hickerson, cited in Ronald Satz, *Chippewa Treaty Rights: The Reserved Rights of Wisconsin's Chippewa Indians in Historical Perspective* (Madison: Wisconsin Academy of Sciences, Arts and Letters, 1991), p. 1.

6. Benton-Banai, *The Mishomis Book*, pp. 74–76.

7. Edmund J. Danziger, Jr., *The Chippewas of Lake Superior* (Norman: Oklahoma University Press, 1978), p. 14.

8. This and the following three paragraphs are principally indebted to Frances Densmore, *Chippewa Customs* (St. Paul: Minnesota Historical Society, 1979), pp. 133, 173; pp. 124–128; pp. 89–95, 125, 150, 174, 179; p. 52. The reference to the Dance of Ghosts and the Northern Lights comes from Danziger, *The Chippewas of Lake Superior*, p. 15.

9. The Potawatomi expanded into the Lake Michigan area in the seventeenth and eighteenth centuries and became middlemen in the fur trade with Europeans. Some Potawatomi were removed to west of the Mississippi River in the 1800s. The remaining Wisconsin Potawatomi remained landless until 1913 when they received a small 14,439-acre reservation in Forest County in northern Wisconsin. The Menominee, residents here long before the arrival of French explorer Jean Nicolet in 1634, were forced onto a reservation in central Wisconsin by their own 1854 treaty with the United States. The Oneida, part of the League of the Iroquois, withdrew

from New York in the 1800s to find a new homeland to the west. The Stockbridge came west with the Oneida and, in Indiana, the Stockbridge joined the Munsee, originally a band of the Delaware Native nation. The Brotherton from New Jersey also went west to Indiana and when negotiations for land there failed, they came with the Oneida and Stockbridge-Munsee to Wisconsin. The Brotherton mostly assimilated into the Stockbridge-Munsee or European population in Wisconsin and have no land or sovereign status (although they did once have a reservation on Lake Winnebago, and some Brotherton today are asking for a reservation again). In 1856, the Menominee gave the southwest corner of their reservation in Shawano County to the Stockbridge-Munsee. The Oneida's reservation (today, twelve square miles, but only about two thousand five hundred acres tribally held) is near Green Bay, Wisconsin. The Wisconsin Winnebago were also victims of the longstanding removal policy, losing land in 1829, 1832, and 1837 negotiations with the United States. In 1874, remaining Winnebagos were removed to Nebraska. Almost immediately some began returning to Wisconsin and were permitted to homestead western Wisconsin. Today, the Winnebago are reestablished in Wisconsin. See Nancy O. Lurie's booklet, *Wisconsin Indians* (Madison: State Historical Society of Wisconsin, 1987).

10. Satz, *Chippewa Treaty Rights*, pp. 13–31. The Chippewa received about eight cents an acre for 11 million acres. Satz notes some Chippewa leaders felt they were granting timber rights to the pine but not deciduous forests. Also noteworthy is the fact that interpreters for the treaties were paid employees of the U.S. government and that among the witnesses to this treaty were well-known traders waiting to exploit the timber wealth of the northern territories.

11. This proposal was made by Gouverneur Kemble, a foundry owner and Democratic congressman from New York. This Lake Superior region would become the world's leading copper producer by the 1890s. This story and other information in this paragraph is also indebted to Satz, *Chippewa Treaty Rights*, p. 33.

12. Satz, *Chippewa Treaty Rights*, pp. 34, 37, 38, 44.

13. Cited in Professor David Wrone's unpublished paper, "Economic Impact of the 1837 and 1842 Chippewa Treaties," (History Department, University of Wisconsin–Stevens Point, 1989). Wrone goes on to say, "The ores of the Mesabi [Range in northern Minnesota, gained in the 1854 treaty] enabled the steel mills of Pittsburgh to flourish, the copper of the Keewanah [Michigan's Upper Peninsula] poured into wires made the telephone system possible. Power sites created paper mills, the fish a natural recreational paradise."

14. Satz, *Chippewa Treaty Rights*, p. 56.

15. Minnesota territory was anxious to get the Chippewa congregated there in order to gain the considerable business of trading with and administering annuities to the Chippewa. The Minnesota territory legislature had also gone on record opposing Chippewa hunting and fishing rights on ceded lands, thus presenting the United States and Minnesota's Whig Party friends in D.C. with the opportunity to kill two Chippewa sovereignty rights (land in Wisconsin and gathering rights in ceded territory) with one stone. See Satz, *Chippewa Treaty Rights*, pp. 53, 57.

16. Satz, *Chippewa Treaty Rights*, pp. 64–67.

17. It was not until 1934 that the Sokaogon and St. Croix bands finally obtained their homeland reservations.

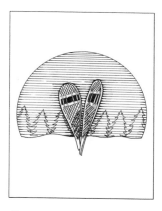

ONABANI GISISS
(Moon of the Crust on the Snow)

The Fallout of the *Voigt* Decision
Anti-Indian Backlash in Wisconsin, 1983–1987

Walt Bresette

NORTH AMERICA'S INDIGENOUS PEOPLE have been long subsumed by larger nation-states. Remnants of indigenous rights are often blurred by the size and power of state, provincial, and national borders and by domineering societies. Yet the concept of indigenous sovereignty remains aglow. This turns into reality when people, in whatever era of resistance, act out elements of this indigenous sovereignty.

The vestiges of sovereignty and treaty rights were to continue after the treaty era's end in 1854, but only because the Chippewa had taken action at considerable effort, risk, and expense. The ninety-some-year-old Chief Buffalo was only among the first of many *Anishinabe* to have to organize just to make the United States live up to what little it had promised on its end of the one-sided land deals.

From Sovereigns to Domestic Dependent Nations, 1600–1954

The several Indian nations [are] distinct political communities, having territorial boundaries, within which their authority is exclusive, and having a right to all the lands within those boundaries, which is not only acknowledged, but guaranteed by the United States . . . Indian nations had always been considered

23

as distinct, independent political communities, retaining their original rights, as the undisputed possessors of the soil from time immemorial . . . The Cherokee nation, then, is a distinct community, occupying its own territory, with boundaries accurately described, in which the laws of Georgia have no right to enter, but with the assent of the Cherokees themselves, or in conformity with treaties, and with the acts of congress.

—John Marshall, Chief Justice,
U.S. Supreme Court in *Worcester v. Georgia* (1832)

The fate of the Lake Superior Chippewa has been that of most other indigenous people. Those who have survived the half millennium of occupation, disease, and warfare continue to struggle for identity. "Indian" policies, although changing over time, were applied consistently to over three hundred distinct Native peoples within U.S. borders. We all became "Indians," a homogenizing term that gave the English-speaking colonialists an easy categorical handle.[1]

Within this five hundred year history of occupation and resistance, the United States has recognized some inherent Native rights. Supreme Court Chief Justice John Marshall in the early 1830s called Native groups "domestic dependent nations." In *Cherokee Nation v. Georgia* (1831), they sought to protect their territory from incursions by Georgia residents, but the court said that the Cherokees could not sue Georgia because they were not a foreign nation. In another case, *Worcester v. Georgia* (1832), Marshall said

The Indian nations had always been considered as distinct, independent political communities . . . [A]nd the settled doctrine of the law of nations is that a weaker power does not surrender its independence—its right to self-government—by associating with a stronger, and taking its protection. A weak state, in order to provide for its safety, may place itself under the protection of one more powerful, without stripping itself of the right of government, and ceasing to be a state.

Here the Cherokee successfully argued that the state of Georgia was without jurisdiction in their attempts to sell land within the Cherokee's lands.

While these rulings stripped indigenous people of external sovereignty (e.g., the ability to establish official ties outside the United States, make treaties, or trade internationally), it recognized internal sovereignty. And although assaults on remaining sovereignty continued, led immediately by then-President Andrew Jackson, the legal precedent was set.[2] Yet, the response to the Cherokee cases underscored the damaging effects of shifting U.S. policies. It set the stage for the implementation of the 1830 Indian Removal Act.

This legal distinction regarding sovereignty is one of many examples of "Indian" law and U.S. policies toward Native nations. Along with legislative and administrative policies, the three branches of government have spoken often of Native rights. In the case cited above, by recognizing tribal self-government, interference by state governments over internal tribal matters is legally rejected. The late 1970s case started by the Tribble brothers from Lac Courte Oreilles Reservation is another affirmation of this judicial view. Nineteenth century Chippewa treaties preserved what little was left of *Anishinabe* land and sovereignty. One hundred fifty years later, ceded territory provided a land base for harvesting rights and subsistence living, and the affirmation of the Chippewa as major players in resource management and economic development.

But as others struggling for rights know, the United States is fickle and can turn a cold heart and a blind eye to political minorities when convenient. While Indian law is well established within the U.S. judicial system, each new administration develops its own "Indian" policy, moving with economic and popular tides, sometimes shifting radically over the years. Congress regularly writes and rewrites legislation affecting Native rights.

As more power shifted from the British to the United States, "Indian" affairs also shifted in importance and design. If the colonial period (1600–1776) was determined by economic interests that saw the tribes treated as sovereigns, then the post-revolutionary period embraced a conquest doctrine. Thomas Jefferson sought to turn Native people into "whites" through Christian missionizing and education, and by shifting the concept of "property" from a communal to a private idea.

The late 1700s and early 1800s saw the United States consolidate power over, and confiscate land from, eastern Native nations. Many tribes were forced west, shifting Native alliances and territories and increasing the competition for land and resources. Andrew Jackson, who became president in 1829, declared the "civilizing" policy a failure. On the heels of successful warfare against the Creek in Alabama (1814–1815), he began the movement that led to the Indian Removal Act (1830), which provided monies for the president to "negotiate" with eastern tribes for their removal west of the Mississippi. As whole tribes like the Cherokee were displaced and the "frontier" states militarily secured, U.S. policies shifted like the changing landscape. In 1849, Indian Affairs moved from the Department of War to the Bureau of Indian Affairs (BIA) within the Interior Department. Treaty making was halted in 1871, shifting to unilateral legislation. Thus laws affecting Native rights were passed without any Native participation.

The General Allotment or Dawes Act (1887) favored the special interests that sought to reduce Native lands and to develop lands that were retained. The following Allotment Era resulted in the loss of 100 million acres of treaty lands. The allotment act gave the president authority to allot 160 acres of tribal land to each tribal head of household, 80 acres to tribal single persons over eighteen and orphans, and 40 acres to each other single tribal person over eighteen. After allotment, surplus lands were sold to the United States, which then opened them to settlement.

By the turn of the century, physical and psychological assaults ended any remaining organized military resistance by indigenous people. In 1924, Congress unilaterally declared that all "Indians" were now U.S. citizens, although this act did recognize some of our Native sovereignty and "domestic dependent status." Tribal citizenship remained unaffected. Native Americans thus have a unique kind of dual citizenship—we are members of our respective states, provinces, and other nations as well as members of our tribes and villages.

In 1934, the Indian Reorganization Act (IRA), also known as the "Indian New Deal," became law. The legislation ended the allotment policy, but undermined traditional rule by maintaining fiscal relationships only with those tribes that adopted constitutions modeled after the United States. Nearly all tribes today have these IRA-styled governments, continuing strains within communities that gave deference to clan leaders, traditional elders, and religious institutions.

In 1954, Congress passed Public Law 280, which gave states the option to assume jurisdiction over certain criminal acts within "Indian Country." Wisconsin was one of the states that opted for this jurisdiction, thus adding confusion and further diminishing internal sovereignty. This law encouraged both assimilation and termination policies, moving tribal members to urban centers and giving states unusual jurisdictional authority. Here in Wisconsin, the Menominee tribe was "terminated," losing their reservation status and becoming a county, although they lobbied and regained reservation status from Congress during the Nixon administration.[3] Hundreds of other tribes lost status across the country and all communities lost members to the anonymity of urban ghettos.

Congressional legislation and legislative inaction affected individual Native rights as well as the sovereignty/jurisdictional arena.[4] While we became "citizens" in 1924, in part because of Native involvement in World War I, Native veterans of World War II and the Korean War were denied many rights on their return home. Notably, while Native rights were being denied or unilaterally changed, none of the so-called "equal rights for everyone" groups (that so quickly emerged in Wisconsin to oppose Indian spearfishing) were around. And it wasn't until 1978 that the Indian Religious Freedom Act was passed by the U.S. Congress, after nearly two hundred years of direct religious oppression.

Backlash in Wisconsin: Court Decisions Fuel a Storm of Anti-Indian Outcry, 1983–1987

"The problem with you Chippewa is that you're supposed to be assimilated or dead," Nancy Lurie said sarcastically at a speech she gave at Northland College in Ashland, Wisconsin, in the mid-1970s. "By surviving you messed up their plans." Remembering the often quoted speech by Nez Perce leader Chief Joseph who said he would "fight no more forever," she quickly added, "he didn't say he wasn't going to sue." Lurie, an anthropologist and curator of the Milwaukee Public Museum, said that treaties were allowed to be signed because the policy makers assumed that the Native people would not survive the various social, political, and military assaults in the offing.[5]

When the Tribble brothers and LCO, in essence, sued the state of Wisconsin for their dormant off-reservation rights, others of us were forced to take another look at our sovereignty and our historical place on the continent. In 1974, Fred and Mike Tribble had responded to new information (through new access to the educational system), responded intuitively to older messages from tribal elders, and embraced the changing social realities won by African-American civil rights leaders and others seeking their legitimate role in today's society. LCO and the Tribble brothers challenged Wisconsin's game laws, arguing that fishing rights guaranteed by treaties signed in 1837 and 1842 superceded state authority.

But when the federal courts agreed in the 1983 *Voigt* decision, the state of Wisconsin and its citizens revolted. They reacted as if manifest destiny had been overturned. Opponents argued that the court rulings were anomalies, which should be ignored or overturned. State and federal leaders were reminiscent of Andrew Jackson when earlier court rulings upheld Cherokee sovereignty in Georgia. In short, the state sought to win back in the political arena what it couldn't win from the Chippewa in court.

At the time of the 1983 *Voigt* decision, I was a reporter at WOJB Radio preparing for my five o'clock newscast. UPI rang its bells. I went out to find the new message, and the lead paragraph shouted the news that a three-judge panel had "given" the Chippewa *unlimited* hunting and fishing rights. I read that lead and I said, "They can't do that. No three judges anywhere can give anyone unlimited anything. It's not what they do." But I was with the only news agency in the state, if not the nation, who didn't run that story.

The next morning a Wisconsin Department of Natural Resources (WDNR) spokesperson said the only thing that would be left in northern Wisconsin after the Chippewa were done would be water skiing. After we Chippewa go out and rape the lakes, take all the deer, whatever it was they thought we were going to do. On the heels of that official reaction, which became state policy in the eyes of the public, certain Wisconsinites recognized opportunity and took advantage of it. Soon anti-Indian organizations formed whose sole purpose was to abrogate Chippewa treaties. They put out material suggesting that we Chippewa were worse than acid rain for the fishing in northern Wisconsin.

The *Voigt* decision, along with other Native claims across the United States and Canada, became epicenters of the legal rumblings across the continent. Although such rulings were predicated on longstanding judicial

Walleyes [also known as walleyed pike] range from minnow size all the way, some of them get to be up to twenty pounds. Walleye is a member of the perch family.

The unique thing about a walleye, aside from the fact that they're very good eating fish, the unique thing about them that sets them apart from all the other fish in the lake is that their eyes shine. The easiest way I could say it is if you look at a star, you can see the brightness of that star in the blackness of the sky. When you shine a light in the water and there's a walleye there, often times their eyes will be shining that bright. They have a real sparkle to them, a real shine. . . .

Sometimes when you're going along the lake shore, it's very dark and you're standing up on the bow of the boat shining your light off into the distance and it's calm enough, you can see the walleyes moving. You can see all these little eyes just swarming around.

They're relatively easy to find. Even if you're going to a new lake, all you have to do is keep going along the shoreline until you see those eyes sparkle. They're usually right up in the shoreline all the way to the deepest part of the lake. But that time of year [two to three weeks of spring spearing], they're up in the shallows. When you see these eyes, you get ready. Often times, they're moving . . . all different stages of movement. Some are just laying there, some are moving towards you, some are very fast. But you see the eyes, you can get an idea of where the rest of the body is.

It feels real good to be out there. Some of these lakes, after one hundred years, one hundred fifty years, we're just beginning to go back and spear lakes that probably our ancestors speared on. It gives me a strong feeling.

—Nick Hockings, LdF spearfisher,
interview with Rick Whaley,
July 13, 1991

and constitutional principles, the sudden reality of court rulings often disoriented the political, cultural, and economic status quo. And while the physical landscape remained unchanged, a sense was brooding that fundamental change in social relations, resource management, and development ethics was about to happen.

The First Off-Reservation Spearfishers:
Racial Slurs and the Threat of Violence, 1984

Every April on northern lakes the walleye and other fish spawn as the ice gives way to the warmth of yet another spring on the region's three thousand lakes. It is time for the *Anishinabe*, the Chippewa, to begin food production, once more teaching the children how to fish. When the walleye signal, it is time.

Legally, Chippewa can spear all year, but deep water spearing is difficult. Between 1909 and 1983, this ancient ritual was limited to waters within the boundaries of the six federally recognized "reservations" of the Lake Superior Chippewa. But with the January 1983 ruling, the U.S. Circuit Court of Appeals affirmed the right of the Chippewa to once more fish in their traditional territories: the northern third of Wisconsin, the western portion of Michigan's upper peninsula, and the northeastern part of Minnesota. Off-reservation harvesting became a reacquaintance with the land once owned but ceded to the United States in the nineteenth century.

The first spearers venturing off-reservation were met with racial slurs and the promise of mob protests and terrorist violence as they practiced once again their harvesting rights in ceded territory. Because of the intimidation and the protest violence that ensued through the rest of the decade, only those who were willing to risk their lives were able to spearfish—everyone else was unable to reclaim their rights. Like *de facto* segregation in the South not so long ago, *de facto* abrogation of treaties reigned in the North. This backlash against traditional Native activity would set state and federal politicians against the Chippewa. It would also spawn non-Chippewa support that stood with the *Anishinabe* spearers and families as they faced the mobs annually at the boat landings. "It looked like the Little Rock of the North," as Suzan Shown Harjo, an executive director of the National Congress of American Indians, would later say.

Official pronouncements on the court case came in 1984 from the state, the WDNR, and elected officials of the six Lake Superior Chippewa tribal governments. The WDNR's George Meyer said that if the Chippewa were allowed to harvest deer in their own season, little old ladies in tennis shoes would be afraid to walk in the woods of northern Wisconsin. The WDNR's official line was that Chippewa spearing could deplete the fish on popular walleye and muskie fishing lakes and that the Chippewa probably could not manage the enforcement end of their fish and deer harvest. Tribal officials said that self-regulation with their own system of wardens deserved a chance, and they would seek federal dollars for this. Then-governor of Wisconsin Tony Earl and William Horn, deputy secretary of the Department of Interior, both said treaties couldn't be abrogated; people needed to get along. Meanwhile, the Boulder Junction town board chair told the department of interior's Mr. Horn in a letter, "If a person's livelihood [from the $92 million tourism industry in Vilas and Oneida counties] is threatened, the more likelihood there will be violence and hostility."[6]

Another voice quickly emerged from among the anti-Indian "sportspeople" —hunters and fishermen who were neighbors of the Wisconsin Chippewa. Paul Mullaly of Hayward, Wisconsin, was arrested in fall 1984 for carrying an uncased hunting gun in his car. Claiming Chippewa from LCO would not be arrested under the same circumstances, Mullaly formed Equal Rights for Everyone (ERFE) to protest Chippewa treaty hunting rights.[7] Though the Chippewa deer harvest was very small in numbers, their season was longer by a few weeks than the regular hunting season in Wisconsin. Mullaly found a sympathetic

CHIPPEWA RESERVATIONS
IN WISCONSIN

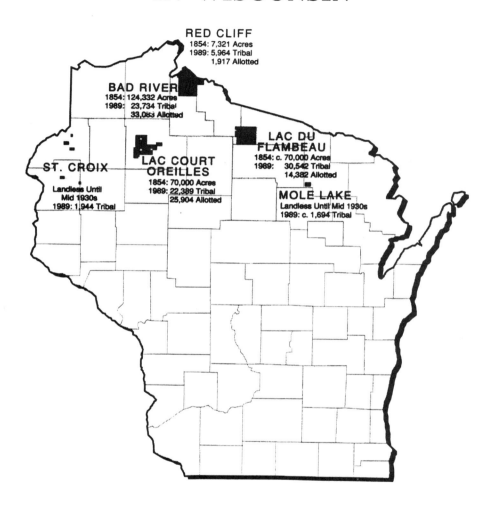

RED CLIFF
1854: 7,321 Acres
1989: 5,964 Tribal
      1,917 Allotted

BAD RIVER
1854: 124,332 Acres
1989: 23,734 Tribal
       33,083 Allotted

LAC DU FLAMBEAU
1854: c. 70,000 Acres
1989: 30,542 Tribal
       14,382 Allotted

LAC COURT OREILLES
1854: 70,000 Acres
1989: 22,389 Tribal
      25,904 Allotted

ST. CROIX
Landless Until
Mid 1930s
1989: 1,944 Tribal

MOLE LAKE
Landless Until Mid 1930s
1989: c. 1,694 Tribal

Map By Sean Hartnett

From Ronald N. Satz, *Chippewa Treaty Rights: The Reserved Rights of Wisconsin's Chippewa Indians in Historical Perspective* (Madison: Wisconsin Academy of Sciences, Arts and Letters, 1991). Reprinted with permission. Data from Lurie (1987) and the Bureau of Indian Affairs, Great Lakes Agency in Ashland, Wisconsin. Compare tribally held acres in 1989 to the acreage originally provided and the number of acres alloted (individually held) after the establishment of each reservation.

audience among other white hunters and there soon appeared bumper stickers that read, "Shoot an Indian, Save 25 Deer," and flyers advertising rules and points for a "First Annual Indian Shoot." ERFE President Mullaly railed against Native sovereignty, saying the reservations would become havens for crime and cripple America with drugs. He warned that allowing the exercise of treaty rights could prove a dangerous situation for northern Wisconsin.

ERFE established chapters in a number of cities in northern Wisconsin and held meetings in Minnesota also, although their claims of 4,000 members in 1984 and 31,000 by 1985 were grossly inflated. The Lakeland ERFE chapter featured Jack Sorenson, who sold advertising for a TV station in Rhinelander, and Larry Peterson, a paper mill worker. Peterson also founded and led another backlash group with the foreboding acronym, WARR (Wisconsin Alliance for Rights and Resources). WARR's propaganda championed "states' rights" and individual citizens' rights to be treated equally. The rhetoric of violence burned so intensely that the FBI was called in to investigate whether some resort owners might be implicated in threats to "kill Indians if they came to certain lakes."[8]

In 1984, the Adhoc Commission on Racism in Wisconsin loudly condemned WARR and ERFE for their racism and violent threats against Chippewa people and rights. To distance themselves from Mullaly and from these charges of racism, the anti-treaty forces formed Protect Americans' Rights and Resources (PARR) in 1985. PARR sought to appeal to sportspeople, farmers, resort owners, and off-reservation businesses and chambers of commerce, to oppose "Chippewa special rights" and the perceived economic destruction resulting from Chippewa hunting and fishing. PARR claimed no affiliation to ERFE, but many activists, including Sorenson and Peterson, just switched memberships. In 1987, WARR handed over its treasury and mailing lists to PARR—the new "civil rights" group of the anti-treaty cause.[9]

What lay ahead at boat landings where Chippewa speared in the late 1980s would be the fulfillment of this prejudice and threat.

Washington State: The Roots of the Modern Anti-Indian Movement in the 1960s and 1970s

The modern era's anti-Indian movement in the United States got its start in Washington state in the 1960s and 1970s.[10] Non-Indian owners of reservation property are a common phenomenon on reservations across the United States these days. Nationally, over half a million non-Indians own land on Native reservations. This land is called allotment land, bought under U.S. allotment programs, or alienated land. On some U.S. reservations, non-Indians outnumber indigenous holders of the land by a 3 to 1 ratio. Historically, the United States sold land on reservation to non-Indians, without the consent of tribal government, often promising white buyers that reservations would become a thing of the past. As tribal governments began to exercise more

jurisdiction over reservation policies in the 1960s and 1970s, non-Indian land owners felt increasingly in competition with tribal members for limited resources and land inside reservations. When Native nations began to battle over control of natural resources off-reservation (fish, deer, rice) under the auspices of Native treaties with the United States, the anti-Indian movement of today solidified.

In the late 1960s, the Quinault Property Owners Association (QPOA) on the Quinault reservation and Association of Property Owners in Port Madison Area (APORPMA) on the Suquamish reservation where non-Indians are 80 percent of the population and own 60 percent of the land formed in Washington state to battle tribal governments over reservation policies on taxation, zoning, construction, land use, and economic development. George Garland and Betty Morris of QPOA and Pierce and May Davis of APORPMA headed the small but vocal opposition to tribal sovereignty, and in 1976, were involved in creating the pseudo-national Interstate Congress for Equal Rights and Responsibilities (ICERR). The Lummi nation in Washington state was a target of their political complaints as well as the Blackfoot, Salish, Kootenai, and the Crow nations in Montana. ICERR attempted to link on-reservation non-Indian landowners with off-reservation non-Indian sport and commercial fishermen, who they hoped were similarly opposed to tribal, treaty-protected fishing rights.

In 1973, fourteen tribes, with the U.S. government on their side, sued the state of Washington to prevent the state from taking salmon or steelhead without tribal consent and to prevent the state from enforcing its fishing laws against tribal members. Federal District Court Judge George Boldt (a Republican and Eisenhower appointee) ruled that the tribes had retained such fishing rights in the six treaties western Washington tribes had signed with the United States in 1854 and 1855. This *Boldt* decision widened the circle of political and economic opposition to Native fishing rights. Washington state's Attorney General Slade Gorton, loser of many legal battles with the Washington state tribes, legitimized the white "civil rights" backlash of ICERR and others by challenging Native peoples as "super citizens . . . with more rights than others."

Through the late 1970s and 1980s, ICERR portrayed itself variously as a civil rights group for non-Indians, a civil libertarian organization of whites and non-tribal Indians, or a blatantly anti-Indian organization, depending on the circumstances. Whenever possible, the movement recruited Native people who had severed their ties with their culture and tribal governments. Helen Sanders (a.k.a. Helen Mitchell or Kirschling) was a former Quinault tribal council member who owned allotted land on both the Quinault and Chehalis reservations. She also ran an extensive timber cutting operation and was as dismayed as non-Indian reservation land holders at the reassertion of tribal, community interests. She and other "assimilationists" served well the anti-Indian cause by providing Indian faces to attack Native sovereignty and treaty rights.

After 1983, the burgeoning anti-Indian movement picked up critical support from well-connected, conservative elements in Washington state— organizer Barbara Lindsay, lawyer David Yamashita, Carol and Tom Lewis, fundraiser Allan Gottlieb.[11] And, most notably, state senator Jack Metcalf lent expertise to the movement against Native rights by linking the anti-Indian backlash with anti-tax, states' rights, anti-Federal Reserve, and white supremacist sentiments. Metcalf became financial supporter and advisor to Salmon-Steelhead Preservation Action for Washington Now (S/SPAWN), formed in 1983 by the same activist core that created QPOA and ICERR.

S/SPAWN emphasized protecting salmon and ending reverse discrimination in appealing to farmers, loggers, fishermen, and laborers in the midst of a recession. In 1983, with the help of Senator Metcalf and lawyer Yamashita, S/SPAWN drafted Ballot Initiative 84, which argued that Native sovereignty status ended with the 1924 Citizenship Act and called on the state to resist federal court decisions affirming Native fishing rights. Since it didn't receive the necessary signatures to make the ballot, S/SPAWN returned in 1984 with the new and improved Initiative 456, reversing the rhetoric and calling for "state policies respecting Indian rights"—meaning state laws to override federal court rulings—and equal rights for all, including treaty Indians. The measure made the fall 1984 ballot and passed narrowly. While it had no effect on the federally affirmed fishing rights of the Quinault, Suquamish, Nisqually, Kllalam, and other Northwest tribes, the backlash referendum victory did signal the U.S. Congress that there were voters out there who favored the destruction of U.S. treaty obligations to Native nations. By 1985, S/SPAWN was aggressively promoting the idea of a presidential commission to study the effects of federal Indian policy on non-Indians and non-tribal Indians.

This anti-Indian fishing rights movement engendered solidarity work for Native rights in Washington state. Richard La Course chronicled the *Boldt* backlash for the *Yakima Nation Review*. He and Joe DeLaCruz, president of the Quinault tribal council and a president of the National Congress of American Indians, hired Gummi Johnson as a consultant. I first met Gummi when I went to Washington state in the late 1970s to support a group called National Coalition to Support Indian Treaties (NCSIT).[12] The second time I met Johnson was in the mid-1980s when he developed a pro-treaty strategy for the 1984 election campaigns and to counter Initiative 456. Gummi was a political consultant, formerly with the Republican Party, but one who believed in the value of the treaties as something that conservatives ought to honor. Based on information we and the Washington tribes put together with the work he had been doing, Gummi published the report *First Our Land, Now Our Treaties*, a key treatise on the modern anti-Indian movement. I learned much from this monitoring and the education/election campaigns there, and sought to use, in some way, these models for work in Wisconsin.

The Washington state backlash that exploited economic fears and anti-Indian bigotry sought national allies as well and reached out to the anti-treaty movement in Wisconsin. The Wisconsin backlash groups, WARR and ERFE, were sponsoring organizations for S/SPAWN. Both ERFE's Paul Mullaly and WARR's Larry Peterson looked to Washington state anti-Indian organizers for expertise and tactics. In February 1985, the Wisconsin Counties Association, the new Washington state Attorney General Ken Eikenberry, and a host of anti-Indian organizations did a massive lobbying effort in Washington, D.C., to support the idea of a presidential review of Indian treaties. This notion became the main theme for the first national convention of Protect Americans' Rights and Resources (PARR) in Wausau, Wisconsin, in 1987. Economic recession, racism, and political opportunism provided the same soil in Wisconsin for the local anti-treaty forces in the 1980s.

The Three Crucial Cultural Forces
Strengthening the Anti-Treaty Cause, 1983–1987

The First Force Aligned Against Chippewa Rights: Misinformation

Northern Wisconsin still makes its modest living from farming, logging, paper mills, and small industries that engendered secondary businesses and small communities around them. Vacationers to northwoods cottages and lakes have spawned the summer tourism and winter recreation that now rivals the traditional industries of northern Wisconsin in importance, and gives a needed shot in the arm to overall economic survival. The economic slump, which has actually been a rural depression for many recent decades, intensified the economic fears of European-Americans, exacerbated social tensions, and overwhelmed those voices of tolerance for Indians and our rights. Public ignorance of Chippewa culture and history and the campaign of misinformation by political opponents of treaty rights further inflamed the situation. The government's lack of economic planning and investment in northern Wisconsin coincided with the state's outright opposition to Chippewa rights and co-management of resources. While the state worked behind the scenes against Chippewa treaty rights, the non-Indian sportsmen, resentful of the perceived "special rights" of Indians, took center stage, protesting and intimidating the Chippewa by whatever means they could muster.

The scare headlines began with the "unlimited rights given Chippewa" headline following the 1983 *Voigt* decision. It continued into the next phase of the court rulings issued by Judge Barbara Crabb, who took over the case following Judge Doyle's death in 1987. In *LCO IV*, Crabb ruled that effective tribal regulation of the harvest precluded state regulation except to conserve a particular species or if there were a risk to public health or safety. In *LCO V* (1988), Crabb issued the "100 percent ruling"—that because "a modest standard of living" could not be gained from harvesting all the ceded territory resources, the Chippewa had the right to 100 percent of the harvestable quota of fish or deer.[13] While this never meant the right to harvest all of one species of fish in a given lake, many newspapers fanned the flames of prejudice with warnings of an end to walleye sportfishing for anglers.

The misreporting took Wisconsin down a dead-end road where there was no escape, no room for accommodation or compromise. Creating an atmosphere of fear and uncertainty, it suggested that the Chippewa were a threat to the "lifestyle" of northern Wisconsin residents and businesses. People were led to believe that the federal courts had "given" the Chippewa something special, something different from other citizens, and given it to them because they were poor, racial minorities. The court ruling was viewed by many northern editors as a temporary setback that would somehow be overturned or changed. Press throughout northern Wisconsin promoted the backlash's false hope that some future action by the courts or by legislation or by the state or federal administration would make this unwanted change disappear.

The initial reports by themselves were not entirely to blame. The reporters went to the same Wisconsin public schools as everyone else, which teach little Native American history, and even less about Wisconsin tribes and their histories, cultures, and treaties. Curriculum projects or higher education debates of Native issues were electives at best, something you learned about if you wanted to be an anthropologist or archeologist. Editors and reporters were unable to see the subtleties of the court rulings and to place them in any kind of historical context. Wisconsin citizens were ill-prepared to deal with victories or justice for minorities. In the case of Native victories, they were psychologically hindered because of the beliefs that Indians have long been defeated. The press, trained by the same institutions that have trained the public, simply could not understand and therefore was unable to report the facts. Native history is viewed as a thing of the past. People prefer to deal with dead Indians rather than live ones, especially if live ones have achieved any sort of recognition that establishes Native peoples as equals in power.

Misinformation threw hardwood fuel on the backlash fire. When Chippewa spearers took their year's allotted quota of fish from Star Lake on one night in 1988, WDNR Secretary "Buzz" Besadny decried the Lac du Flambeau spearers. "This goes to show that the Chippewa cannot manage the resource," Besadny crowed following the Star Lake spearing. Although the lake was not overfished by the Chippewa, Besadny's comments suggested overfishing, further inflaming an already militant anti-Indian north. These comments came just prior to a large rally by PARR in the city of Minocqua. Receiving uncritically information from WDNR spokespeople, the press reported Besadny's comments as fact. The reality was rather that a strict quota existed for each lake the Chippewa speared, one agreed to by both the state and the tribes, but because of the increasing intimidation and potential violence by anti-Indian protesters, the traditional method of small groups which fished many lakes seemed dangerous. LdF spearers decided that it would be safer to fish together, lake by lake. So even though the Chippewa indeed took the entire quota in one night, since they would not return to that particular lake, it was not overfished. It was simply fished more rapidly than anticipated by the WDNR. Nonetheless, the Chippewa received bad press because the quota system was not properly explained to the public.

Initially, anti-treaty groups produced their own pamphlets and held news conferences condemning the court ruling and calling for Congress to abrogate or modify the treaties. Since no other groups or institutions except the state were a part of the public debate, these anti-Indian groups became the de facto spokespeople for the sports groups and for other white citizens of the state. Media quickly elevated the anti-Indian groups into a prominent and therefore legitimate stature. PARR leaders were called and asked for a comment whenever a treaty or fish or tourism story would appear in the press: "Chippewa greed will deplete the resource. . . . Chippewa don't need the fish. . . . Those fish are wasted, thrown away in dumps or along the roadside." The state, who in reality was the other side against Chippewa rights, then assumed falsely the public role of mediators in what the media now called a racial dispute.

Where there was more open-minded media coverage (e.g., in Hayward near LCO, due largely to WOJB radio which aired all sides), there was less trouble at the boat landings. Where the information available was narrow in scope, there was trouble, as in the Minocqua area. Larry Greschner, an editor of *The Lakeland Times* in Minocqua and later a PARR official and PARR newspaper editor, legitimized the anti-Indian group he had helped form, and no one in the mainstream raised concerns about conflict of interest. Media members sympathetic to PARR and other reporters, by omission or ignorance of Chippewa culture and treaty history, created an abundance of anti-treaty coverage.

So, misinformation and calculated misreporting was the first force. It worked primarily because the other educational institutions had also failed to inform the public of the cultural and legal history of Native people. The state of Wisconsin also sent the wrong message to the public, suggesting that this legal anomaly would somehow be overturned and the status quo would resume. This first force, which initially confused the public, quickly began to anger them: misinformation built the anti-Indian movement. The anger against the Chippewa by a confused public was quickly woven into a tacit state policy. This policy was prelude to the second force: the attempt to win back at the boat landings what the state was unable to win in the courts.

The Second Force: Intimidation

Misinformation fell on receptive ears and was turned into hateful insults and threats thrown back at spearfishers and their families. Intimidation became the second force acting against Chippewa rights. In 1984, a flyer appeared in the employees mailboxes at the Ashland County Courthouse calling for open season on "Smokes" (Chippewa Indians). In the mid-1980s, LdF adult baseball teams were banned from northern Wisconsin league play because of resentments over off-reservation spearfishing (the excuses given were minor complaints about LdF playing field conditions, and, in one incident, playing the same aggressive style as the visiting off-reservation team). It was not unusual for insults and slurs to be pitched at LdF players by some non-Indian spectators. After Paul Mullaly lost a state senate race in 1984, ERFE faded and PARR began organizing large rallies against Chippewa treaty rights. Their tactic was to convince people that the treaty rights of the Chippewa people were threatening the resources; that the court rulings were an affront to "equal rights," and that through protests, the treaty rights could be changed. Despite racist protest signs and Indians hung in effigy, both common at PARR lake rallies in late 1980s, the Wisconsin backlash also had its non-tribal Indians, e.g., Hiram Valliere and Verna Lawrence, fronting the "equal rights"/smash the treaties effort.

PARR listed sixteen chapters in Wisconsin and was first identified as part of a larger national network in the 1985 report, *First Our Land, Now Our Treaties*, by C. Montgomery Johnson and Ann Quantock.[14] The report outlined the evolution of the national anti-treaty network and its ten-year plan to bring the issue of Native American treaties before Congress. The plan entailed focusing on local and state levels along the northern tier of the United States and building to a cumulative effort to shift the position of Congress to abrogate or modify the treaties.

State senator Dan Theno (R.–Ashland) and U.S. Congressman David Obey further legitimized the anti-Indian groups by downplaying the dispute's racial overtones, suggesting the real focus of the anger was over the illegitimacy of the treaties and that the anger wasn't being directed against the Chippewa but at the unfairness of the court ruling. Yet it was the Chippewa who were being taunted and threatened and then stoned, not the federal courts.

Obey also worked behind the scenes to silence treaty advocacy from any tribal organizations. I was public information officer with Great Lakes Indian Fish and Wildlife Commission (GLIFWC) in 1986 when Obey attacked Chippewa treaties through letters to the editor in northern Wisconsin newspapers. I sent a series of responses to the newspapers, challenging Obey's threat of sanctions against the tribes, which earned me a brief argument from Obey at a GLIFWC meeting that year. My next run-in with Obey occurred because of a Radioactive Waste Review Board meeting when state and federal officials were trying to site a high-level radioactive waste site in northern Wisconsin. When my turn came, I spoke to the crowd instead of the board, challenging the hypocrisy of politicians (including Obey) who supported nuclear production but not waste storage in their districts. Additional challenges from the other citizens there forced state senator Joe Strohl to shut down the meeting. The next week I was called before GLIFWC supervisors and fired. Congressman Obey not only got a letter notifying him of my firing, I believe he instigated it out of fear of my advocacy of treaties as the best environmental protection for all citizens in northern Wisconsin.

The anti-Indian protesters worked in tandem with state and federal policies of economic and political intimidation. First, misinformation was used to rile up the public—then the Chippewa were warned by government officials to "use restraint" in the exercise of treaty rights because "the public was so riled up." This technique was used most effectively by the lead negotiator for the state of Wisconsin in the mid-1980s—George Meyer, head of the WDNR's law enforcement division.

Following the initial ruling, Meyer headed up the state team that negotiated "interim" agreements with the Chippewa. The interim talks were to "provide a meaningful exercise of treaty rights" until there was a final decision from the courts. And, according to Meyer, they were also designed to begin preparing the public for the full exercise of the ceded territory treaty rights. In reality, they were used to keep the public confused and riled while new strategies to negate rights were being developed.

Through the effective use of media, the WDNR was able to keep the tribal negotiators off balance, leaking hard negotiating points to the press, which in

This "poster" was found in an Eagle River, Wisconsin, bar and also seen on car windows at boat landings. It's a clear picture of the violence associated with the protest of treaty rights.

turn put pressure on the tribal negotiators to soften their positions. Through selective use of the media whose editors sided with the state, Meyer was able to effectively characterize the Chippewa as resource terrorists. (In 1985, according to reporter John Sherer, the WDNR threatened three journalists with arrest if they went out in the spearing boats to do a story on this *new* Chippewa activity.) It was Meyer's job to find some moderate Indians so that he could wrest back control of the resources for the real people of Wisconsin. This Wisconsin "Ollie North" played both sides against the middle, but in the end aided in convincing the public that while the courts have ruled for treaties, "it is not something that they favor," and that they (the courts) will do whatever they can to reclaim control.

In many ways, Meyer represented the white male sports ethic during those initial years. Although he was an attorney and fully understood the legal position of the Chippewa, he was unable to translate that knowledge to an emotional level. Unable to accept what was legally correct, he was always searching for a way to regain the pre-1983 status quo. Had the WDNR instead opted to lead the citizens toward acceptance of the legal rights of the Chippewa, much of the subsequent intimidation and violence would have been minimized and certainly better controlled.

The Third Force: Scapegoating Wisconsin's Economic Fears

The next question for the Chippewa and our allies became, "Why have protesters turned so quickly to violence, to racism, to quick economic or social fixes?" "What are the underlying forces at work that allow these symptoms to continue?" Racism was merely a symptom that thrived in the atmosphere of misinformation and intimidation. The third—and probably most intractable —force at work in northern Wisconsin was the economy.

As national urban and industrial economic trends shifted, the consequences were felt across rural America. The same forces at work destroying rural America are at work in northern Wisconsin. Urban sprawl, real estate speculation, and agribusiness—rural gentrification—have displaced small, family farms. We have not just lost so many small farms. We have lost a part of rural culture and rural values. The forces behind this displacement find little value in rural culture. In fact, it's seen as sentimentality in the way of progress. Like the gentrification of old neighborhoods in urban centers, gentrification is occurring in rural America as real estate speculators, corporate marketeers, agribusiness, and timber interests bear down on communities.

Resort owners were facing recession times, but it was not from Chippewa spearing. New trends were emerging in vacationing—fewer fishing trips and more families seeking fancier accommodations or entertainments, for example, or the conversion of resorts to second homes. A 1981 Wisconsin Tourism Industry study said that resort problems were shown to increase with the age of the resort. Those that appear to be having the most significant problems, however, were built prior to 1930. Twenty-five percent of these resorts were shown to have declining occupancy trends. This may be attributable to the declining quality of these resorts due to their age and the fact that over 60 percent of their owners have not made any improvements or done upkeep since the resort was built.[15]

But this report didn't gain currency until the late 1980s. Before that, all that was heard in press, political, and anti-treaty circles was the serious impact Chippewa spearing would have on the livelihoods of Wisconsin's small resort owners.

The story Rick Whaley heard from a PARR member who ran a resort near Boulder Junction, Wisconsin, illuminates some of the connections between racism and economics. The man and his wife had fled Poland as a young couple, moving to France where he trained as a master in French cooking. They emigrated to Chicago. In the 1980s, they bought a resort on Boulder Lake, a Class A muskie lake in ceded territory. "Did you ever work with niggers?" this owner asked Rick while he was vacationing there in 1987 with his extended family, including his African-American daughter. "Well, I have," the immigrant went on. Remarks followed about how they won't give you an honest day's work, live on welfare, and steal. "Just like the Indians up here," he said. What was unusual about this couple as PARR recruits and resort owners was that they came so far to arrive at this relatively privileged and prejudiced position on America's social ladder. Not one generation in the United States, they were already living the American small-business dream, and hating those ethnic groups here for centuries, groups whose own rights and dreams are still not realized.[16]

Every logo seen on the new and widening highways heading into northern Wisconsin is a tombstone for small business, mom and pop resorts, and for rural culture and values. Maids are told that the reason they can't get the needed raise or the insurance plan they were promised is because we, the Chippewa, are disrupting the resort-tourism economy. Sportsmen and women are told that the reason the bag limits have been reduced is because of the Chippewa. Yet no one protests about fish too contaminated to eat, or Mercury Marine Motors, which kills tens of thousands of fish a year in the Fox River Valley.[17] Mom and pop resorts are told that money is tight and the expansion loan they need for their resort is not available, but if they wanted to sell a buyer could be found. Though lending institutions are not into the business of risky small business lending, real estate speculation in the developing northwoods gets a good return. Unable to afford to maintain their equipment or insurance, small loggers are increasingly squeezed out of the large-scale timber operations by multi-nationals. But loggers are *told* that the Chippewa claim to timber rights has frozen the market and that is why they are getting lower stumpage and fewer jobs. Counties are doing wholesale timbering, throwing out previous management plans, to get as much money out of the timber before the Chippewa have a chance at it. It is no wonder people at the boat landings want to throw rocks. People feel the heat of changing economic times, but because of misinformation and intimidation, they cannot see the forest for the trees.

The Chippewa were scapegoated because those responsible for environmental protection and resource management failed in their duties. When the courts affirmed the property interest of the Chippewa in natural resources in northern Wisconsin, those government officials and agencies were reluctant to shift policies and give the Chippewa their rightful role in co-management of resources. This reluctance was tied to mismanagement, especially in light of the mercury- and PCB-poisoned fishery in Wisconsin.[18] Refusal of co-management was also tied to existing sweetheart relationships with both the sports industries and with multinational timber interests. And it was tied to institutional racism, which prevented the state bureaucracy from accepting Native people as equals, with shared power.

Executive and legislative branches of government here in Wisconsin were responding to short-term economic gains and trends. Tied to corporate and large special-interest monies, elected officials were quick to use the supposed economic threat of Chippewa spearing as an excuse to cover failed government economic policy. Vulnerable small businesses were quick to seek easy answers without seeing the expense of long-term loss. Tribal officials and many tribal members, like their counterpart protesters who were poor or middle class, were vulnerable to misinformation, intimidation, and the influence of power, regardless of its source. Consequently, nearly everyone looked at the symptoms, searching for answers at the boat landings. It was another dead end. The problem was much larger than a handful of Chippewa spearing a few boatloads of poisoned fish. The larger problem required honest scrutiny, impossible in the midst of impending violence, of all that had an impact on the region's environment and economics. Without such a policy or plan to develop such a policy, the Chippewa remained the target. If we were forced off the lakes, like farmers were forced off the land, then rural culture would be lost. And if the Chippewa were no longer in the way, then the rest of rural culture in northern Wisconsin would soon follow.

Rural gentrification was one of the underlying forces that allowed the overt racism and violence to fester. But racism was a method that could be used only in an economic environment where people's tools and jobs were being threatened. Racism was used to deflect what was coming down the pike anyway, in economic trends or resource management policies. The anti-Chippewa backlash became just another form of community violence, violence turned against oneself, one's family, one's neighbors. And it became clear to Chippewa and their allies that the social healing and political solutions we sought also meant we had to address economics for ceded territory as a whole.

Butternut Lake, 1987

The initial efforts to intimidate the exercise of off-reservation rights between 1983 and 1987 had failed. Violence escalated however as the spearing seasons unfolded. Large mobs, often fueled by the liquid courage of nearby resort bars, traveled nightly to the boat landings. Rock throwing, sexual and racial taunts, gunshots, assassination threats against tribal judges, and boat ramming and boat swamping all became annual scenes that Chippewa spearers faced as they exercised their legal, constitutionally protected rights. By 1987, northern Wisconsin became a literal battleground: one group fighting to keep the Chippewa from exercising their rights; the other, the new warriors, not responding to the taunts and violence, but maintaining a degree of nonviolent resistance that was Gandhian in nature. With the crisis at Butternut Lake a turning point was reached for us, and we began to organize for intertribal and mainstream support.

Deep in the northwoods lay small driveways where spearers would back their vehicles and boat trailers in, unloading their fishing boats onto Wisconsin's walleye lakes. Some landings stand next to lake homes and private property, or in small towns like Minocqua. Most boat landings are out of town where rural county roads snake down to small parking lots by scenic inland waters. A small clearing around the driveway and parking lot, and the dark forest surrounding this, usually set the stage for the boat landing dramas to come. Out on the lakes at night, shining brightly (to the naked eye or gun scope), would be the white light of the spearer's headlamp as it searched the waters for the famous reflection of walleyed pike.

Netted by hilly woods and cottage homes, Butternut Lake lies about halfway between Lac du Flambeau (to its east) and Lac Courte Oreilles (to the west) in Price and Ashland counties in northwest Wisconsin. Lac du Flambeau spearing coordinator Tom Maulson anticipated trouble at Butternut Lake because it was in an area PARR had been organizing. He knew LdF would need support from other reservations, so he asked me and others to come there in 1987. The police and WDNR wardens were at the boat landing when spearers arrived. Nominally, the police turned away protesters but anti-treaty people parked down the road and streamed in through the woods. Soon a drunken mob, primed by misinformation and prejudice, was hurling insults and rocks at the Chippewa for two hours. Two Chippewa elders, Maggie Johnson and Shirley Miller, were pulled off of a truck and thrown to the ground. Few arrests were made and no convictions resulted. The anti-Chippewa hysteria had culminated in the most organized muscle flexing of the protest movement, and—with no state or local legal follow-up—they declared Butternut Lake their first boat landing victory.

Butternut Lake 1987 made it imperative for us to build, the way Washington state had, an intertribal and mainstream support for a pro-treaty politics in

Wisconsin. The police weren't going to help. Neither were most state politicians. Were there people who would do something about misinformation's false witness against Chippewa neighbors? Would citizens, if not the state, respond to the rock throwing and intimidation of more promised violence? And who would step forward with some kind of vision of reconciliation and economics that made sense to northern Wisconsin?

Notes

1. Canadian policies, although similar, have some differences as they apply to Native people, including our Chippewa relatives.

2. Jackson, president from 1829–1837, said defiantly of the Supreme Court ruling, "John Marshall has rendered his opinion. Now let him enforce it."

3. Behind the push to make the Menominee reservation a county was a desire to privatize and "modernize" the successful and sustainable lumber mill there, and to gain access to the Menominee's extensive and well-managed timber lands.

4. An interesting sidebar to P.L. 280 was the legalization of liquor sales to "Indians." This was viewed by some as an extension of full citizenship to Native people —tribes could now choose to regulate liquor sales or continue to ban it themselves. Others viewed it as a setback, a return to "chemical warfare," i.e., an invitation to alcohol dependency.

5. Lurie was an expert witness in a landmark case (*Gurnoe*, 1972) where the Wisconsin Supreme Court upheld Chippewa fishing rights in Lake Superior.

6. Information in this paragraph is from the *Milwaukee Journal's* series on treaty rights by reporters Dennis McCann and Don Behm, October 14–17, 1984.

7. Rudolph C. Ryser, "Anti-Indian Movement on the Tribal Frontier" (Center for World Indigenous Studies, P.O. Box 82038, Kenmore, WA, 98028. April, 1991), p. 29.

8. *Milwaukee Journal*, December 7, 1984, cited in Ryser, "Anti-Indian Movement," p. 30.

9. Ryser, "Anti-Indian Movement," p. 31.

10. This section is directly indebted to Rudolph Ryser's valuable booklet, "Anti-Indian Movement on the Tribal Frontier," cited above. Used with permission.

11. Gottlieb, a convicted tax felon, is head of the Citizens Committee for the Right to Keep and Bear Arms in Washington state, and a member of the board of directors of the American Freedom Coalition, a Rev. Sun Myung Moon front in Washington, D.C. Gottlieb is a fundraiser for national anti-environmental and anti-Indian rights causes.

12. NCSIT was designed as a tribal government-controlled support group, primarily funded by churches and non-Indian allies. I rejected this as a model for the Midwest because I didn't want any support group controlled by tribal governments.

13. For fish, this was to be regulated by *total allowable catch* which meant about 7 percent of the adult fish in a given lake was set aside for tribal harvests. 28 percent was for the sports fishers, and 65 percent was left for maintenance of the fish stocks.

The Chippewa have never come close to harvesting what they would be allowed in this ruling, taking about 4 percent of Wisconsin's total walleye annual catch and less that 1 percent of the state's deer harvest. The tribes negotiated a series of interim agreements with the state WDNR to set walleye harvest levels each spring. In March 1989, Crabb ruled in *LCO IV* that a stricter measure, *safe harvest level,* would be used to determine the number of fish spearers and anglers would share. Tribes set 60 percent of the maximum as their quota for spearing lakes, but rarely took this much, thus keeping lakes open for anglers.

14. PARR chapters in Wisconsin included Park Falls, Wausau, Ashland, Minocqua, Sturtevant, Wabeno, Green Bay, Plymouth, Land O' Lakes, Rhinelander, Stanley, Butternut, Abbotsford, Neenah, and Antigo, and one near Ontonagon, Michigan. PARR also continued to build organizational and national legitimacy through its Washington state and ICERR connections. Listed as associate members of PARR (in vol. 1, no. 4, Spring 1987, PARR newsletter) were the Jemez River Basin Water Users of New Mexico; the North Dakota Committee for Equality, in New Town, North Dakota; the Port Washington Property Owners, of Suquamish, Washington; Concerned Citizens Council, in Winnebego, Nebraska; All Citizens Equal, Polson, Montana; Totally Equal Americans, in Ponsford, Minnesota; Alaskan Constitutional Legal Defense Fund, Anchorage, Alaska; Saginaw Valley Steelheaders, Saginaw, Michigan; the Manono County Landowners Association, Sloan, Iowa; and the Landowners Against Negligent Claims, Wagner, South Dakota. C. Montgomery Johnson and Ann Quantock, *First Our Land, Now Our Treaties* (Hadlock, WA: Montgomery, Johnson and Assoc., 1985).

15. Wisconsin Department of Tourism (Madison, 1981), quoted in Jim Thannum, "1990 Chippewa Spearing Season—Conflict and Cooperation—The Two Wisconsins," p. 17 (Odanah: GLIFWC, 1990).

16. By the early 1990s, this couple had sold their Boulder Lake resort and bought a new establishment in Wisconsin Dells, formerly sacred land to the Winnebago and now greener pastures for the tourist, weekend partyers, and dog racing crowd.

17. Mercury Marine tests their boat engines in the Fox River, creating carbon monoxide emissions from the incomplete burning of 1200–1400 gallons of gasoline a day. Fish die at a rate of 37,000 per season in the 1.25 kilometer-stretch by their plant. No state laws govern carbon monoxide poisoning of water and no tests for this apparently exist, except testing the blood of suffocating fish. Kenneth S. McIntosh, "Mercury Marine Killing in Fox River," *Green Net,* April–May 1992. See also Charles Friederich, "Firm blamed in Fox fish kills," *Milwaukee Journal,* September 7, 1988.

18. The Wisconsin DNR had issued (October 1988) warnings on over 100 lakes and rivers in northern Wisconsin where game fish were contaminated with mercury. Lakes and streams in southern Wisconsin had fish advisories because of PCB contamination.

PART II

Spearfishers and Witnesses

The Beginning of a Nonviolent Coalition

ISHKIGAMIZIGE GISISS
(The Sap Running Moon)

Witness in Our Own Backyard
*The First Year the Witness Joins the
Spearfishers, 1988*

Rick Whaley

THE REACTION TO *VOIGT* by non-Indians in northern Wisconsin was "like a train hitting a wall—that's the social dynamic," said George Meyer, head of Wisconsin's Department of Natural Resources (WDNR) Division of Enforcement. In one of the first years of spearing, WDNR wardens had to hold back protesters at North Twin Lake. To get ready for the following year's spearfishing, the WDNR sought to involve local law enforcement at the landings. "You should have heard the language at the first meeting about protecting Indians," said Meyer, "but they [northern Wisconsin sheriffs] agreed to do it."[1] The WDNR also sent out hundreds of letters to civic and religious leaders and sports folks saying the resources, under the agreement between the state and the Chippewa, would not be harmed by spearing, and asking people to help keep the peace.

But the media coverage in 1987, especially the headlines on how many fish were being speared, heated popular resentment to the boiling point, brewing trouble for the closing night of spearing. Here is Meyer's account of the 1987 Butternut Lake incident:

[WDNR had] one sheriff's deputy and ten conservation wardens. Early in the night there were about two hundred people who had been drinking for about three to four hours that night. They were anti-Indian types from Park Falls. And out on the breakwater, Chippewa spearfishers were putting their boats into the water and non-Indians approached. We had been trying to calm them down by walking [through the crowd], to get them to clean up their act because there were young children. . . . A four-year-old's father had been spouting some of the most evil rhetoric you'd ever want to hear. And I remember this four-year-old pulling on his Daddy's pants leg saying, "Daddy, Daddy don't say those things." His reaction, to his wife, was "Get the kid out of here. . . ." We [WDNR] weren't successful in trying to dissuade the situation. . . . The eleven law enforcement officers and I put our bodies in the way [when protesters approached the breakwater] to prevent the non-Indians from going at the Indians.[2]

Meyer thought the three main causes of the difficulty were prejudice, Judge Crabb's 100 percent ruling, and the view that special rights cuts against the grain of the American concept of equality. Meyer argued that, overall, the state's role was to recognize the treaties and recognize the needs of those non-Indians affected by the treaties.

Chippewa activists and tribal negotiators saw the state of Wisconsin as the primary political mover against treaty rights, with the hostilities brewing at the boat landings as a nasty spin-off that the state had helped engender. To northern Wisconsin audiences, Meyer appeared to take a "treaties are the law, *but . . .*" stance that gave sport hunters and fishers, and northern editorial writers, the impression that the state's annual interim agreements with the Chippewa on off-reservation deer and fish harvests were but necessary stopgaps until political pressure or the courts reversed treaty rights. While the state of Wisconsin argued vociferously in appealing the *Voigt* decision that these treaty rights didn't exist, the state also made overtures offering the Chippewa money if they would limit their exercise of off-reservation rights. "As a tribal member, I attended the [Red Cliff] tribal meeting in January [1988] where the [Atty. Gen.] Hanaway proposal was outlined to tribal members," said Walt Bresette in February 1988. "The framework of the proposal [was] this: the state of Wisconsin will acknowledge that treaty rights exist if tribal members agree to limit the exercise of those rights . . . If the tribes accept that framework *then* detailed negotiations will ensue. If you give up spearing rights, as an example, you'll get more compensation than if you give up other rights . . . articulated by Judge Doyle."[3]

The Beginning of the Nonviolent Witness

On January 2, 1988, Walt Bresette spoke to seventy people at a "Peace on Earth Social" sponsored by Our Communities Are Up to Us and the Upper Great Lakes Green Network at Pentecost Lutheran Church in Milwaukee. The Peace on Earth gathering was an annual, community-based event in the Sherman Park neighborhood designed to celebrate the holidays and look at the true meaning of peace on earth and good will to others. It was hosted by myself (Rick), my wife Ellen Smith, Charles Crawford, Lillian Karkoski, Sierra Powers, and Bea Blank. At this Milwaukee meeting, Walt talked about the fear and anger he felt as the father of three young children when he saw protest signs that said "Save a Walleye, Spear an Indian." Walt emphasized the dangers of violence spearers and families faced in 1987 and would face again come spring 1988.

Walt told of a late 1987 awards ceremony sponsored by the Wisconsin Community Fund where he listened to Congressman Robert Kastenmeier talk about failed U.S. policies in Central America. Walt had been reminded of another time when people sought help, and a group in Madison joined the Black Hills Alliance. At that same time of support for the Black Hills, Native people were under attack for commercial fishing on Lake Superior and Lake Michigan. Exxon was beginning to make noises about a major minerals development in northern Wisconsin near one of the Chippewa Reservations. Why did people choose to go so far away to show support for others? At that awards ceremony in 1987 and again now in 1988, Walt implored, "You don't have to go all way to Nicaragua to witness, you can witness in your own backyard." He asked people to come north to the spring boat landings in a manner similar to the Witness for Peace in contra-attacked areas of Nicaragua.

Following the Peace on Earth social, supporters and interested people met and talked. We formed the Witness for Non-Violence for Treaty and Rural Rights in Northern Wisconsin. Sierra Powers and John Okolowicz were elected co-spokespeople for the Witness. University student Jim Young and retired professor Don Rasmussen joined the steering committee. Dorothy Thoms, Anita Koser, and Dick Watkins of United Indians became the first Native American witness supporters in Milwaukee. Dorothy and Anita, who had taken a course on Chippewa treaties from Roger Thomas (director of the Indian Community School in Milwaukee) in the early 1980s, also joined the Witness steering committee.

The Witness responded first to this issue of violence and racism. "We were driving up north with my father," remembered Sarah Backus, a nursery school teacher/director, "when my daughter [Samantha Whitefeather] saw a bumper sticker that said something about Indians. She said, 'Catch up, Grandpa. I want to read it. It says something about me.' We caught up to the car and read it. It said something like 'Save Two Walleyes, Spear a Pregnant Squaw.' My daughter was crushed. . . . That's why I got involved. This is about my kids and their future." We in the Witness set out to inform ourselves of treaty history and court cases, fish statistics, spearing's impact on tourism, and other environmental and economic issues in rural, northern Wisconsin.

Within two months of our formation, the Witness joined with the Lutheran Human Relations Association, southeast Wisconsin ministers, and Native American activists in protesting the second national PARR Convention in Racine, Wisconsin, February 18–20, 1988.

And we had much success. Two hundred people marched to protest PARR's presence in Racine that weekend. PARR had hoped to further the anti-treaty cause in Wisconsin and nationally. The convention's featured speaker was David Yamashita, an attorney from Washington state who helped draft Initiative 456 and the proposed presidential commission to review U.S. treaties with Native nations. The convention created the Citizens Equal Rights Alliance (CERA), the new national umbrella for the anti-Native rights movement. But unlike the 1987 PARR national conference in Wausau, Wisconsin, which PARR pronounced a huge success, attendance at the second convention was, for them, disappointingly low. Larry Peterson declined the chairmanship and PARR's vice-chair didn't even show up.[4] PARR tried to walk the line between putting on a non-racist face to lobby government officials, on the one hand, and, on the other, dealing with increased demands from within to escalate the boat landing protests.

What About the Fish?

The Sentinel Sports Show in March of 1988 provided the Witness with its first opportunity to look deeper into the issue of fish. Sponsored annually by the *Milwaukee Sentinel* newspaper in Milwaukee, the show features activities and exhibits to promote vacationing, fishing, hunting, and motorboating in northern Wisconsin.

The northern Wisconsin press had continued to trumpet the perception that tourism was declining because of off-reservation harvesting, and WDNR emphasized declining tourism as a legitimate concern of non-Indians in the northwoods.

The Witness put together a leaflet emphasizing the commonality of Native Americans and European-Americans in Wisconsin: a love of the land, a concern for resources and the impact of pollution, a sense of fair play, family traditions, and opposition to racism and violence. We found out about the fish harvest from WDNR and the Great Lakes Indian Fish and Wildlife Commission (GLIFWC), which was mandated to keep strict records of this harvest. We discovered, and put in the leaflet, that Chippewa spearers in 1987 took only 2 percent of the state's walleye fish harvest and 1.5 percent of the state's muskie (muskellunge) fish take. This represented only 26 percent of what they could have legally taken under the negotiated quota with WDNR. Chippewa hunters harvested off-reservation 2,837 deer, about 1 percent of the state's total and far less than the number of deer killed by automobiles every year in Wisconsin. A 1987 survey by Jack Grey at University of Wisconsin Extension found that only 8.3 percent of northern Wisconsin tourists said they came to fish, but it remained unclear what impact off-reservation spearing or the protests had on numbers of summer tourists.

Equal Rights vs. Property Rights

The Witness also began to look into the question of equal rights versus treaty rights. When the Chippewa, in the 1800s, ceded the land that is now the northern third of Wisconsin to the U.S. government, they retained the right to hunt, fish, and gather wild rice on off-reservation land as well as on the reservations. This arrangement is akin to the property rights tradition where one could sell or lease one's land to another party, but still retain water or mineral rights on that land. The federal courts have upheld and continually reiterated that Chippewa off-reservation harvesting rights are, in fact, property rights and entitled to protection as such.

The property right to harvest off-reservation, guaranteed in the treaties that excluded all Chippewa mineral rights, was not a question of "equal protection of the laws" (14th Amendment) or equality of opportunity. Protester arguments that Chippewa rights were "special privileges" or "unequal rights" were really attempts to put Indians back on the reservation and break up their

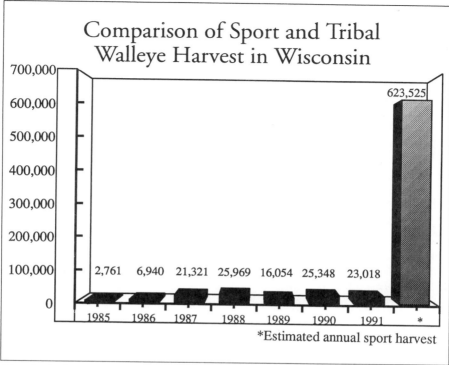

Comparison of Sport and Tribal Walleye Harvest in Wisconsin

623,525

700,000
600,000
500,000
400,000
300,000
200,000
100,000
0

2,761   6,940   21,321   25,969   16,054   25,348   23,018

1985   1986   1987   1988   1989   1990   1991   *

*Estimated annual sport harvest

Note: Angler harvest column at right is the estimated *yearly* angler take, to be compared to the separate yearly spearing harvests.
Source: Great Lakes Indian Fish and Wildlife Commission (GLIFWC).

political rights, if not the reservation system itself. Beyond the differences about rights was the fundamental question: Does (white) America honor its word or would it merely break another treaty when some found its conditions inconvenient? Felix Cohen, the renowned scholar on American Indian law, had called Native rights the miner's canary of American democracy. Like the canary taken into the mines to forewarn miners of the presence of toxic fumes, the rights of Native people in Wisconsin were sagging and the signal to do something was apparent.

The 1850 Presidential Removal Order, which occasioned Chief Buffalo's great sojourn to Washington, D.C., had given the protest movement grounds for denying any and all Chippewa rights in modern Wisconsin. However, President Fillmore, in 1852, had agreed to rescind the Removal Order and end all attempts to remove the *Anishinabe* from Wisconsin. The outpouring of support then for the Chippewa staying in Wisconsin, including prominent European-American citizens and the state of Wisconsin itself, sealed the agreement. The Chippewa also made the right to permanent reservations in Wisconsin a condition of the

1854 treaty negotiations that yielded that last of the mineral-rich lands to the United States.[5] By restricting spearing to the reservations, the modern anti-Indian backlash, with the state of Wisconsin on its side, sought to deny the validity of off-reservation rights laid out in the treaties.

Sovereignty

PARR Chairman Larry Peterson expounded that Native American sovereignty was a fabricated concept and that Chippewa treaty rights were created by "ludicrous court decisions" catering to Indian greed. PARR regularly cited Chief Justice Marshall's 1831 reference to Native tribes as "domestic dependent nations" to deny the existence of sovereignty or obligations to Native nations today. While Chief Justice Marshall did note this "peculiar" relationship—tribes are nations within a nation—Marshall and the U.S. Supreme Court ruled that the Cherokee Nation constituted "a distinct political society" that was capable of managing its own affairs and had "unquestionable rights to their land." According to Marshall, the domestic dependent status of Native nations did not preclude treaty making by tribes with the United States or lessen America's obligation to uphold treaty commitments.[6]

Stan Webster, an Oneida Nation member and then director of the Wisconsin Indian Resource Council, spoke at a February 20, 1988, Witness public meeting in Milwaukee. Stan reiterated the constitutional basis for the sanctity of treaties. The U.S. Constitution gave the federal government the prerogative of treaty making: Article II, Sec. 2 (the President with consent of Senate makes treaties); Article I, Sec. 8 (Congressional authority to "regulate Commerce with foreign Nations, and among several states, and with the Indian tribes"); and Article I, Sec. 10 (prohibits any state government from entering into treaties). Most importantly, Article VI of the Constitution states that "the Constitution, and the laws of the United States . . . and all Treaties made, or which shall be made, under the Authority of the United States, shall be the supreme Law of the Land." This article accords treaties respect equal to that given federal laws and superior to state laws. They thus preempt state laws or constitutions should a conflict arise. This law formed the basis of the government-to-government relationship between the Native nations and the United States.

Webster quoted the following passage:

> Indian nations made treaties with the United States just as they had with each other long prior to white contact, as they did with other European powers. The Indian nations viewed treaties as covenants, as moral statements which could not be broken unless by mutual consent. Tribes were recognized as independent, sovereign, separate nations, and treaties made with them were negotiated between equals as with any foreign nation.
>
> The purpose of these intergovernmental contracts was not to give rights to the Indians—rights which as sovereign nations they already possessed—but to

remove from them certain rights which they already had. In treaty making, tribes were the grantors and the United States the recipient, and rights were granted to the United States **by or from** Indian nations. Treaties limited only the **external** sovereign powers of Indian tribes—tribes agreed, for example, not to make treaties or go to war against foreign nations. Treaties did not affect internal or self-governing powers of Indian nations. Furthermore, rights to land, water, hunting, government, etc., which were not expressly granted away by the tribes in a treaty, or taken away by a later federal statute, were reserved by that tribe, and did not diminish with the passage of time or changes in technology.[7]

Nonviolent Witness Training

Sheriffs in northern Wisconsin announced in late March 1988, that they would be trained in riot-control techniques in preparation for the expected protests at Chippewa spring spearing. Press in Wisconsin talked about the "treaty problem" and what could be done to solve it. PARR leaders disclaimed the racism and violence of the previous year's Butternut Lake incident, but plans were being laid by protest militants to disrupt spearers while they were out on the lakes. Stop Treaty Abuse–Wisconsin (STA–W), formed in 1987 to fundraise through sales of (anti-) "Treaty Beer," began to coalesce the most aggressive strategies and rhetoric against spearing rights. Politicians not already outspoken against treaties remained silent, with a few exceptions like Milwaukee state representative Marcia Coggs, who spoke out publicly for Chippewa rights. In such an atmosphere, what kind of nonviolent model would be effective for what the Witness was about to embark upon? What particulars did we have to figure out for ourselves in our struggle? And could we intervene without escalating tensions and making life worse for Chippewa and European-Americans in northern Wisconsin?

Pledge of Resistance trainer Marylou LaMonda, peace activist Bea Blank, and I put together the initial witness trainings we needed in March and April of 1988. The Witness was not planning civil disobedience challenges—one of our roles was to make sure that assault and battery laws as well as Chippewa rights were being upheld. We wouldn't carry signs or wear political pins, so that we might encourage dialoging when possible, instead of creating arguments or a counterdemonstration. Like the Witness for Peace in Nicaragua, we hoped to be a peaceful, nonconfrontational presence in the midst of tension (or worse), documenting what happened and trying to shed light on the situation. Like the Big Mountain Witness in summer 1986, where hundreds of national volunteers helped prevent the forced relocation of the Dine (Navajo) from the Joint Use Area, we hoped to bring enough people north to prevent the extinguishing of Chippewa treaty rights because of mob violence and intimidation.

The goals of the first Witness training were: to do something about the boat landing violence; to build a broad base of statewide support for treaty rights; to establish trust with the tribes; and to bridge with local Native American issues (e.g., support for trust status for the Indian Community School in the face of neighborhood opposition, and support for the Indian Summer Pow-Wow's alliance with environmentalists). Clergy and Laity Concerned (Eugene, Oregon) shared the guidelines for supporter sensitivity toward Native culture, which were developed by the Big Mountain Legal Defense/Offense Committee. Witness trainings used role plays based on the hassle lines we'd seen in the "Practice of Peace" video, developed by Phyllis and Richard Taylor of Philadelphia, founders of Witness for Peace. We stressed the need for group discipline and individual centering so witness participants would not strike back or flee rough situations. Where the Big Mountain solidarity effort prepared people for a desert witness, we had to prepare people for the logistics of very cold, late winter weather.

The Witness was asked: Why go up north when there is more violence in Milwaukee in a week than anti-treaty protesters can promise in a whole year? Our position was that while the causes of violence in the cities are systemic— poverty, drugs, joblessness—the violence is random. Organized hate groups were not operating with the tacit support of government officials going out at night and openly attacking African-Americans. If the governor would not invoke the hate crimes law to stop people from *shooting bullets* at spearfishers, why would he ever use hate crimes laws to protect women from violence or Black students on campus from harassment. If treaty rights were negated by mob violence and state inaction, we would all suffer from the momentum of growing social backlash politics.

The commitment to the principle of nonviolence came first and foremost from the Chippewa spearers stance of nonretaliation and their call for allies. People at the Witness trainings also called upon their religious backgrounds (such as the story and tradition of the Good Samaritan), their politics (nonviolence is one of the key values of the Greens), or their personal sense of neighborliness and fair play. Part of the training was devoted to a circle of sharing in which people talked about other historical examples of nonviolent, political action: Gandhi's Salt campaign; Milwaukee's open housing marches; the day Sojourner Truth stopped a lynching by singing to the lynch mob. Neighborhood block club leader Charles Crawford told of the time in Kansas when he, inspired by the then-current work of Dr. Martin Luther King, Jr., refused to sit on the Black-only side of the bus station waiting room. He persistently took down the cord separating the two races, until he was arrested. Like those struggles of the past, our witness sought to empower those who participated, empower those oppressed by mob violence and prevailing state policy, and touch the hearts of others, including those acting as opposition.

What would we do if protesters charged to attack us? Take the blows. Don't fight back. Fall to the ground if necessary. Should we hold hands or put arms around each other for protection? Witness (and PARR re-enactor in the training role play) Sarah Backus said, "If I saw witnesses holding hands in a circle, it would feel like 'us and them.'" Were we trying to win arguments at the landing? We wanted to share information we were learning about fish and treaties, but not convey an attitude of having an answer for everything. We were more interested in absorbing anger and in listening and learning from people there. We would not try to dialogue with anyone who was drunk. If the police told us to leave because we were illegally assembled, what would we do? We were not seeking arrest, but knew it might happen if police arrested everyone at a landing, or told us to leave but not the protesters.

One of the key political questions was: would we still do our witness if the tribes did not invite us to come? This remained a difficult question, even through the spearing season, since tribes and churches that supported treaty rights did not then endorse the Witness. We decided to go because Bresette had urged us to and because we knew that other European-American supporters in northern Wisconsin were also going to try to get to landings this year. We went because racism is a problem created by whites and we, as political European-Americans, needed to take a stand on this environmental and justice issue affecting us all. Hence, it was critical for us to find someone, some group in ceded territory to host us—to open the way for us politically, not to mention guide us to the lakes and landings in the far outreaches of northern Wisconsin.

Treasures: Finding Allies and Hosts, The Northwoods Connections

Driving north and stopping at a local tavern and asking, "Where are the Chippewa spearing? We're the peace people from Milwaukee," didn't seem like such a good idea, so we searched for the northwoods connection to what was happening (and where these spearing lakes were). Despite the predominately anti-spearing sentiment, several small pro-treaty organizations had formed in support of Indians' rights. Through the pro-treaty and Green grapevine, we had heard the story of Linda (Cree) Dunn[8] and a handful of people trying to get to Butternut Lake in 1987. The police had stopped them on the road and said they weren't allowed at the landing. All the while, PARR protesters had streamed in through the woods to create the first of many protester near-riots.

After this incident, Linda and others formed Citizens for Treaty Rights (CTR) in the fall of 1987. Linda had recently moved to the Eagle River area, not far from Minocqua and Lac du Flambeau, with her forester husband and their children. "I believed in what the treaties said," she asserted. "Even if I didn't believe it, I would still do something about the scenes at the boat landings. I can't believe neighbors would stand by and let the Chippewa be badgered and bullied for exercising legal rights. If you don't stand up [to] this, then it will be done to someone else's rights."

One of the first activities CTR participated in was a Thanksgiving 1987 feast on the Bad River Reservation where Chippewa and European-Americans enjoyed food and listened to Chippewa drumming together. The Thanksgiving Feast was hosted by Support Treaties Organization of Peoples (STOP), the first grassroots treaty organization, founded by Katie Lemieux and based on the Bad River Reservation. She had worked with the American Indian Movement in the 1970s and hooked up with Walt when he was picketing Governor Thompson on his visit north in early 1987. Walt remembers Katie telling him, "You looked pitiful." So Katie joined Bresette and local Greens in their next action—a takeover of the Ashland City Council to protest the council's anti-treaty resolution in summer of 1987.

On April 10, 1988, CTR helped organize a tree planting ceremony at Lac du Flambeau for the Day of Renewal and Reconciliation. CTR presented LdF with a Peace Quilt they and other supporters made. In attendance at this event was Rose Mary (Robinson) Korbisch who had formed with Theresa Selenske and Gale Demlow the first non-Indian treaty support group, Orenda (from the Iroquois word for "spirit" or "life"). These rural homemakers from the Birnamwood area in central Wisconsin had gone back to college and had studied treaty rights for a debate in one of their courses. Their interest in Native American cultures and their support for treaty rights continued beyond the classroom as they studied further and held information meetings in their community.

Rose Mary had also served on the jury that convicted Posse Comitatus leader James Wickstrom.[9] Her interest in white supremacy movements such as Posse Comitatus and the emerging treaty rights issue lead her to a PARR meeting in 1986. "That summer PARR was invited to . . . the sportsman's group in Langlade County, to a meeting," she recounts. "So I went up."

> Larry Peterson [was there] and this man from Rhinelander was introduced as a treaty expert. . . . I took notes during the meeting and made little sounds here and there, when they talked about welfare [and Indians]. I said, "Well, that isn't right," so I questioned that—there was maybe thirty people there and I think twenty-five of them were PARR people already. But this man got up, and he was talking about the 1884 Intercourse Act . . . that federal law that there is to be no intercourse between Indians and non-Indians. And he said, "If that's the case, why are there so many little dilutes running around." And I just lost it. I couldn't believe it. I couldn't believe that anyone could be so ignorant. . . . And I got up and I let them have it with both barrels [verbally]. When I got done, an older gentleman stood up, and he was sitting on the side, and he said, "Why

don't you go back to the reservation where you came from?" I got up and said, "I thought this was equal rights and protect the resources. This is all treaty stuff. Why don't you do some reading and find out the truth?" I had to go through the bar area to get out 'cause I was so mad by that time I didn't know where the outside exit was."

The three women in Orenda, known to spearers as the three amigos [sic] from Antigo, had been at the boat landings in 1987 where the storm of prejudice and protest was beginning to gather.

Experienced ally help also came to this Wisconsin indigenous struggle from people involved in support work for Indian refugees from the undeclared wars in Central America. Blake Gentry and Laurie Melrood worked with the Madison Border Support Group and had been to the Chippewa reservations with indigenous families from Guatemala—Quiche (pronounced *key chày*) and Cakchiquel (pronounced *kokcheekol*) refugees. Blake, along with Bob Kasper of Madison Earth First! and Lenny Kanter, would come to witness what was happening to indigenous people in 1988 in northern Wisconsin. Blake co-founded and worked with Madison Treaty Rights Support Group (MTRSG), formed in October 1987, in part to monitor and counter PARR's efforts. MTRSG was doing educational work around the federal court trial and the role the state was playing against the Chippewa. In 1988, they approached Bishop Desmond Tutu, when he visited Wisconsin, with concerns about the treatment of the Chippewa.

Shortly before spearing was to start, Linda Cree of CTR took three Milwaukee Witness coordinators (Sierra Powers, Bruce Hinkforth, and myself) to meet with LdF tribal judge Tom Maulson, who was also an important spear-fishing leader. We explained what the Witness was and what we hoped to do and asked for his okay. Judge Maulson welcomed the idea. He also recommended that, yes, we wear armbands at the landings so the spearers would know who was friend and who was foe. Later, at a meeting during the Tree of Peace weekend with other spearers and soon-to-be witnesses, Maulson articulated the spearers' position: "This is our right. If we don't use it, we'll lose it. You [witnesses] are not fighting this for us. It's for our kids and grandkids. You are not going to make it worse for us." In late March, Citizens for Treaty Rights extended the formal invitation to the Witness to come north in 1988 and be part of the off-reservation, nonviolent, observer presence at the boat landings.

An eagle flew over the Lake Minocqua boat landing on Sunday morning April 17 as Walt Bresette lead a talking circle for members of CTR and witness participants at the Upper Great Lakes Green Network Gathering. It was the day before LdF's two week spearing season opened. People shared their hopes for a peaceful spearing season, the wish for understanding with their neighbors and, for one downstater, "a chance to return to the part of the state I grew up in, to come back as more than just a tourist, and learn a little and give back a little to places I remember fondly."

STOP, Orenda, CTR, border support people, and other northwoods Native, peace and Green activists were the first of many organizations and individuals that joined with the downstate Witness to go to the landings to be in solidarity with nonviolent conflict resolution and the honoring of treaties.

The Boat Landings

Despite the difficulties the previous year, Chippewa spearers returned to Butternut Lake to open the 1988 Lac du Flambeau spearing season Monday, April 18. This time police blocked off the parking lot with yellow crime tape and allowed only spearers' vehicles in to unload their boats and equipment. (The only vehicles allowed to stay in the parking lot were vehicles of the one hundred police present.) In the middle of the lot was a giant spotlight to be used once it got dark. As the sun set, protesters, Chippewa families, and witnesses parked our cars along the road that led to and past the boat landing. Those arriving later had to walk in a half mile or farther in darkness on the road with only a few police.

A handful of CTR members and a few of us Milwaukee witnesses who stayed over from the Green Gathering joined journalists, including Walt Bresette, and a growing crowd of protesters. "You're taking notes on us?" a young man said to me. I put away my notepad and talked for a while with this laid-off mill worker. He was worried about the impact of spearing on this lake and about the tourist economy in general. Another protester came over briefly to our conversation to angrily say that spearing wasn't the sporting way to take fish.

Later in the evening, as the darkness and the cold set in hard, young teens from Park Falls came in to stand menacingly near the Chippewa families down by the lakeshore. Carrying on the tradition from 1987, they heckled spearers with remarks about their long hair: "Look at the braids on that one." Two young Chippewa women came down to talk to a relative next to the witnesses and not far from the clutch of Park Falls teenagers. "Someone tried to run us over on the road," they said excitedly. "He sideswiped a van too. The police got him."

According to press accounts the next day, Dean Crist, STA founder and treaty beer entrepreneur, had clipped the sideview mirror off of a spearer's van parked up on the road: "The van was struck by a pickup truck that witnesses [on the scene, not treaty witnesses] said had earlier just missed hitting two teenage Chippewa girls."[10] Crist was arrested for disorderly conduct, reckless operation of a vehicle and hit and run to an attended parked vehicle.[11] Protester John Bablick, Jr., of Butternut, driving slowly, had hit a sheriff's deputy, knocking the deputy onto the hood of the car. He was only charged with disorderly conduct. That night witnesses walked with Chippewa families who asked to be escorted back to their cars.

The confrontations and intimidation tactics of protesters escalated as the two-week spearing season progressed. Gunshots were heard on Little St. Germain Lake (April 21) as the Chippewa speared. That same night a bottle rocket was exploded over boats on Big St. Germain Lake in an effort to intimidate spearers. Protesters took to boats this year for the first time to create wakes to unbalance spearing boats and disturb spawning beds, so the Chippewa could not harvest all they wanted (and were entitled to). Tom Maulson complained mightily to the WDNR to do something to stop the lake harassment during opening night at Butternut Lake, but George Meyer of the WDNR's enforcement division said the protest activities were not illegal.[12] On April 21, the state of Wisconsin denied the Lac du Flambeau tribe's request to clear the lakes of protesters whose sole purpose was to disrupt spearing. The state WDNR added more wardens and some citations were issued to boat protesters (e.g., Plum Lake, April 21, and Big Arbor Vitae Lake, April 24).

On Sunday night, April 24, PARR held a rally at a tavern near Big Arbor Vitae Lake where Chippewa were to spear. Joining PARR and STA–W leaders there was former Iran hostage, Kevin Hermening of Wausau, a Republican candidate for the 7th congressional district against David Obey. According to a CTR witness there:

> It was crazy. Crowds of people were following the Chippewa everywhere they went, taunting them on shore, on the docks. The police were there but could barely restrain the crowd. You didn't know what was going to happen. Fifty to seventy people following the spearers around . . . making fun of the tobacco ceremony at the beginning . . . and saying things like, "When you get all those fish, you can get off welfare."
>
> The spearers gather together on the dock and sing "My Country 'Tis of Thee." The crowd doesn't know what to do with that. They back off. Then along comes Kevin Hermening waving an American flag with a crowd of PARR protesters behind him. . . . He gets in a boat [with Crist] and goes out on the lake to confront spearers. There's three DNR boats and four spearing boats. Wherever the unprotected spearing boat is, the protester's boats race over to and harass.[13]

Different traditions about fishing did motivate some of the protesters in 1988. The same CTR witness said, "It's a question of manhood, the number and size of fish taken." He reported an exchange where he asked a protester if he wasn't concerned about the mercury in the fish. The protester screamed back at him, "But these are trophy fish!" However, it was clear that racism was fueling the protests every step of the way. "Squaw," "timber nigger," and "red nigger" were common insults hurled at the boat landing protests. A radio

I'm not a racist, BUT . . .

PARR and their arguments:

I'm not a racist, but Indians should give up their culture and be part of the 20th century. (cultural racism)

I'm not a racist, but those treaties were made over a hundred years ago and we don't have to keep our word to Indians. (political racism)

I'm not a racist but Indian unemployment of 50–80% (economic racism) is their own fault. (prejudice)

I'm not a racist, but Chippewa taking 2% of the walleye in Wisconsin are more of a threat to the environment than the Sportsmen who take 98%. (how racism is used to cover real threats of acid rain, toxic waste and nuclear dumps)

I'm not a racist, but white folks are angry so the Chippewa should back up on their rights. (the DNR's institutional racism and their legitimization of PARR)

A Chippewa woman at a 1987 PARR rally was given an application to the Ku Klux Klan. But PARR is not a racist organization.

Rick Whaley, Witness for Non-Violence
Milwaukee, WI

commercial sponsored by PARR ridiculed Native drum (sacred) music and warned that violence could be the result of Chippewa spearing. Linda Cree of CTR heard a youngster with a protest family at Butternut Lake tell a Chippewa elder, "God made us white. You don't belong here."[14]

When the season closed, the Chippewa had harvested 25,969 walleyes (which would end up being 4 percent of the state's total walleye take that year—anglers would take an estimated 672,000 walleyes or the other 96 percent). They'd also taken 158 muskies, 167 bass, 59 northern pike and 2 sturgeons (less than 1 percent of the state's 1988 totals of these other species). Newspapers throughout the state, along with members of Wisconsin's congressional delegation, continued to push for a "negotiated settlement" to the treaty rights problem. At Cass Lake Reservation in Minnesota, tribal members occupied tribal headquarters for a month in an unsuccessful attempt to reverse the Minnesota-Chippewa settlement. Walt Bresette argued in his speeches that the Minnesota and Wisconsin Chippewa tribes were being played off against each other: Minnesota tribes were told to sign the agreement or else they might have Wisconsin's troubles at the boat landings. Wisconsin bands were told, "Look at Minnesota. They settled and got money and no trouble." In a March 15, 1988, letter to Minnesota's DNR, George Meyer bemoaned Wisconsin's "extensive costs, adverse court decisions and much publicized social conflict" due to treaty rights. "[T]here is little doubt," Meyer went on, " that if such problems could be avoided through early negotiations such as yours, that is by far the preferable course of action."15

Evaluation and Feast

Intimidation could have lightning-flashed into violence, but no spearers or witnesses were seriously injured during the 1988 season. The protester mob tension did not break loose into riots. Whether the Witness presence made any difference we cannot measure, but Chippewa families were glad to have company at the landings and escorts back to their vehicles. On numerous nights in 1988, some lakes had spearers and a handful of protesters, but no police present. On these nights, the presence of witnesses seemed to turn the protesters into observers and may have deterred the most determined. We dialogued with some protesters, but the best impact we had was on the public dialogue in the media based on the eyewitness interviews we gave to reporters.

Looking back at the spring spearing, we realized that two of the tensest times were Sunday protests when the downstate witnesses had returned home, leaving a handful of CTR and Orenda members to cover the landings. It would be imperative to have people stay for long weekends or even take a whole week off in the following year's spearing Witness. The Witness also needed to become more serious about fundraising, obtain better maps of the counties and lakes, and get more ministers to the boat landings. We ruminated on what could be done in 1989 about the on-lake harassment. Could we bring witnesses out in boats, or build enough pressure to get the state to stop it?

I wrote a six-page spearing/witness report and the Milwaukee Witness distributed five hundred copies of it in Milwaukee, Madison, and northern Wisconsin to Chippewa tribal leaders, witness activists, the press, and clergy. It summarized findings, made lobbying recommendations, and highlighted, despite the tensions, the possibility of unity in northern Wisconsin—the common need to protect the beautiful woods and resources from the ravages of pollution and waste dumping, and to prevent violence and inflammatory rhetoric against the Chippewa that could wreck the tourist economy for both Chippewa and off-reservation towns.

The Milwaukee Witness continued to work on the issue of trust status for the Potawatomi and the Indian Community School in Milwaukee, in the face of neighborhood opposition to Indian gambling that was to fund the school. That summer, Witness members sent out a call to start a Milwaukee Greens group in order to reach a broader audience and find local issues and constituencies for justice and ecology concerns. Dorothy Thoms and Anita Koser threw a giant feast (of venison and walleye and desserts) to thank witnesses for the work and announce they were moving back from Milwaukee to their hometown, Lac du Flambeau.

The Black Hawk Vigil: The Importance of Allies

The 1988 spearing season was over, and our initial evaluation and regular post-season activities were well under way. Activist friends of the Witness and Walt Bresette went on a "Black Hawk Vigil" that November that would end up providing a rich opportunity for many of us to rethink and reaffirm our connections with the many indigenous people's struggles and environmental and justice issues confronting Wisconsin, and the world, that year.

Blake Gentry of Border Support; Bobby Bullet, a singer/songwriter originally from Lac du Flambeau and now a pipe carrier in the *Anishinabe* tradition; and Linda Maloney, who organized spiritual gatherings with Bobby, began retracing the trail of the Black Hawk War, doing pipe ceremonies at each stop Black Hawk and his people made on their tragic journey in 1832. They would end their travels at the Thanksgiving Day Vigil, to be joined by Walt, by many from the Wisconsin Greens and Honor Our Neighbors Origins and Rights (HONOR), and by witnesses from the 1988 boat landings, including myself.

Linda, Blake, and Bobby started their remembrance in Rock Island, Illinois, where the old Saukenuk village once stood. They built a fire by the Rock River, did a pipe ceremony and were given a journey staff by Indian Alliance people there.

In the 1820s, European-American settlers began encroaching on Sauk and Fox lands (now northern Illinois) in violation of the 1804 treaty signed by the United States and some members of the Sauk nation.[16] Settlers fenced off Sauk and Fox cornfields, burned wigwams, insulted Native women and beat Native men, and ploughed up Sauk and Fox burial grounds. These grievances went unaddressed by white authorities. "We are told," Black Hawk, a war chief with the Sauk and Fox, said, "that white people want our country, and we must leave it to them!" Forced west across the Mississippi River with other Sauk and Fox villages in 1831, Black Hawk came back across to his homeland on April 6, 1832, with one thousand people (including four hundred warriors) to replant their fields and assert their rights. "My reason teaches me that land cannot be sold," Black Hawk said in his autobiography. "The Great Spirit gave it to his children to live upon, and cultivate, as far as is necessary for their subsistence, and so long as they occupy and cultivate it, they have a right to the soil . . . Nothing can be sold, but such things as can be carried away."

The 1988 journey traveled north by car, alongside the Rock River and past the fifty-foot cement statue of an Indian face that came to be known as the Black Hawk statue lying in the bluffs above the river near Oregon, Illinois.

The three sojourners did a pipe ceremony for the European-American soldiers and Sauk and Fox people who died at Stillman's Valley—a stark marble spire is now monument to the forgotten soldiers who died there.

When Black Hawk realized he would not get the help he felt promised by the Winnebago, the Potawatomi, and the British, and would face certain annihilation unless he returned west of the Mississippi, he sent three unarmed warriors carrying a white flag to Major Isiah Stillman's Illinois militia's camp. Stillman's men captured the emissaries and killed one of them. They then chased the five observers Black Hawk had sent to watch the peace mission, killing two. Enraged at this response, Black Hawk took forty of his warriors and charged Stillman's encampment and routed the drunken militia.[17] After the Battle of Stillman's Run, Black Hawk, the warriors, and families retreated north into Wisconsin (territory), heading for the marshes of the Lake Koshkonong area where they hoped to find safety and forage for food. Facing starvation in the marshes where there were only roots, grasses, and bark to eat, Black Hawk's group moved continually west, stopping twice in what is now Madison, Wisconsin. One day, a man stayed behind to mourn his dead wife and pursuing U.S. troops found him seated on her grave and killed him. The same fate befell those Sauk too sick to travel or who tried to surrender. Black Hawk's group fled further, to the northwest side of Lake Mendota.

A plaque on Bascom Hill at the University of Wisconsin, scene of anti-Vietnam war battles with police of the sixties and seventies, marks the path of Black Hawk's people on their way out of the area. In Madison, Guatemalan refugees (Cakchiquel Indians) joined the 1988 ceremonies. Laurie Melrood of Border Support remembers:

> I thought that if the Guatemalans came and joined this journey and this reliving of a sorrowful time for indigenous people, it might be a way for them to talk about their own stories and to let people know about the bonds that existed between [them] . . . They sent their elder, Don Domingo, who was a man in his sixties who had been through a horrifying exile experience from the Guatemalan mountains into Mexico. Their spirits were just taken by this [event]. It wasn't that they [just] understood it. They were in it again, especially the old man. He stared at the trees and seemed almost in a trance. Through the day, he recounted to us what it had been like to be exiled from Guatemala . . . how their centuries-old way of life had been ravaged by the government.

West of Madison at Wisconsin Heights on July 31, 1832, Black Hawk's forces gave battle with the numerically superior U.S. company led by Col. Henry Dodge (a lead miner and later Wisconsin's first territorial governor). Atop a white horse on a sandy bluff over looking the battle, Black Hawk directed his warriors in what was actually a diversion while the rest of his party escaped to the Wisconsin River and across it. Sauk and Fox losses were between six and eighty, while one soldier was killed. The rest of Black Hawk's men crossed the river and, by night, constructed crude rafts and elm bark canoes and sent some of the families and warriors downriver in hopes of reaching the Mississippi and safety in Iowa. (These people were captured or killed by troops waiting for them at the mouth of the Wisconsin River.) In the early hours of the next day, Black Hawk's lieutenant called from a tree near the U.S. forces that the Sauk and Fox wished to negotiate a surrender. This second attempt to surrender went unheeded.[18] The main body of Black Hawk's party then retreated west, through the hills of southwest Wisconsin trying to reach the Mississippi River where the Bad Axe River joins it.

The 1988 Thanksgiving Day Vigil, at what is now ignominiously called Victory, Wisconsin, was sponsored by Wisconsin Greens and Honor Our Neighbors Origins and Rights (HONOR). Witnesses from the spring 1988 boat landings were there. Area ministers and farmers joined with descendants of Sauk and Fox in the talking circle and pipe ceremony. Laurie Melrood remembered the stories of her own family from the Kiev area of the Ukraine, killed in the Nazi massacres of Jews in World War II. Walt Bresette told of coming back from spearing at 4 A.M. one morning. His wife had been frantic with fear. "I thought you were dead," she yelled at him and then broke down crying. The Guatemalan Indians who had relived their own terrible flight and survival through pine mountains of their land, shared gifts with Bobby Bullet and talked of their work in resurrecting and carrying on their culture. After the circle, people climbed the great bluff beyond the highway. Here we read from Black Hawk's autobiography, and reflected while looking out over the valley, the river and Battle Island. Below us was the valley where the bone-white birches grow, their bare branches raised to the sky.

On August 1, 1832, Black Hawk and his people reached the Mississippi and Bad Axe Rivers. The militia steamboat "The Warrior" had come up river to meet them. Black Hawk again sent the white flag of surrender, but the gunboat fired relentlessly for two hours on Sauk and Fox.[19] The next day, General Atkinson with Colonel Dodge and 1300 soldiers moved in from the east, forcing Native men, women, and children into the river to be shot, drowned, or killed—at Atkinson's instigation—on the other side by Sioux enemies of the Sauk and Fox. More than five hundred Sauk and Fox were killed in the campaign against Black Hawk, most of these at the Bad Axe massacre of 1832. "Rock River was a beautiful country," Black Hawk said a year before his death in 1838. "I loved my towns, my cornfields, and the home of my people. I fought for it."

Black Hawk's justified struggle to regain his people's homeland failed because his own nation was divided on whether to back his cause and because only a few individual allies stepped forward to help. Without organized support from his hoped-for allies, Black Hawk was at the mercy of the U.S. policy of land usurpation. This policy was backed by U.S. military force, and fed by European-American fears, prejudice, and ignorance of the culture and land ethic of indigenous peoples. Our vigil at Bad Axe on the Thanksgiving after our first year's witness was reminder of the importance of finding allies in our struggle, too.

As the Americas, north and south, near the twenty-first century, it is obvious that the wars against Indian peoples are not over. Indigenous people are being massacred in the rain forests of Guatemala and Brazil. Native people in the United States were killed in the struggles of the 1960s and 1970s and are risking their lives again in the 1980s and 1990s just to exercise rights they have long held. Nonviolence is not merely a strategy for the boat landings. It is a philosophy for living together today. It is also a way of reconciling with a heritage of violence, whether as victim or as oppressor, by remembering together the tragedies, the real losses of life and culture for many peoples. The Bad Axe Vigil on Thanksgiving Day, 1988, was also an opportunity for today's Black Hawk trail sojourners and the witnesses to remind ourselves where we came from—our political as well as ethnic heritages. It was a day to be inspired and recommit ourselves to the healing we still needed to do in Wisconsin in our lifetimes.

Notes

1. George Meyer, at Witness for Non-Violence public meeting for Black History Month, February 20, 1988, Milwaukee, Wisconsin. Meyer also said at this meeting, "I have no problem with [Witness] representatives being at the boat landings. At a state meeting of law enforcement last week, this question came up. We know there'll be pro-treaty groups there. Do we have a problem with that? The sheriffs don't have a problem with that. The WDNR doesn't have a problem with that. It may lead to better dialogue at the landings."

2. Ibid.

3. Walt Bresette, at Witness public meeting in Milwaukee, in rebuttal to George Meyer's points just mentioned February 20, 1988.

4. Information in this paragraph is indebted to Rudolph Ryser's booklet, "Anti-Indian Movement on the Tribal Frontier" (Kenmore, WA: Center for World Indigenous Studies, April 1991.)

5. Ronald N. Satz, *Chippewa Treaties* (Madison: Wisconsin Academy of Science, Arts and Letters, 1991), pp. 61–69.

6. Satz, *Chippewa Treaties*, pp. 111–112.

7. Webster was reading from "The Constitution and Indian Law," from the *Washington Newsletter of the Friends Committee on National Legislation* (FCNL), Aug.–Sept. 1987. The article originally appeared in longer form in *Grapevine,* a publication

of the Joint Strategy and Action Committee, a North American interdenominational agency.

8. Linda Dunn changed her name to Linda Cree in 1990 and is referred to by this name in the rest of the book.

9. Posse Comitatus is a semi-religious (Christian identity), far-right organization spouting violent anti-Black and anti-Jewish rhetoric, which capitalized on the growing farm crisis in both the Midwest and the West during the 1970s and 1980s. Wickstrom was arrested with a cache of arms on his property and charged and convicted of impersonating a government official (for declaring Tigerton Dells a county and himself a judge).

10. *Milwaukee Sentinel,* April 19, 1988.

11. Crist spent the night in jail and posted a $1000 cash bond rather than promise to stay away from landings. "Chippewa spearers ask for help," *Milwaukee Sentinel,* April 20, 1988.

12. Dennis McCan, "Treaty critic charged; spears are stymied," *Milwaukee Journal,* April 19, 1988.

13. Tim Kaiser, interview with Rick Whaley, March 29, 1988.

14. At LCO, spearing lakes were quiet, but three times in 1988 WOJB (the public radio station) at LCO had their billboards defaced. The last time the spray painters said "What would Sitting Bull think? Welfare hogs and sister rapers."

15. George Meyer, Wisconsin Department of Natural Resources, letter to Steven Thorne, Deputy Commissioner, Minnesota Department of Natural Resources, March 15, 1988.

16. The following section is based on: Donald Jackson, ed., *An Autobiography: Black Hawk* (Urbana and Chicago: University of Illinois Press, 1990), pp. 54–56, 101–111, 120, 134–140; John M. Douglas, *The Indians in Wisconsin's History* (Milwaukee: Milwaukee Public Museum, 1954), pp. 43–46; Blake Gentry and Laurie Melrood's retelling of the 1988 journey, personal interview, December 26, 1991, Milwaukee; William T. Hagan, *Black Hawk's Route Through Wisconsin* (Madison: State Historical Society of Wisconsin, 1949), pp. 20–29; Richard Kenyon, "Hearing the echos of Black Hawk," *Milwaukee Journal,* September 15, 1991; William Stark, *Along the Black Hawk Trail* (Sheboygan, WI: Zimmerman Press, 1984), pp. 60–61, 119–124, 154; and Walt Bresette's and my recollection of the 1988 Thanksgiving Day Vigil.

The Sauk and Fox were allied but distinct tribes designated by the United States as "the united Sac and Fox" in this 1804 treaty, which no Fox representative signed. This treaty gave the United States, from its point of view, 50 million acres of land in exchange for $1000 annuities to the Sauk signers. Subsequent treaties, in 1816 and 1825, sought to reaffirm this 1804 agreement. Black Hawk and others disputed the 1804 treaty: It had been signed by four members of the nation at a meeting in St. Louis that had been set up under another pretext. The Sauk and Fox councils had not discussed the treaty for land cession ahead of time nor sent appropriate leaders/delegates to such an important negotiation. Black Hawk (not one of the original signers) and some of the 1804 signers also interpreted the annuities, or annual cash payments, as gifts (which their former allies, the British, had been known to give), not as a payment for land. Black Hawk refused annuities after he found out the United States considered them payment for Sauk and Fox land.

17. Abraham Lincoln was in the burial brigade for victims of the Battle of Stillman's Run. He enlisted in the militia to fight Black Hawk but was discharged early. Zachary Taylor, later the twelfth U.S. president, was second in command to Atkinson in the campaign against Black Hawk.

18. The troops could hear but not find the messenger, Neapope, who, by some accounts, was speaking in Winnebago, in hopes that Winnebago allied with U.S. forces were there to translate. The call was either not understood or ignored. Other individual Winnebagos had allied with Black Hawk and some may have provided canoes for the fateful escape downstream.

19. The commander of the gunboat, Captain Throckmorton, claimed that he thought that the white surrender flag was a hoax. It is clear, however, from statements by General Atkinson and policy directives from the Illinois territorial governor at the beginning of the Black Hawk campaign, and from President Andrew Jackson during the "Black Hawk War," that retribution and the political gain of ridding the area of "hostiles" once and for all, was the policy and point of the pursuit and massacre of the Sauk and Fox. See Jackson, *An Autobiography: Black Hawk,* p. 135 footnote.

4

WABIGONI GISISS
(The Budding Moon)

Mentors and Allies
Coming to Leadership as a Native American Activist

Walt Bresette

MY EARLIEST TRAINING CAME from my family. My folks were both very much individuals within our rather homogeneous community. Both maintained relative independence from the travails of our poverty-stricken, rural reservation village. Dad was a freelance lumberjack, had a garden, and always raised a few animals. Mom endured both Dad and her seven sons without going crazy. She also worked outside the home when extra money was needed. They built a secure home that was always open to us regardless of what situation we got ourselves into. During my rebellious teenage years and my searching young-adult years, they not only let me be, they would really listen to me. When I became political, they'd never speak against me, but would be supportive of me personally.

Mom's sister Toddy, Victoria Gokee, emerged as a leading political force in Native issues just as I was reaching puberty. She was one of the first women tribal chairs in the nation—certainly here in Wisconsin. In some ways she was before her time. It was through the efforts of her and her colleagues that today's tribal government infrastructure was built. Then, there were no budgets, only commitment and drive, and she had an abundance of both.

Her kitchen attracted both traditional people and newer would-be activists in the movement for Native rights. As youngsters we sat in on the discussions and were recruited to help in a struggle then not clearly defined. She taught us mostly through her tenacious convictions about what was right for "Indian" people. She'd make us do some of her work, researching and typing reports, knowing that we'd read them and have to become familiar with the issues. While she was often short on tactics, she was rarely wrong on the issues. She led with her heart and relied on the trust and friendship of others to pick up on the issues she initiated.

Victoria was always talking about treaties, and the Indians and white people, whenever we would go to Madeline Island. I'll remember it forever. As a youngster, one of my first nonviolent actions came during a volleyball game at her house. We were teenagers, eighteen, nineteen years old; I had come back to visit. We saw a tree falling about an eighth or quarter of a mile from her house. We all looked at each other and said, "That tree shouldn't be falling. What's going on at Yellow Springs?"

So we all jumped in our separate cars—there were five of us. It looked like there were a whole bunch of people going. And we all sped off and pulled into this pine grove. People (off-reservation loggers on alienated land) were in there cutting trees. We got out and said, "Well, this is our grove. You're cutting trees down. This is the reservation. We have treaty rights, you know."

We had a standoff. In the end, we were right, but we didn't know it. We were just bluffing our way. And we stopped the cutting of that pine grove. Those were the kind of things Victoria did. You know, she'd kind of act, and ask questions later—see if she had the right to do it later. She was my early mentor. She was always great on issues, but it was difficult for her to maintain support for what she was doing.

During these early years, I also remember the first stirrings of institutional change. Veda Stone, a European-American woman now in her eighties living in Eau Claire, Wisconsin, opened educational doors for many of today's leaders. I remember attending one summer session for Indian youth when I was twelve or thirteen years old at University of Wisconsin–Eau Claire that Veda organized. I thought they got the wrong list and that some other poor (smart) souls were left back at the reservations. I remember being in a dorm feeling out of place and somewhat fearful of what was expected of us. And then this huge Oklahoma Indian walks in, funny accent, a guitar at his side and big cowboy boots. Clyde Warrior was one of the gentlest people I'd ever seen. He sat down and talked to us in a way no one had ever talked to us before. His air of confidence and larger-than-life presence filled the room. He made us feel comfortable, even got us excited about the weekend gathering. I'd never known there were Indians like that. It was strange looking up to an "Indian."

Victoria Gokee at Madeline Island pow-wow, Memorial Day, 1988. Photo by Amoose.

Finding Love While Running from Self-Doubt

The roots of my activism were also in the political atmosphere of the 1960s and the 1970s. My involvement came at the tail end of the Vietnam War, after I had served four years in the army as a noncombatant with an electronic intelligence unit. I spent most of my time in Japan monitoring the Cold War. Although affected by the social unrest at that time, when I left the army in the fall of 1968 I was naive and lost, looking for a place to be rather than searching for a revolution.

The path I took was that of someone looking for safe, familiar surroundings —new or old. It was not a journey of a committed idealist who knew where he wanted to go. I did not as much want to change the world as I wanted to understand where I fit. Then and into my late twenties, I feared I didn't belong anywhere. With a BIA (Bureau of Indian Affairs) grant I moved to Chicago to study advertising art, more as a way of buying time than looking for a profession. Although I attended some of the antiwar actions, I got my first taste of activism with "Indian" issues.

My uncle Leo LaFernier, now an official with the Red Cliff tribal government, lived in Chicago's Uptown—one of the non-Black poor areas of town. It was one of the relocation centers for Native people that the United States used to assimilate Native populations in the 1950s. Similar centers exist in other major cities. Instead of creating a cadre of middle-management former "Indians," Uptown became an urban ghetto for those unable to find their way back home. They shared the deteriorating tenements with poor whites from Appalachia as well as newer refugees from the Caribbean, South and Central America, and later from east Asia.

With my confusion I fit in well with the Uptown atmosphere. It was good to have family there, although I wanted to get my own footing. I felt guilty contributing to Uncle Leo's already overcrowded apartment. He had his own family but always seemed to make room for others who needed help. At any time, even now, you can find extended family members or friends crashed and recovering at Leo and Shirley's house or apartment. He was my mom's youngest brother and in some ways became an older brother to those of us who passed his way.

Leo was friends with Mike Chosa and Betty Jack, a brother and sister who were also living in Chicago but came from the Lac du Flambeau reservation. These two became my first teachers on the road to political activism. Betty, who now works in northern Minnesota in the drug and alcohol recovery field, was a forceful woman amidst the men. Her knowledge and intuition came from the land and the people it grew. Her brother Mike remains an brilliant tactician who was then at the center of growing Native activism. He was a student of Saul Alinsky, noted organizer and author of *Rules for Radicals.*

For me it was a great time, looking in, standing at the periphery, marching and chanting. Once we were all arrested for not ending a drum ceremony— Mike told the police it needed to go all night. We danced into a waiting police wagon, high on our collective rejection of authority, and knowing that within a few hours Operation Breadbasket or the Black Panthers would bail us out. For me it was a party that didn't seem to end.

The most memorable event for me came one day when a reporter showed up at a camp we had set up outside of Wrigley Field. He wanted to do a story about Native rights. Mike had organized an action to protest slum landlords following the eviction of a Menominee woman who had nine children. When that reporter started to ask questions about treaty rights and I turned to have him talk to Mike or Leo, no one was there. I was the only one available —everyone else had gone to yet another meeting. When the reporter continued to direct questions at me I was devastated. I had no answers, I knew no strategy, and I had little experience even to bluff my way through. I was embarrassed and angry and felt cheated. My inflated ego, built vicariously on others' knowledge, immediately crashed. I had no answers and I understood for the first time that I didn't understand what I was doing. The party was over.

Fortunately, my embarrassment was so great that I couldn't let the event go. I became determined then to find out what this treaty business was all about, to find out whether there was any substance to the claims made by the Mike Chosas of this world. I started a long, painful journey to find myself and where I, as an "Indian," fit into this larger world.

The Menominee Takeover—1975

In 1975, Menominee activists took over the Alexian Brothers abbey near the reservation at Gresham, Wisconsin. They demanded the unused building be turned into a health center for the Menominee reservation. Some local whites wanted to force them out with guns and many politicians warned of a repeat of the 1973 Wounded Knee confrontation at Pine Ridge, South Dakota. The state of Wisconsin called out the National Guard and sent them to Gresham until a negotiated settlement was reached.[1] I was in Madison working at the university when the abbey was taken over. The Native community met and we decided that we needed to do something in solidarity. So we decided that we would do a peaceful, nonviolent sit-in at the state capitol, and stay there until there was a peaceful resolution at Gresham. We would talk with legislators and others as they went to work each day. We set up camp at the state capitol.

I remember it was in February and it was very cold. It was below zero. Sitting there freezing my ass off, thinking to myself, "What the hell am I doing here? I mean, if I'm going to do this for the Menominee, shouldn't I get a better handle on my tribe?"

That really was a turning point in terms of my returning north. I decided I needed to understand my tribe first, to get a grip on who I was. So, that next summer, I went home to talk to the elders and to read the history of my tribe. And that began a process for me of more deliberately reacquainting myself with the Lake Superior Chippewa.

The La Pointe Treaty Commemoration—1979

A lot of things came from that reacquaintance with my people. One of those things was, eventually, the concept of reunification. How, I wondered, and discussed with different people, did we (the *Anishinabe*) get separated, and how could we—or should we—come back together?

When I was working for Great Lakes Intertribal Council as their public information officer in the late 1970s, I saw the 125th anniversary of the 1854 La Pointe treaty coming up.[2] I began going to the Chippewa tribal members of the Great Lakes Intertribal Council, asking them if they would be interested in doing some kind of commemoration around the 1854 treaty. My thoughts were to use this event as part of a process of reunification. A beginning process. I didn't tell them that. Just wanted to throw a party.

"Well," they said, "yeah, that's a great idea. Do something with it." But there wasn't much enthusiasm. So it was really disheartening, disappointing. Sandra Brown and I and two or three others did the planning and it basically took off as a cause. And we began doing publicity and a variety of things, not really knowing if it was going to happen or not.

Well, in the end, it happened. We held a three-day gathering. Two of those days at Red Cliff; one on Madeline Island. We did a two-day treaty conference at Red Cliff where we brought in people from around the country to talk about the treaties, treaty rights, and the history of the tribe. We brought in storytellers, we brought in linguists, we brought in people from all over. On Sunday (it rained all prior to that) it was awful. It was cold. It was absolutely, utterly miserable. We were in this little community building at Red Cliff. Then the sun broke through and it was the most beautiful day that it could ever be.

On that third day, people came to Madeline Island and we had ceremonies and we had a pow-wow. The elders came, drums were made, and ceremonies were led by Archie Mosay and Tom O'Connor and it was wonderful—a wonderful day, and people came together and talked about the island in a way it hadn't been talked about in a long time. We talked about history differently. The island had kind of an aura different than the mainland. What happens on the island is kind of unrelated to what happens to us on the mainland. There are a number of activists, Sylvia Cloud, for example, who only do island stuff—reclaiming parts of the island and reviving the importance of the island among different people—because they view the island as a sacred place.

I remember Basil Johnston came, and he said when he left Canada—he was up in the bush—he told some of the people where he was going. He said he was going to *Mo-ning-wun'-a-kaun-ing*. And they said, "Oh yeah. That's where the *Megis* Shell was last seen. . . . Good, you're going to that sacred place." So he told the story. The people in the bush knew that this was a sacred place.

So, that was what happened in general terms. It was an idea that, in a sense, was fulfilled. It was a dream that we accomplished. But we didn't accomplish what we were after, which was what we thought would be the beginnings of a reunification process. It didn't happen.

Learning from Tribal Governments

If reunification from within was not possible, larger economic forces were at play that required unified Chippewa position-taking in Wisconsin. By the early 1980s, northern Wisconsin/ceded territory was seeing mineral company exploration, government attempts to locate a nuclear depository, and a federal struggle with Wisconsinites over Project ELF—an underground antenna system linked to contact nuclear first-strike submarines, to be buried in the northern forests.

There was a meeting early in this decade that twenty to twenty-five Midwest tribes came to in Eau Claire, Wisconsin. I remember that one of the main issues was James Watt's appointment as secretary of the Department of the Interior. Vern Bellecourt of the American Indian Movement (AIM) was there and gave some incredibly good speeches about Watts and the agenda he and Reagan had.

At that meeting I remember Jake Whitecrow, then the national director of the Indian Health Board. Jake was invited to talk about Indian health concerns. However, during one of the general sessions, I remember him taking off his "health" hat and saying that he simply wanted to address the people from other experiences that he had had, particularly as it applied to environmental issues. He prefaced his remarks by saying that he was a member of the Indian Policy Review Commission, which I believe issued a report in 1975 or 1976 that was an update of the old Kennedy report that was focused primarily on education but had broad ramifications. This was the latest Congressional report and Whitecrow was one of the citizen members. He also prefaced his remarks by saying that he was a member of the council from his tribe, one of the Oklahoma tribes—I think it was the Ottawa. He recalled his Oklahoma political days with the tribe, when they were either reluctant to give oil leasings or oil and mineral developments were coming before his tribe and there was resistance to it.

I remember his deep booming voice warning, "If you have something they want, they are going to get it. And they are going to get it however they choose to get it. First," he said, "they will simply try to convince you that this is the correct thing to do and if you don't change your mind, based on that, then they will start threatening you. They will threaten you in a variety of ways, and if that doesn't work, they will bribe you. They will give you money. They will give you sex. Or give you booze. Or give you whatever you want. Whatever they think will change your mind. But in the end," he said, "if you have something they want, they will get it." He went on to caution the tribes to be prepared and always on guard and vigilant against some future unknown, particularly as it applied to environmental issues.

In the end, the tribes that gathered passed resolutions against Project ELF, against high-level nuclear waste dumping in the region, against minerals development, against a whole variety of ecologically unsound developments that would pose a threat to the environment or in some way intrude upon their sovereignty and treaty rights.

These Wisconsin tribal dynamics paralleled the energy policy politicking that was afoot nationally in the 1970s and 1980s. I remember going to a National Tribal Chairman Association (NTCA) meeting in Denver in the late 1970s.[3] It was the time of Jimmy Carter's presidency and the era of synfuels and domestic energy exploration. All the mega-corporations of the planet, it seemed, came to this meeting. These industry people would come to these meetings and just wine and dine the tribal chairs. But at this time, the Coalition of Energy Resource Tribes (CERT) was just assuming its control of reservation uranium and coal deposits. That's when Peter McDonald (longtime Navajo tribal chairman) left NTCA and took over control of CERT. Begun in 1975 as a confederation of twenty-five energy-rich Native American nations, CERT coordinated control over resources estimated to be half the U.S. uranium reserves and one-third of all western U.S. low-sulphur coal.[4] It became kind of an Indian OPEC (Organization of Petroleum Exporting Countries). The National Congress of American Indians and NTCA diminished as soon as CERT established itself as a large economic force and the tribes became easy targets to be picked off by a number of these huge corporations.

It was a scary time. I remember this guy from Alaska who came in with this raggedy slicker. But he was one of the richest of the new village corporation characters, and it was pimping and prostituting like I'd never seen. The old geezer pulled out this piece of coal shale and began crushing and extracting the oil from the coal. He said, "Hey, look at this," and he flicked his lighter and lit it like a torch. It was a scene I looked back upon and knew what Jake White-crow's warning was all about.

Other tribal leaders also played a mentoring role for me. Hillary Waukau, an influential Menominee tribal figure, always found time to be with the Chippewa and anyone else working on nuclear waste and other issues that affected us. Norbert C. Hill (Oneida) took some of us at Great Lakes Inter-tribal Council under his wing. Whenever an issue was brewing in Washington, D.C., he would drag some of us leaders-in-training out with him to go lobbying. Eugene Taylor, former chairman at St. Croix, was a person I looked to as a barometer of how things were generally in Indian country.

At one time I did think about running for tribal office. In fact, I was extremely confident that at some time I would run. I saw myself as an official in tribal government. That was during the late 1970s. However, at the time one of my former classmates actually became tribal chair. I was so happy for him. I felt as if, "Wow, we've arrived. Things are going to be different. I don't need to do this organizing now. It's taken care of." That was when Tommy Joe Gordon was elected tribal chair at Red Cliff, and people like Rick St. Germaine were being elected at LCO, Joe Corbock at Bad River. It was my age group, my era. But it was extreme disappointment at Red Cliff. I assumed I would have access through just the age relationship, but that didn't happen. The issues were viewed quite differently once one got into office.

Just when I thought that things were going to change, I changed. And I came to the conclusion that it was the nature of the office itself, the nature of the process itself, that was wrong. It didn't have what was needed in order to have the kinds of things we talked about in the Native activist circles. I began giving up hope of tribal government being anything more than a caretaker institution during that period. And I deferred further thoughts of joining it until after I turned fifty.

Black Hawk's War Club

During the 1980s, I did media consulting work for the National Congress of American Indians (NCAI), a large lobbying group comprised of tribes from the

United States. I was asked to come to their national conferences and assist with media relations, help with press conferences, do press releases and some reporting of the proceedings. The first conference I went to was in Tulsa in 1980. At this Tulsa meeting, Robert Holden, who was working on nuclear waste and other environmental issues for NCAI, introduced me to an elder Lakota from Pine Ridge who he had brought to the meeting to address Department of Energy (DOE) officials. His name was Peter Catches, and Robert had said that he had adopted Peter as a grandfather. Robert felt that it was important that DOE as well as other officials begin to hear more from the traditional members of our communities. I remembered Peter as a dapper dresser with fine features and a very self-confident air about him.

When I got to my second NCAI annual conference, also to do public relations, this time in Tampa, Florida in 1986, I saw that Robert had once more brought Peter Catches with him. While running the media office, I received a call from an elderly woman who said she wanted to talk with the Indians. I told her she had gotten the Indians, but which ones did she want to talk with. "The ones from Illinois," she said. I took her number and said I'd get back to her. She seemed like a hundred other calls I'd received from curious folks wanting to somehow get in touch with themselves vicariously by doing something with Indians. I took her message to the caucus room for the tribes in the Great Lakes, where I knew most of the delegates. They politely told me that they had more important business to deal with and that I should handle the old lady. I told Robert who, in turn, talked with Peter who announced that we should go see her. She lived in St. Petersburg, across the bay from Tampa. We arranged to visit with her that evening. It was a distraction I really didn't need or look forward to dealing with, although the idea of getting out of the hotel was exciting.

Earlier in the afternoon we were scheduled to do a live talk show with a local radio station—one of a number of media events. Robert said that the delegates who were scheduled to do the radio show were tied up and that Robert and I plus one local Floridian would have to handle it. So off we went, to discuss the important national issues of the day facing Native people in the United States. It was a well-listened-to radio show in a very large market. The host had a good reputation so we looked forward to making some inroads with the public. The strangest thing happened, however, when we got to the radio station. The host, who had been briefed about the various issues, turned out to be a history buff with a special interest in a former chief of the Sauk and Fox named Black Hawk. It was the only thing he wanted to talk about. It took all our skills to get him to talk about the issues facing Indian country. We all knew a little about the Black Hawk wars in Illinois and Wisconsin, but none of us knew these stories in any great detail. We were a little upset over the direction he wanted to take the talks and were glad to get out of the station and back to the hotel.

Later that day Robert, Peter, and I headed for St. Petersburg to meet the elderly woman who said she wanted to talk to the Indians. When we arrived at her small bungalow, she indeed was waiting for us. It was very much like going into the home of an aunt we hadn't seen in a long time. We visited for a while and then settled into the purpose of our visit. She sat down and picked up a club made of dark wood. It was rounded like a ball with a geometric carving around its circumference. The handle was twenty inches long, with more etchings near the end of the handle. She held it in her right hand and would cradle it in the palm of her left hand, sometimes bringing it away and striking it back on her open palm. It looked weird, this old lady with this unusual-looking club.

She told us that the club was the reason she had called. It was her husband's dying wish that the club be returned to "the Indians." Her husband had died a number of years earlier; we found out that she was in her early nineties, although still very alert and agile. She said she knew the club didn't belong in a museum and when she heard that the Indians were going to have this gathering in Tampa she hoped she could fulfill her husband's wishes. She said her husband got the club from one of his grandfathers. It had been handed down to him from his father and his father's grandfather. With the club came this story as I remember it told to us by the woman from St. Petersburg:

> My husband's ancestors had a farm in Pennsylvania and one day a soldier arrived at the farm. He was on his way home from a war in Wisconsin and asked if he could stay at the farmer's house overnight. They did put him up and fed him. In return for their hospitality the soldier gave them some gifts, including the club which the soldier said was war booty. The soldier told my husband's great-grandfather, the farmer, that the club belong to Chief Black Hawk.

After she finished her story she handed the club to me. I was sitting closest to her on the left and Robert and Peter were on my left. We were on a couch and she was on a chair.

"What do we do now?" Robert almost mournfully asked.

"Well, I can't touch it, I'm a medicine man," said Peter.

"You mean it's real?" said Robert.

"Damn right it's real," chimed in the old lady. "Had it tested at the university and they found blood on it and everything."

It was a bizarre scene, yet funny in a surreal sense. I clung tightly to club, trying to pick up the unknown meaning of it all, looking closely at it as though I were some kind of official club inspector, trying to look like I knew what I was looking for. "It used to be longer," the old lady said to me, "but part of the handle got sawed off quite a few years ago." We visited for a while longer and then left her bungalow to head back for Tampa.

"That old lady's gonna die tonight," said Robert, "The only thing keeping her alive was that club."

Robert continued talking, confused about what we were going to do with the club. Peter and I ignored him as we walked to the car, yet he had a point: what were we going to do with the club? Robert was driving and Peter got into the front seat also. I and the club got in the back of the car for the trip over to Tampa under the now darkening skies of Florida.

"I've got it," I yelled excitedly to Robert. "I give you the club to take back to your office in Washington, D.C., and at the next annual conference you arrange a special ceremony and return the club to the Sauk and Fox."

"Yes!" Robert gleefully agreed. We breathed a collective sigh of relief and continued toward the hotel.

Just as our excitement turned to quiet reflection, Peter turned to me and said, "No! That club was given to you for a reason and now it is your responsibility to find out why and to find out who this Black Hawk was and to find out why he did the things that he did." I immediately froze in response to the simple directives given by Peter. I turned into a child, not really understanding what was being said but also not wishing to challenge by asking what he meant.

My adult mind reeled. "What?" I thought. "What the hell does he mean 'find out why Black Hawk did the things he did?' Don't give me this medicine man stuff I've run into too often; this ambiguous 'you'll know' bullshit." I didn't know, didn't have the foggiest notion of what he was talking about. I wanted details, directions, phone numbers, dates, times. Not, "you'll know" and "you must find out." But, instead, I sat silently in my confusion.

"It's like getting a sacred pipe," Peter added later. "You must use it like that." That was the last time I talked with Robert or Peter about the club or the woman who gave it to us. We finished our conference and each headed back to our homes. I left Tampa excited yet confused.

The club came home with me. I sought its meaning and its power as I carried it with me to Veteran's Day ceremonies with Vietnam Vets Against the War, to schools and to boat landings, and to the Bad Axe Vigil on Thanksgiving, 1988, still searching, for what its role or final resting place should be today.

Learning from Grassroots Activism: AIM

The Red Power movement was preceded by a youth movement in Indian country, led by people like Clyde Warrior and Gerald Wilkerson with the National Indian Youth Council.[5] These were people who challenged authority. They began the process of organizing young people to get the tools to create our own authority, tools to reclaim our own role. So it was an academic American Indian movement that spawned the other American Indian Movement (AIM), founded in 1968. AIM came along when we were at war in Vietnam and women were starting to stand up for their rights. It followed the Black civil rights movement. This intellectual struggle in America and in Indian country was going on at the same time as the major organizing efforts and famous confrontations of the 1960s and 1970s.

All of the 1960s social movements that were creating friction began to burst. For us, 1969 was the Alcatraz occupation. The year 1972 was The Trail of Broken Treaties march from Alcatraz to Washington, D.C. In 1973 came Wounded Knee. There, AIM responded to the call from the Oglala Sioux Civil Rights Organization and traditional Oglala chiefs to support their demands for an end to Chair Dick Wilson's corruption and on-reservation repression of his critics. AIM leaders—including Clyde Bellecourt, who refused to carry a gun throughout—were part of the courageous seventy-one-day standoff there. The Wounded Knee occupation secured AIM a heroic, larger-than-life image for many Native people and gave them the mantle of grassroots militancy leadership for the next decade. In 1977, the International Indian Treaty Council, started by AIM, spearheaded the United Nation's Geneva (Switzerland) Conference on Discrimination against Indigenous People of the Western Hemisphere.

In the 1970s the Wisconsin Indian Resource Council (WIRC) was involved in consciousness-raising with churches, doing sensitivity training, and trying to bring church support to Native issues. WIRC was church supported, although they were not church affiliated. They used the funding arms of the various churches who were concerned about peace and justice issues. WIRC was predominantly Oneida based.[6] Lloyd Powless and Royal Warrington of WIRC were the Midwest contacts for The Longest Walk in 1978. They organized a send-off to Madison to join The Longest Walk and many of us went to Madison to be part of that send-off. The only thing that I remember was the day that we walked into Madison—we marched down East Washington Ave. to the capitol. A number of us gave talks. It was really bizarre. The state capitol has four main entrances. We were on the one facing east toward Washington Ave. A Hispanic group was next door and every other door was someone doing something different. It was also a day they were having a parade of airplanes around the capitol square. That was organizing in the 1970s. The Longest Walk finally arrived in Washington, D.C., in mid-summer only to find that President Carter was off in Europe lecturing the Soviet Union on human rights for dissidents.[7]

Then, in 1979, I was publishing a small monthly when Red Cliff tribal members took over the tribal offices there in protest against the then-current leadership. That same weekend, two Chippewa had died in an attempt to take over the Red Lake tribal government in northern Minnesota. Rumors that AIM was heading for Bad River escalated the tensions and polarization within this Wisconsin Chippewa community.

Within days, in fact, AIM arrived under the leadership of Clyde Bellecourt, who clearly aligned with those out of power. Up until then I had not met any of the AIM leaders, and was as swept away by their reputation as anyone else. However, I quickly noticed that while they did great organizing and had dynamic rhetorical skills, the community quickly deferred its power to this outside force. "Eugene Bigboy is no different than the Shah of Iran," Bellecourt reminded the gathered forces in the community center at Bad River. Tumultuous cheers followed as the crowd was energized by this outside hero. While I knew Eugene and had been as critical as any other of tribal leadership, I didn't quite see where he fit as the equivalent of the Shah. Later I found out that Bellecourt had never met Bigboy. As the excitement rose, the momentum swung and eventually the Bad River tribal government was ousted. Fifteen years later remnant factions and animosity still remain from this divisive struggle at Bad River.

My problem with AIM was that they were great organizers, but poor teachers. They came in and lanced wounds that needed lancing. Then they left, often with the sores still dripping. The core leadership that created AIM was blessed with the vision, but lacked the ability to transfer power to those they sought to liberate. The great struggles and victories of the 1960s and 1970s generated few new leaders within the high ranks of AIM. And while a few of the initial AIMsters left on other roads, the main characters remained and filled the vacuum rather than recruiting new leadership or evolving newer ways to address newer situations. Although this feeling may reflect more of my own impatience, the true test of this concern will be when graduates of the AIM survival schools attempt to assert their role as new leaders.[8] The 1989 Chippewa spearing season would bring our alliance-building efforts back to these creators of the modern American Indian movement.

Finding More Allies

Just as Tom Maulson had known LdF needed supporters at Butternut Lake, I knew that for other landings and for overall political victory, the Chippewa needed many allies. This networking had begun in earnest for me already in 1978, when I became public information officer for the Great Lakes Intertribal Council, and carried through my years at WOJB Radio and as editor of the *Masinaigan* newspaper at Great Lakes Indian Fish and Wildlife Commission.[9] It continued when I became an independent businessman and organizer.

Bob Albee was one of the key allies and advisors to me and others in Wisconsin on Indian solidarity issues. He saved the LCO *Journal* by publishing it out of his house for a while, came to the 1979 La Pointe gathering and recorded everything, and worked on the 1984 Ad Hoc Commission on Racism in Wisconsin. He had been working in public television and came up to LCO to do a program on the Honor the Earth Pow-Wow during the time Gordon Thayer was chair. Gordon was one of best chairmen around. He was the one who brought together all the Chippewa tribes after the *Voigt* decision to deal with the gathering public rage against Indian rights. Gordon wanted a little AM radio station at LCO and he kept asking Bob questions about radio. "For the money you're going to pay," Bob told him, "you might as well go for Corporation for Public Broadcasting money." WOJB Radio was born and Bob never went back.

Albee and I worked together at LCO attempting to shift the theory of tribal sovereignty into some kind of practical reality. Albee, a political science major who went into special education teaching and the Peace Corps for a time, always viewed himself as somebody who could provide the tools, knowing people would use them. He was also a brilliant tactician. He and Paul DeMain (later editor of *News from Indian Country* newspaper) led the campaign that undermined Paul Mullaly and his Equal Rights for Everyone (ERFE). Bob and Paul organized a group of people called Smerfs for ERFE. They got these little Smerf T-shirts and would go to ERFE meetings and laugh while everyone else was just so serious about stopping Indian rights. It was wild.[10]

Albee also worked with Gordon Thayer on LCO's brilliant $2 bill campaign. The Wisconsin Counties Association weighed in early against the *Voigt* decision and Sawyer County, where LCO is, was no exception in their opposition to off-reservation rights. LCO's Thayer and allies wanted to demonstrate that if people were going to attack the tribe, they needed to understand that the tribe spent money in the area's biggest off-reservation town, Hayward. So LCO issued every pay check in bundles of $2 bills. For weeks and weeks, there were $2 bills circulating all over the county showing how much everyone benefited from LCO's role in the local economy.

As if ERFE weren't enough, we had to deal with the ELF, too. I was working, on behalf of the tribes, against the U.S. Navy's Extremely Low Frequency (ELF) project—a massive underground antenna system in Wisconsin and northern Michigan that transmits commands to every U.S. nuclear weapons submarine. The Great Lakes Intertribal Council and the St. Croix Chippewa had gone on record opposing this nuclear first-strike radio station. Through this work, I met Tom Hastings, an anti-ELF, nonviolent provocateur. Tom was arrested for his anti-ELF actions while he went with me to witness at one of the first Butternut Lake incidents in Ashland County. According to Tom's account:

> The ELF facility sits smack in the middle of the ceded territories of the Lake Superior *Ojibwe* and was built over the directly expressed opinion of their leadership. Its waves affect the migratory habits of birds and affect rapid cellular growth, thus very probably enhancing the speed with which cancer passes through its latency period. Federal Judge Barbara Crabb, the same judge who heard and ruled on so many *Ojibwe* treaty rights, issued an injunction on January 31, 1984, proscribing any further construction of ELF in Michigan and any further "upgrading" of the Wisconsin facility. Within a couple of months the appellate court in Chicago lifted those injunctions based upon the Navy's claim of "national security."

The bench warrant [that led to my arrest at Butternut Lake] was for my lack of appearance in court to answer to what had been deemed crimes: spray painting five signs at Project ELF with new identification such as "Global Auschwitz," "Planetary Jonestown," "Bhopal for the World," "Nuclear Command Center," and "Danger: Nuclear First Strike Trigger." I did the spray painting on April Fools Day.[11]

During this time, I worked on other issues as well. When the Department of Energy came looking for a nuclear waste site in northern Wisconsin, Chippewa and environmentalist allies harangued them for nineteen hours straight at hearings in Ashland. I worked with Linda Cree and the Headwaters Peace Group on early mining concerns, and first met Wisconsin anti-mining activist Al Gedicks during the Black Hills Alliance.[12] This early anti-mining networking would prove valuable later when we discovered how treaty rights had an impact on plans for more mineral development in northern Wisconsin (for more on this see chapter 8). When Soviet troops were massing on the borders of Poland in 1981, we went to Ashland and did a Christmas vigil against Soviet intervention in Poland. We hooked up with Northland College and the Sigurd Olson Institute, which were both doing education and outreach on Native American culture and concerns.[13]

Tom Saunders of the Farm Unity Alliance did as much as anyone in showing me the value of establishing networking relationships between rural America and progressive multi-racial efforts like the Rainbow Coalition. Tom got me to come down to Jesse Jackson's farm rally for the Wisconsin primary in 1984 and made me aware of agribusiness's effort to foist the bovine growth hormone on dairy farmers.[14] This work with farmers and rural environmentalists started me thinking about what's happening in rural America today and where Native rights fits in with what is happening to our neighbors as well.

I joined the Journey for Freedom campaign that was done around the 1986 state elections, organized by Dennis Boyer and the Labor Farm Party of Wisconsin. We kicked it off with a Holly Near concert in Duluth, Minnesota, and came across Wisconsin, traveling by car, canoe, bike, and foot. At one point, people biked through the nuclear power plant grounds on Lake Michigan. Folksinger Larry Long did a concert at the Stockbridge-Munsee Reservation (just southwest of the Menominee Reservation). Along the way, we proposed, more as a rallying cry than a strategy, I think, a march through the sometimes unfriendly city of Minocqua. At Lac du Flambeau, we did a press conference that only three young women from the reservation came to. There were more press there than participants. The women said, "We've been waiting a long time for [someone like] you. When are we going to march through Minocqua, like you promised?" We organizers took a look at each other and said to ourselves: we'd better do this. They pulled out the eagle feather staff, and off we went. I realized then that this is what I was looking for: people rising, standing up for a cause, like these three young women.

At each place, I stopped to listen and learn and make allies. And as I responded to those openly responding to me, each issue became a window to someplace else I could go to promote the meaning of treaties in the ceded territory.[15]

Dennis Boyer left the Labor Farm Party to promote the formation of local and regional Green groups throughout the state, first with the Upper Great Lakes Green Network (founded in November 1987) and then Wisconsin Greens (founded in autumn of 1988). Boyer, Frank Koehn (now a county supervisor in Bayfield County) and I were the early Greens trying to figure out how to broaden the treaty alliance and the larger movement.

In the winter of 1986 to 1987, Boyer set up a public meeting at a union hall in Milwaukee where I first met Rick Whaley. He had grown up in ceded territory (though he didn't know it was), and, like me, was returning to childhood roots carrying similar social and environmental hopes for northern Wisconsin. He and his wife, Ellen Smith, had come out of the National Organization for an American Revolution, an antiracist formation of African-Americans who had recruited, in the 1980s, European-Americans like Rick and Ellen. Their work with Creek-Chicano activist Roberto Mendoza, the national Greens, and the North American Bioregional Congress would also give the Chippewa treaty rights struggle early national allies. Coming from this antiracist and organizer training background, this couple came up with the Peace on Earth event that spawned the Witness group in Milwaukee.[16] The rest would become all of our history together.

"Speaking with My Grandson: An Analysis of the Treaty Rights Issue" (A 1988 Speech)

In organizing, one can travel a narrow road and come to view one's issue as preeminent. But one overriding conclusion in my work is that all struggles are related and many methods are transferable between issues. Our current witness-for-nonviolence training material and many of our strategies come out of the Southern civil rights struggle and other nonviolence campaigns. Building alliances is about understanding oneself, believing in our own self-interest and cause, and then recognizing the common interests that exist between disparate groups. We ally not because we are "alike" nor to remake each other or to force compromise or correct tactics. We ally to affirm each other's strengths and to call upon that which we need but don't have ourselves. If we are to build even stronger alliances for our common goals, we must accommodate and encourage our personal and cultural differences, while tolerating our natural weaknesses, and thereby solidify our political partnerships.

I'd like to end this chapter with the text of a speech I gave that is an example of the speech-making I do regularly around the issue of treaty rights and spearing. It shows the form of some of my activism these days, thanks to the years of mentoring and alliances that have nurtured me. It also gives a sense of the emotional impact of the crisis. This speech was given at a public meeting in celebration of Black History Month on February 20, 1988.

I've been a witness myself to the past five years of confusion in northern Wisconsin, confusion over broad rights and concerns over natural resources. I'm not sure yet, in my own mind, why someone probably needs to die before we resolve this. I'm not quite sure why. I have some ideas, but I think that my ideas are too limiting. I think we need to broaden the discussion to include everyone in the state of Wisconsin. So the challenge is to our perceptions of what the issues are.

I was talking to Sierra [a Witness spokesperson] on the phone about a week ago, right after the Minnesota Chippewa tribes signed an agreement to give up their rights [like] the Chippewa rights in northern Wisconsin. We were talking about this upcoming meeting and I was emotionally distraught when she called. I don't know if she realized that. I didn't know what to do. That signing was like a death knell to what's going to happen here in Wisconsin. And as we were talking I did a flash forward, like one of those things you do in novels or the movies. I did that, right on the phone. I mean it was incredible. And there I was an old man. And there was a young man there next to me, and he was my grandson. I don't have any grandchildren, yet. And he looked at me and said, "Grandpa, do you remember when you had treaty rights?" And I nodded. And he said, "How come they sold them? Who sold them? And what's left for me?" And I cried on the phone. Because I tried to imagine what kind of an explanation I could give this child. I reached inside of my heart, inside of my mind, and couldn't find an answer.

It's as though Martin Luther King [Jr.] went to the mountain, saw the vista out there and went back and negotiated with the goddamn racists in the South and said, "Yes, you can call us niggers. It'll only cost you a million dollars. No, we won't sit in the front of the bus, but you gotta pay us $500,000. No, we won't sit at the lunch counter, but that will cost you two and a half million dollars." That's what happened in Minnesota. That's what's going to happen and that's what's being negotiated right now in Wisconsin [at Mole Lake]. It is illegal. It is immoral. It is abrogation of treaty rights through intimidation. It is de facto abrogation of treaty rights.

They're not gone yet, but they're really close. Why? It's because of the atmosphere. It's because of the disregard of the Constitution. It's because of the abdication of the responsibilities of the elected leadership of the state of Wisconsin and of our federal delegation. It's precisely because of the illegal, immoral blackmail and extortion by state and federal officials, which are forcing tribal members to sit at a "negotiating" table to forego our rights. It's illegal. [Treaties are] the supreme law of the land.

David Obey [7th congressional district], or Bob Kasten [Wisconsin U.S. senator], or James Sensenbrenner [9th congressional district], or [Governor]

Tommy Thompson or [attorney general] Donald Hanaway, has no right, no authority to bargain for my rights. I know he doesn't have enough money. But he has no right to bargain for those rights. Yet he's doing it and he's being allowed to do it. If I were to say, "I'm going to give you a housing project in Milwaukee. All you gotta agree is not to be so damn mouth-y about this racism stuff that's going on. That's the trade-off. We might even let you name the damn bridge—Father Groppi bridge—if you want. But just stop this racism business. We'll give you houses. We'll keep Chrysler in Kenosha. Just stop with this racism business. That's all you have to do. But if you don't, if you insist, you can forget about economic stability. You can forget about health, housing, medical care."

We used to have buffalo here in Wisconsin. I remember I traveled to the Southwest and I had this yearning in my heart when I was there. There's something there that was missing here. . . . Our buffalo, which is the pine, are gone. Our identity, which is a woodland identity, was slaughtered, is slaughtered. All of the spirits associated with a woodland culture w[ere] devastated. A holocaust occurred in the Great Lakes that was part of our identity. And so, we've never mourned, we've never mourned the loss of our identity. Instead, we look at the books of Wisconsin and we see the big piles of wood and the big people standing on the piles of wood celebrating the building of Milwaukee and Chicago, [all] over the loss of our identity of our homeland. The pine was our buffalo. And that's what's missing. And we need to yet mourn that. And we need to stop mourning things we shouldn't be losing in the future.

The PARR people are not the problem. They're a symptom of the problem. The problem is the state of Wisconsin, as the leaders of the citizenry. They're the leading anti-treaty organization in the state of Wisconsin. They have deliberately and consistently attacked the credibility of the tribes and the validity of the treaties. Until that changes, we will continue to have a fight with our families in northern Wisconsin. The PARR people are our kin. They're us. There ain't any foreigners out there. . . . This is a family dispute that's going on in northern Wisconsin.

The problem is they've been told that the problem is the Chippewa. Having problems at your resort? Having problems with the fish? Having problems with the economy? Having problems with tourism? Having problems? It's all the Chippewa's fault. So they turn to us and say, "If you guys would just behave yourselves or go away or go back to where you came from or whatever it is, then the problems will be solved." [PARR's] hurtin' and they have legitimate hurts and complaints. They've been told it's the Chippewa. They've been lied to. And therefore we're having this big fight.

In trying to understand the underlying causes of the battles in northern Wisconsin, the doubts that the Chippewa had about our rights remained nearby. Again and again, victims doubt themselves, wondering if indeed what we were doing was wrong. Wondering if we had indeed brought the violence upon ourselves. Wondering if we were the evil threats that the state and the other anti-Indian groups said we were. Yet, the facts remained clear. The rights were reserved and were not contrary to other rules of land law. The arguments over their age, always mentioned by the media reports, disintegrated when examined. These treaties were younger than the Bill of Rights, yet no one ever suggested that this should be thrown out. There seemed to be no lack of summer tourists since spearing began off-reservation, undercutting the argument that it would devastate this element of the northern economy. There wasn't an honest biologist in the country who could show that the Chippewa posed any threat to the resources. Yet, the anti-Indian movement and the state policies persisted.

After careful study of the protesters, filtering through the blatant and overt, listening to the emotions and feelings, it became clear that most of those at the landings really did believe that the Chippewa were the problem. Despite the legal, economic, and biological facts, protesters were ready to strike out at their neighbors, like inner-city looters burning down their own stores and neighborhoods, exasperated and angry with no answers. The Chippewa became the northern scapegoat of shifting economic and environmental realities. The court ruling of 1983 simply quickened the time in which residents would have to face these new realities. And they were not prepared and they hung rigidly to simple answers, simple enemies. The protesters were indeed threatened and their lifestyle was imperiled, but it was not the Chippewa who posed the threat. European-Americans were victims of failed or nonexistent economic and environmental policies. They were victims of educational institutions that left them socially and historically illiterate. And, they were victims of new interests finding their way into the northland.

So, we need to go back to our communities and find out what the real problems are. I'm willing to risk my treaty rights. I'm willing to say: if it is the Chippewa and if it is even spearing that is really the problem, I will forego, the operative word here, I will forego those rights. But I won't do it until we do a health assesment of the resources in northern Wisconsin. So that there's at least a year-long study where we can evaluate the relative health of the resources and we can look at all of the impacts [on] natural resources. So we can assess and determine: Do the paper companies have any impact on the natural resources? Does the motor boating have any impact on the contaminants in small lakes? Does the sports industry and all the paraphernalia associated with it have any kind of peculiar interest and impact on the natural resources? I'm willing to risk and give up my treaty rights if in an objective forum it's proven [Chippewa spearing is the problem].

Notes

This chapter on mentors and allies is based on Walt Bresette's writings and Rick Whaley's interviews with Walt in December 1991.

1. The Menominee Reservation is located in Shawano County in central Wisconsin. Despite exchanges of gunfire in the first days of the thirty-four day occupation, the National Guard kept out of sight of the abbey and kept local non-Indians away. The state of Wisconsin, Menominee Tribal Government, and the Menominee Warriors, who led the occupation, eventually negotiated a peaceful settlement to the situation.

2. The Great Lakes Intertribal Council is made up of representatives from several Wisconsin tribes, not just the Chippewa. Originally it was a Community Action Program (CAP) program set up to funnel federal poverty programs to Native communities in Wisconsin. It also serves as a quasi-lobbying group for tribes in Wisconsin.

3. NTCA was an organization not only for tribal officials, but rather open to any tribal member. Pat Locke, who was matron/mentor of NTCA, thought I was an up-and-comer and encouraged me here and later by her example. She did bilingual education in Canada and once did a conference presentation on education as war.

4. CERT became an "Indian energy think tank," inventorying energy reserves and analyzing strip mining laws and environmental regulations. The federal government provided money to CERT for development studies primarily focused on synfuels (e.g., coal gasification), mining, nuclear parks, and non-renewable resource extraction on Native U.S. reservations. See Winona LaDuke, "Selling the Indian Nation," *Workshop In Nonviolence (WIN)* magazine, February 1, 1980.

5. Clyde Warrior and Gerald Wilkerson are figures in the book *The New Indians,* by Stan Steiner (New York: Harper and Row, 1968). Years later, when I was in the army, I remember reading Clyde Warrior's obituary in *Time* magazine. He was one of the three mentioned that week. He died too young, only thirty years old.

6. Sharon Metz, later director of HONOR and key ally of Chippewa treaty rights, was a Democratic state representative from Green Bay and therefore represented the Oneida as well. Her contact with WIRC made her an early ally of Native causes.

7. Through the auspices of WIRC, we met with the editorial boards of the *Milwaukee Sentinel* and the *Milwaukee Journal,* among the most influential editorial boards in the state. We met in Racine at the Johnson Wax Company offices and charged them with biased reporting and blackouts on The Longest Walk, which they denied. Later in 1990 when I heard that *Wa-Swa-Gon* lawyer Lew Gurwitz and spearing coordinator Tom Maulson and Witnesses were going to meet with the *Milwaukee Journal* and *Sentinel* editorial boards, I remembered these earlier efforts.

8. As noted by Peter Matthiessen in his *In the Spirit of Crazy Horse* (New York: Viking Press, 1983, 1991), the AIM survival schools were "an attempt to help young Indians adjust to the white society without losing what was most valuable in their own culture, and to offset the distorted information about the Indian role in American history" (p. 36).

9. Great Lakes Indian Fish and Wildlife Commission (GLIFWC) began in 1984 when the Great Lakes Fisheries merged with the Voigt Task Force. Federally funded, GLIFWC is the Chippewa intertribal agency created after the *Voigt* decision to manage harvestable resources through biological surveys and planning, monitoring and enforcement, and coordination with the Wisconsin DNR.

10. Paul DeMain, Albee, and others also engineered the takeover of the Sawyer Democratic Party so LCO members were well represented in it, and they and their

sympathizers were the majority. DeMain worked on the campaign of Democratic candidate for governor Tony Earl, who was elected in 1982. DeMain was appointed to Earl's cabinet as Indian affairs advisor.

11. Tom Hastings, letter to Rick Whaley, "Witnessing in the Far North," March 27, 1990.

12. The Black Hills Alliance was formed in 1979 as Lakota and European-Americans in South Dakota joined forces to fight uranium mining and the resulting water depletion and contamination that would impact both communities. The Black Hills Alliance supported the Lakota people's land claim to the Black Hills. A support group in Madison, Wisconsin, did educational outreach for the alliance and brought people to the Black Hills Survival Gathering.

13. Sigurd Olson was the renowned northwoods guide and author of many loving books about this northwoods land we now share. The Sigurd Olson Institute does environmental education and connected up with the Chippewa tribes in this work on environmentalism and cross-cultural understanding. I met Sigurd one time. He told me he had once dated a woman from Bad River, but it didn't work out (and her family was glad).

14. Tom Saunders witnessed at the boat landings in 1989. He died tragically later that summer in a logging accident on his horse farm. His family was given an honor staff at the Labor Day Protect the Earth Gathering that year, and Tom was also honored by the Rainbow Coalition with their Rural Leadership Award for the bridge he provided to farm and rural concerns.

15. The Woodland Indian Arts collective that I put together also kept me in touch with artists and craftspeople on the different reservations in Wisconsin. At an art show in Red Cliff, I first met artists Karen Harvey and Merle Wolford, who would become key allies and facilitators in the Witness, Greens, and anti-mining struggle in Wisconsin. Traveling the pow-wow circuit selling art, tapes, books, and "trinkets" kept us in constant touch with other Indian people and our struggles and visions.

16. The organizer training background in Rick's case comes from the Midwest Academy in Chicago, founded in 1973 by Heather Booth. Midwest Academy's community organizing approach is sometimes referred to as a "neo-Alinsky" and thus they are heirs to the tradition that helped train Mike Chosa.

PART III

Powerful Enemies and Steady Friends

Spearing Gains Increased Attention as a Political Issue

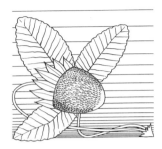

5

ODE IMIN GISISS
(The Strawberry Moon)

When a young Indian man says it's a good day to die, you need to listen carefully. You need to make this witness idea work.

—James Yellowbank
March 19, 1989

Why Are You Involved?
The Second Year of Spearfishing and Witnessing, 1989

Rick Whaley

THE YEAR 1989 BEGAN the full-throttle assault against Chippewa treaty rights by both the racist northwoods backlash and by the major political players at all levels of Wisconsin government. In this year also, the Witness stepped strongly into the public view at the boat landings and, along with other solidarity groups, into the public debate.

Political Assault

On Monday, February 20, 1989, Dean Crist and Al Soik of Stop Treaty Abuse-Wisconsin (STA–W) announced: "It is the intention of STA–W to encourage all its members, as well as all citizens, to use every available means to minimize the slaughter of spawning Wisconsin sport fish by nontraditional Chippewa spearing." The six-point program to disrupt Chippewa spearfishing in the spring included:

- as many citizens as possible coming to the boat landings to legally protest spearing;
- nonviolent civil protests including blocking landings or sit-in protests;
- as many boats as possible to be on the water during spearing and use of "whatever means are available to disrupt the slaughter";
- coordination of lake watch groups to inform residents when *their* lakes are to be speared;
- starting a legal defense fund for the defense of protesters who might be arrested;
- formation of a board of review to decide allotment of funds.[1]

STA–W also announced a walleye decoy contest where members were encouraged to produce concrete decoys to distract spearers (and break spears). The decoys most resembling walleyes would win and be placed in lakes. Said Crist, "The Chippewa are acting out of greed, not need. You do not need to jeopardize the resources in northern Wisconsin because of antiquated treaties."

The state of Wisconsin was pursuing its own course to stop 1989 spearfishing. January 1, 1989, brought the headlines that State Attorney General Donald Hanaway and the Wisconsin Department of Justice had drafted a settlement agreement with the Mole Lake Sokaogon Chippewa. The buyout plan, as the state's newspapers referred to it, offered the Sokaogon $10 million over a ten-year period to give up their off-reservation spearfishing rights and withdraw from the timber harvesting rights and back damages phases of the *Voigt* litigation that re-established Chippewa rights to off-reservation harvesting. Hanaway praised the "lease" agreement as a model for all the Chippewa bands in Wisconsin. (Since late 1988, Hanaway had been threatening Chippewa's legal gambling operations by promising that the state's ability to regulate lotteries and gambling on Indian reservations would "be part of the discussions" over treaty rights.)

Mole Lake tribal chairman Arlyn Ackley defended the proposed settlement and helped gain approval for the buyout from the Mole Lake tribal council. A deciding referendum vote was set for Saturday, January 14. At this time, Ackley was under indictment on two counts of selling cocaine to undercover agents in a sting operation set up by Hanaway's justice department in 1987. Convicted of the drug counts on January 14, Ackley's sentencing was scheduled for February 28, after the results of the settlement vote would be known. That January, Sokaogon tribal members voted overwhelmingly to reject the $10 million settlement. Tribal elders, among others, had counseled against undoing the agreements made in the nineteenth century treaties.

At this same time, attorneys for the state of Wisconsin were in federal district court arguing against what they called the Chippewa's "trust us" approach to their harvesting management plans. The Chippewa plans had, in fact, been highly successful and far more extensive than the WDNR's management of anglers' fishing. In November 1988, the same attorneys, led by Asst. Attorney General Thomas Dosch, were before Judge Crabb saying that the GLIFWC proposals would jeopardize the walleye and muskie populations in northern lakes. The state also claimed that the "safe allowable catch" on speared lakes causes sportfishing to suffer. (See chapter 7 for the Strickland Report and more on the great fish debate.) This was part of the state's potent three-prong strategy: fight the legality of treaties in the courts, fight co-management of off-reservation resources by the Chippewa despite this possibility being implied in Doyle's ruling, and join the public outcry over Chippewa harvests having a negative impact on resources and tourism in northern Wisconsin.

WDNR officials said publicly that if the Chippewa were allowed to spear to their court-allowed limit, the only thing left to do on Wisconsin lakes would be waterskiing. George Meyer, then the state's chief negotiator for the buyout bid, had plenty of negative things to say about the effects of Chippewa spearfishing. Much to the chagrin of treaty activists and Chippewa spearfishers, George Meyer was also the head of the WDNR's division of enforcement, the WDNR's man at the landings, and the person in charge of safety on the lakes in northern Wisconsin.

In early March 1989, northern Wisconsin sheriffs and police chiefs called on the state to enact a mutual aid package to cover financial costs of law enforcement (i.e., policing protesters) in spring, and to send police reinforcements or call out the National Guard "if shots were fired." By late March, Witness trainings had been completed in Madison and Milwaukee, rumors of a new settlement with Mole Lake abounded, and PARR had called on its members to stay away from the boat landings and focus on pressuring the federal government to "resolve the treaty problem."

At the instigation of Congressman David Obey (Dem.–Wausau), Wisconsin's congressional delegation sent a letter on April 18 to all the Lake Superior Chippewa tribal chairmen in Wisconsin. "We are greatly concerned," said the letter, "that the tribes exercise those [hunting and fishing] rights in a manner that does not create a danger to the livelihood of anyone else, or unfairly impinge on the ability of others to also use the resource in a given area." The congressmen, swallowing whole the disinformation campaign of STA–W and the state of Wisconsin that spearing damaged tourism and angling, warned against tribal intentions to engage in a "heavy harvest," though the Chippewa had never taken more than 3 to 4 percent of the state's overall walleye catch in a given year. This letter of congressional blackmail went on to clearly spell out their threat:

> Obviously, if the tribes choose, they can legally exercise these rights *without exhibiting due sensitivity to the needs of other groups.* But, the tribes will then have to appreciate that if they do engage in tribal activities that *needlessly inflame the*

situation and needlessly abuse the rights of other groups to share in the resource, then members of the congressional delegation will certainly have to take into account the tribes' lack of cooperation and their lack of sensitivity in assessing tribal requests for federal grants and projects. (emphasis added)[2]

Every member of Wisconsin's congressional delegation, Democrat and Republican, two senators and nine representatives, signed the letter.

No doubt feeling the squeeze from state and federal officials, tribal government representatives from the six reservations in Wisconsin met with Governor Tommy Thompson that same Wednesday, April 18, and agreed to cut their spearfishing quotas to 60 percent of the safe catch on fifteen northern Wisconsin lakes.[3] Tribal leaders bargained for safety at the boat landings and the governor was reported to have promised safe and separate, cordoned off areas for Chippewa families at the landings; the spearers could launch their boats and park their boat trailers at the landings; he would urge protesters to stay off lakes and landings; and he would make sure backup law enforcement was available in emergencies.

Both STA–W's Dean Crist and Oneida County Sheriff Charles Crofoot announced to the press that they would not be able to go along with such an agreement.

The Formation of *Wa-Swa-Gon*

The most significant political development of 1989 was the formation of the *Wa-Swa-Gon* Treaty Association by Lac du Flambeau spearfishers and supporters in early 1989.[4] *Lac du Flambeau* is the French phrase meaning *lake of the torches. Wa-Swa-Gon* is the *Ojibwe* phrase for place of the torches or spearing. The founding members, and others joining shortly thereafter, joined together to actively promote the exercise of off-reservation harvesting rights and the restoration of traditional *Ojibwe* culture. *Wa-Swa-Gon's* political arena included both their LdF reservation, where tribal government was considering its own buyout settlement, and Wisconsin at large: the press, the public, politicians, and supporters. Serving as host for the 1989 Witness, *Wa-Swa-Gon* issued the invitation for as many witnesses as possible to come to the landings in northern Wisconsin.

The person most branded a radical and militant by both the anti-treaty leaders and by state politicians has been Lac du Flambeau tribal judge, *Wa-Swa-Gon* co-founder, and spearing coordinator, Tom Maulson. Tom is fifty years old, a man with an easy smile, who looks like a defensive end for the Green Bay Packers or like Jim Thorpe might have looked at the same age. Laura Maulson, Tom's wife, is outgoing and energetic; together they run the family businesses—a restaurant, grocery-gas station, a reservation campground (until late 1989), and a bottled gas service. Tom also teaches scuba diving and rents scuba equipment. Dorothy Thoms has said of Laura, "With a wife like that, it's no wonder Tom can accomplish so much."

Their living room is filled with mounted fur animals and water birds. If you had just met Tom without an introduction to Wisconsin politics, you would think he was just another northwoods family man. Except, of course, that his mother is Chippewa. For this, and for being spearing coordinator for Vilas and Oneida county harvests, he is subject to an endless tirade of racial and sexual remarks against him and his family. "We need another Hitler to take care of that Jew Maulson." "Where's Gibby tonight, giving it to your daughter?" "Tom, Tom, the white man's son, spear a fish and away he run."

Maulson is not afraid to go to STA–W press conferences in Minocqua and verbally challenge Crist. In his younger years, Tom was not unwilling (nor is he now) to fight physically if he felt the situation called for it. Except for one incident when a Witness was shot in the kidney with a wrist rocket, Tom has never let anger get the best of him at the boat landings. His sense of humor in the face of the worst harassment, and his raw courage, have led him to wade into the most hostile crowd to dialogue with protesters or just walk through to prove he had a right to go where he was going. Still, even so imposing a figure can look small and vulnerable in an angry mob promising death and retaliation to him and his family.

The Upper Great Lakes Green Network Gathering was scheduled for April 22–23, 1989, to coincide with the opening of LdF spearfishing season. The first witnesses were often the organizers of local Green groups, in Bayfield, Madison, St. Croix, Milwaukee, and Ripon. When Witness and Greens coordinators arrived at the Treehaven Conference near Tomahawk, Wisconsin, Sierra Powers, spokesperson for the 1989 Witness, called Lac du Flambeau. Three witness coordinators, Sierra, Zoltán Grossman, and myself, are invited to a spearfishers' meeting taking place that Friday afternoon at LdF.

The three of us drive another fifty minutes up to the reservation and find the meeting at Tracy's Cafe. Tom is sitting at the lunch counter, apparently chairing a discussion of what to do since the governor has delayed the start of spearing season. The three of us outsiders find a table in the corner near Dorothy Thoms and Anita Koser and listen attentively. We feel honored and humble as those other few whites might have felt at the early SNCC meetings or at an early Malcolm X rally.

"The fish are already spawning. We can't afford to wait."

"He's trying to cut our season by making us wait."

"We ought to go anyway. I don't give a damn what Allen [the tribal chair] says."

"Thompson's trying to push the spearing into [the angler's] fishing season [May 6], so all hell breaks loose on the lakes."

Gibby, playing Malcolm to Tom's Martin, says, "We should have taken care of the protesters when this all started [1987]. Then we wouldn't have this problem now."

Tempers flare against the governor. Tom gets up from his stool and goes to sit at a table with another man I do not know, thereby yielding the floor (and facilitation) to the impassioned testimonials to courage and spearing, no matter what the state does. In a while, the tone of the discussion calms. Tom returns to the lunch counter. "If we fish now, it'll be our own tribal wardens who'll be arresting us, not the state. We should wait until Monday. If the state wants to stop the season, let them arrest us." This strategy prevails.

After the meeting breaks up, we go to Tom's table. I meet Nick Hockings for the first time. "It's like the sacred scrolls of the Jewish people," Nick tells us. "These treaties preserve our culture. They must be used to keep their power." We again extend the invitation for Wa-Swa-Gon *spearers and families to join us at Treehaven for our Saturday treaty discussion and Witness training. The invitation is accepted.*

Treehaven is a conference center and biology/environmental studies field station for the University of Wisconsin–Stevens Point, located in the north-central part of the state. Its environment-friendly, red brick dormitories and meeting places are built into the north side of a forest hilltop with the south, windowed sides facing a beautiful expanse of birch and pine woods. The Upper Great Lakes Green Network (UGLGN) has met there each spring since 1988 in conjunction with Chippewa spearing and the Witness effort. The model for these Green weekends has been to gather people from across the region to support a locally defined struggle. The host local group usually creates an educational event focusing on their issue (or related theoretical topic) and plans a public action to which Greens lend their support and participation. Saturday evening is a cultural event or social time, and Sunday morning is devoted to a Green business (politics and finances) meeting and sharing of other groups' issues and concerns. Past network issues have been toxins in Green Bay Harbor; the military's Project ELF (which extends into Michigan's Upper Peninsula); bleaching paper pulp mills in the Upper Peninsula; incineration in southeast Wisconsin; and stopping Kennecott's plans for an open copper mine one hundred feet from the Flambeau River in Lady-smith, Wisconsin.

Chippewa treaty rights has been the most dramatic and galvanizing of all the Green gathering issues. There is a deeply felt intersection of Native American earth philosophy and traditional practice, on the one hand, with the Green values of ecological wisdom, eco-feminism, and social justice, on the other. Combined with a strong activist sense of intervening in a white populist- and government-created crisis, the treaty rights issue has reached many movement campaigners, young and old, new and experienced, in Wisconsin and the Midwest in general.

The Saturday afternoon at Treehaven begins with a circle introduction and presentations by Dorothy Thoms, Maggie Johnson, Jeff Peterson (chair of Wisconsin Greens), Nick and Charlotte Hockings, Anita Koser, and Tom Maulson. Maggie Johnson is one of the Chippewa elders who was thrown to the ground from the back of a pickup truck at Butternut Lake 1987. Now, in 1989, she expresses her appreciation to witnesses who come to see what is happening.

Tom Maulson warns people about what we need to be prepared for.

What you hear at the landings is ugly—from the men—"We'll sleep with your squaws,"—from one woman protester—"I'd rather fuck a nigger than an Indian." You don't know what violence might happen, to spearers or those who come as their friends. The safety of my family and friends is at stake out there and so are my rights. I know why I'm involved. Why do you people want to get involved?

I remember the circle and fast at the Bad Axe massacre site near Victory, Wisconsin, Thanksgiving Day 1988. Walt Bresette had said, as the burning sage is shown and then drawn over each one there, "You have to be in this for yourself, not to help Indians. What is your story?"

We begin to go around the Treehaven circle:

"I love my Native American daughter. I have to make this racism [we see] and the struggle for rights my risk too."

"This issue is a symbol of my European-American past."

"If the German people had stepped forward earlier, my [Jewish] people might not have suffered."

"I live up here. You can't pigeonhole or stereotype people. Non-racists are at the landings too. . . . Spearers talk to the resort owners [who are worried about making a living]. We are brothers to the protesters, too."

"We're focused on the wrong issue. The mercury in the fish makes most inedible. All life is being threatened now."

"My father was a man of respect and honor. He kept his word."

"It all comes together for me here. . . ." Tears follow.

The emotional bond between Maulson and the witnesses is tangible.

"We can't let PARR rethink things" (i.e., define the politics of northern Wisconsin).

"This is my home. I want people to listen. I want peace in my own family."

Brandon Thoms, Anita Koser's son, relates what it's like to be a Chippewa student at the high school in Minocqua. "You don't know what it feels like to have people keep asking you, 'Do you have a job?' all the time." Brandon and some of the other young adults on the reservation are preparing for spearing for the first time.

Following a Witness training that afternoon, Nick Hockings leads the group in a closing ceremony, telling part of the Chippewa Seventh Fire Prophecy, the story of the new people, from all races, who come together to save the earth. Women at this Green Gathering are invited up to the reservation that evening for a Grandmother Moon ceremony. The men at Treehaven divide our evening watching a video on Chico Mendez and the rainforest struggle, playing pool with some of the teenagers at the conference, and drinking beer with a man we think is an infiltrator who enjoys telling us how risky it would be to go to the landings. We speculated afterwards that this might make a good male ritual for Green gatherings: retell the Chico Mendez story, spend time with the kids at the conference doing something they like, and distract the infiltrator-provocateurs.

"Send Me In, Coach": A Protester's Rambo Placard

Steve Semmelmeyer, the Minocqua Chamber of Commerce president and one sympathetic to the rights of the Chippewa, told a reporter in mid-April that, despite the negative publicity around spring spearfishing, tourism will keep thriving in the area:

> People last year were saying "this is going to kill the summer," and last year was one of the best we'd ever had . . . Out of the 15,000 to 25,000 requests we get every spring for information on our area, we have received five letters [this year] indicating that because of the Indian spearfishing season, these people have chosen to vacation elsewhere.[5]

On the eve of 1989 spearfishing, Semmelmeyer's car tires are slashed and a death threat is made against him.

The St. Croix Chippewa opened the 1989 spearing season on Sunday, April 23, in northwestern Wisconsin, followed a few days later by Lac du Flambeau's opening. As the press veil over boat landing protests began to lift in 1989, these were some of the incidents reported:

> At the Big Eau Pleine Reservoir in Marathon County that LdF opening night, protesters carried signs that said "Welfare or Walleye" and "Spear an Indian, Save a Walleye." One man carried an Indian effigy on a stick. When a spearer yelled back, "it's a harvest," at the crowd's accusation of "slaughter," a protester responded, "In the old days they used to harvest Indians."[6]
>
> Protesters lined rocks along the shore of the channel connecting Cranberry Lake and Catfish Lake, to greet and punish spearers on their way through. Midweek, at the Rainbow Flowage in Oneida County, a gunshot was fired from a protester's car that witnesses had been watching. The license number was given to a police officer but no action was taken.[7]

Despite the gunshot, tire slashing, and threatened violence, Attorney General Hanaway told a U.S. Civil Rights Commission hearing in Wausau that week that the protests had been nonviolent and had caused no injuries. The WDNR took advantage of the situation by choosing this time to announce that the bag limit for hook-and-line anglers on all the lakes open to Chippewa spearing would be reduced from five walleyes a day to three, despite the WDNR's plan since 1979 to reduce bag limits because of angler overfishing.

On April 28, as PARR and STA–W prepared for major weekend protests, news stories broke saying spearfishing opponents had collected $30,000 as a bounty on the heads of Tom Maulson and LdF tribal chair, Mike Allen. That night on Big Arbor Vitae Lake, police protection broke down again. Police stood shoulder to shoulder to hold back the protest mob, as protesters chanted "KGB" and recited the Pledge of Allegiance. Towards the end of the night, police told everyone to leave because spearers had come off the lake at another landing. The next day, the Witness found out that spearers had not come off the lake when we were told, and that when they finally did, they were met by angry protesters and had to remain in their boats for an hour and a half because the police were gone.[8] On the way back to the reservation, Gibby Chapman's car and boat trailer were run off the road. The assailant was apprehended by police but no charges were ever filed.

On Saturday, April 29, Governor Thompson, who spent the first week of the state's civil rights crisis in Europe on a trade mission, traveled to Boulder Junction, Wisconsin, to meet with protest leaders and resort owners. "If I had the right to change the treaties, I would be willing to change them," Thompson told them. But only the federal courts or Congress could do that, he added. A *Milwaukee Journal* article reported:

> Thompson acknowledged Saturday that police had received several reports of bombs being prepared for use against spearers. Nonetheless, the governor requested a scaling down in the use of bomb-sniffing dogs and other high profile security measures at the boat landings, in hopes of easing tensions.[9]

That night at North Twin Lake, 350 protesters and a hail of rocks and ball bearings fired from wrist rockets—sling shots tied to one's wrists—greeted the LdF women and men spearfishers. Police did not arrest anyone who threw rocks at the beginning of the evening because it was too hard to identify who was doing it, according to George Meyer of the WDNR. Later some arrests were made. On Sunday, April 30, PARR led a rally of two thousand people in Wausau and called for the resignation of Wisconsin's entire congressional delegation for not doing enough to get rid of treaties, except for Congressman Jim Sensenbrenner, Jr., who had introduced legislation to abrogate the treaties. Sunday night, spearfishers' canoes were overturned by the wakes of high-powered protest boats on Long Lake in Washburn County. How could Witnesses convey to a state and the public the facts as well as the outrage of what was going on, before it was too late?

Lake Minocqua: Sunday, April 30

Witnesses follow the caravan of spearers to Lake Tomahawk the evening of April 30, where a few spearing boats have put in but are not spearing. The police have put up snow fences to keep protesters away from the parking lot that is the boat landing to the lake. Witnesses, Chippewa families, and protesters are mixed together on two small hills overlooking the landing. Every person coming into these observation areas has to walk single file on a path between the snow fence and low pine boughs. Tom Maulson is standing by the parked spearing vehicles listening to the jeers from protesters as other spearing boats that had not gone out quietly leave the landing.

The boats in the water are a decoy. Tom feels the situation is not safe for spearers or supporters. We get word to leave as inconspicuously as possible and, a few minutes later, Maulson leaves, followed by a gaggle of protesters. Police scramble to get to wherever Maulson is headed before the protesters do. We head for Lake Minocqua to the boat landing in the city of Minocqua, just a few blocks from Dean Crist's pizza parlor.

I know this place. We are just down the shoreline from Bosacki's, a popular restaurant and boathouse in Minocqua. Bosacki's was famous for two incidents in 1988: in one, Mr. Bosacki, the owner, was quoted in the press as saying the spearfishers were like an "invading" army coming on his lake to spear, and in the second, a cocktail lounge singer at his establishment did a derogatory, anti-Indian tune during his evening performance. Bosacki's is where I came as a youngster to watch the water-ski shows. One summer, we saw Dwight and Mamie Eisenhower there on vacation. The crowd gathered along the street and hill above the shoreline just to get a look and wave at the president and his wife. Tonight, now, we have gotten to the landing just before this new crowd, come to stare in hatred, not curiosity, fills the street and hill surrounding the boat landing by a bar and grill called the Thirsty Whale.

We take a position as near to the shore as we can get, alongside the tavern and across the driveway from where spearers and their families have parked their vehicles. The protesters start arriving immediately and take the hill back above the landing and small parking lot. Despite the agreement with Governor Thompson to provide safe and separate places at landings, the scene at Lake Minocqua is wide open. As protesters realize they will not be restricted to their chosen spot, they press down to where we are, carrying signs and yelling. We try to form a human barrier between Chippewa families and protesters. James Yellowbank (from the Chicago Indian Treaty Rights Committee) tries to reason with them. "Can't you see you're being used? The fish are poisoned. The mines are coming. You have more in common with the Chippewa. . . ." The protesters will have none of it.

Things are becoming very tense. The protest crowd has grown much larger. We are easily outnumbered eight to one. We try to find the police commander in charge. Law enforcement officers from various jurisdictions are trying to decide what to do (including deciding who's in charge among them). No, we can't keep protesters out of here, they tell Maulson and the Witness coordinators, as the yellow crime tape goes up holding us all in the tavern side of the driveway. In 1989, Maulson will probably spend more time in the two-week season negotiating at the landings for protection than he does spearing. He finally tells officers he is going to move his people over by their cars.

"No, you can't," he is told.

"We can't stay here," he says and, risking arrest for all of us, lifts up the crime tape and leads us over to the family cars.

Here we find relative safety for a while. Spearing boats are unloaded from trailers as the mob chants "bullshit, bullshit" and "timber niggers!" Anti-treaty signs wave and a three-fingered devil sign is flashed at spearers. Protesters with their boats come in to unload to the cheers of the crowd. Witness Karen Harvey walks out into the driveway, right up to a protester and writes down the number of his boat. "What the fuck do you think you're doing?" he says.

"Taking your boat number," she says, doing police work the police won't do.

I can't decide which is worse—the times when the crowd's chanting crescendos and threatens to unleash a mob, or the times when we stand in the bitter cold with only boat lights in the distance, not knowing what will happen next.

This is the third night of spearing after the $30,000 bounty has been placed on Tom's life. Farther west on the shoreline is a railroad trestle that offers a direct view of our side of the landing. Police say they have checked the trestle for snipers, but will not post any officers there for the evening.

A group of Chippewa women and a number of witnesses have braved the crowd on the other side to go and use the bathrooms in the Thirsty Whale. In the hallway outside the women's bathroom, the bar manager is screaming at the women to get out of there. He tries to come in and pull them out. As the witness and Chippewa women come out in the hall to leave with the men witnesses, the male patrons of the bar create a gauntlet of harassment. "You can shove those drumsticks up your ass!" "Abortionists!" To an older witness woman: "You're one of the ones who serviced the men in World War II." Outside on the Thirsty Whale dock are stacks of splintered 2"x 2" wood sticks, broken off and pointed at the ends, and lengths of pipe ("from the construction," the manager says). Witness coordinators have to negotiate, fortunately successfully, for the right to use restrooms at the temporary law enforcement headquarters, lest we risk life and limb and dignity to pee in a Minocqua tavern.

As the cold and bitter evening wears on, the police make it clear that, while they will keep the protest crowd apart from the Chippewa families and witnesses, they will not prevent individual protesters from coming over to our area. It then becomes the macho test to travel through to our "enemy" side and say something to Tom Maulson. Despite witness pleas to police, anyone can venture in our midst to verbally assault the spearing coordinator and Chippewa women.

I am standing behind Tom Maulson, trying to watch the protest mob, the infiltrators coming over, and the nearby railroad trestle at the same time. A man with a placard suddenly walks up on Maulson's backside and yells, "Maulson, you deserve whatever you get." Tom has turned to look at him at his first shout. After a moment's pause, he turns back away from this indignity, the first time I have seen him refuse to dialogue with a protester. The protester waves his sign at his friends on the other side. They cheer loudly.

Maybe it can work to break the mob's energy to look across the way at the faces of individuals protesting. I see a man with a PARR–Milwaukee sign looking directly at me. I gaze back at him. When I was in high school in Wausau, my father, a Goldwater Republican, asked me if I wanted to take the pretest for the Naval Academy at Annapolis: "You'd make a good officer." Telescoping back in time, I wonder, how many steps is it from playing cowboys to neighborhood fights to Annapolis to Vietnam? Which side of the hill might I have been standing on? The fear that lies beneath all other fears: that I look among the protesters and see my own face, shouting as stubbornly self-righteous and hateful as my northern Wisconsin brothers.

The bitter cold has not only drained me but the protest mob's temper as well. The only excitement comes when a spearer's boat comes in to unload and count the walleyes and the crowd chants and hurls its insults again. As the evening winds on, the size of the crowd begins to wane. A spearer's boat is now being set onto its trailer, getting ready to leave. The phantom friend of "equal rights," Dean Crist, suddenly appears and sits down in front of the Chippewa vehicle. As he is arrested by police, the crowd cheers him and yells at the police. "It's his city," says one of the Chippewa. "He had to do something while we were here."

A while later, Tom tells us that the other spearing boats are going to get off the lake at another landing. We don't know if this tactical maneuver is something he's considering, something he's told police (who have been known to convey spearers' plans to protesters) in order to get protesters to leave, or if it's already happened. We wait a while longer until Tom feels the boats are safely in, then leave with Chippewa families, carefully caravaning back to Lac du Flambeau.

That same night, Sunday, April 30, on Lower Eau Claire Lake in Douglas County, gunshots are fired at Red Cliff spearers, including tribal judge Andrew Gokee. According to the WDNR, the suspect allegedly was shooting into a tree trying to knock branches down onto spearers' heads. On Monday night, May 1, on Catfish Lake in Vilas County, thirty to forty protest boats harass spearers on the lake. When spearers Ray Cadotte and Nick Hockings land on shore, a shower of rocks comes at them. When they request help from the police, they are told, "We're sorry, we can't. There are too many of them."

Storming the Capitol

Monday morning, May 1, Sarah Backus, from the Milwaukee Witness for Non-Violence, met Walt Bresette in Madison for a capitol-storming tour of state legislators. Sarah remembers the events of that week:

I had been coordinating [witnesses] at Lac du Flambeau and it was clear that law enforcement wasn't doing an adequate job. Every night, there were acts of violence from being spit at to gunshots to threats of death. We talked to law enforcement and WDNR at the landings and made daily calls to state government. I talked to Walt, who was having the same problems at Red Cliff, and he said, "Maybe the problem is we're trying to deal with this at the landings and the people [law enforcement] at the landings are not empowered to deal with it. We need to go to the state capitol." Walt was on his way to the Green Earth Festival in Milwaukee [to speak] and said he would stop in Madison to meet me there on my way home. We wanted to see any politician whose door we could find open and tell them who we were, where we had been, and what we'd been through in the last week.

We found a mixed bag. [David] Clarenbach [Dem.–Madison] was sympathetic but said it wasn't his realm. Marcia Coggs [African-American, Dem.– Milwaukee] understood fully and would have called out the National Guard.

She got us in to see Mr. [Tom] Loftus [Dem.–Sun Prairie, Speaker of the Assembly]. Loftus, at that time, felt a negotiated settlement was the way to go. We found this pretty disturbing and Walt said angrily, "We'll bring the first brown body here and lay it on your desk, sir, because we're not going to be selling off our birthrights."

We then went to the governor's office and Walt asked to see the governor. He was out. Walt asked to see Waldo (Buck) Martin [Native American advisor on the governor's staff]. The secretary got up and walked back to another office. She came back and told Walt that Buck was not in and wouldn't be back. Walt had asked me before going up to this desk to wait in the hall, but I was in hearing distance of this conversation. When Walt came out he said to me, "Now you go in there." I went in and asked to see Buck Martin. The secretary got up and went to the back office and came back. "Follow me please." I went in and met Buck Martin in a parlor. . . . How could he not be there when an Indian spearfisher wants to talk to him but he is there for a nursery school teacher from Milwaukee?

I said to him, "I'm very concerned and confused about the level of antagonism and violence against Indian people [in northern Wisconsin] and by the nonresponse of the state of Wisconsin." We met for about fifteen minutes.

Buck said, "There's a lot you don't understand about Indian politics. There's a lot you don't understand about Indian economics. There will be a negotiated settlement and that will take care of everything." He said that spearfishers were militant and rabble rousers and just looking for trouble.

"Can you give me examples?" I said.

"The fact that the press has reported the first two nights' catch was given to elders and those who were unable to leave their homes. I know for a fact that spearfishers have extorted money out of the elders for those fish."

I then showed a little bit more of my hand by saying that I helped clean those fish that first and second night and that women and children went to deliver those fish. I had accompanied them on one of those trips and that no money was offered, expected, or demanded.

Buck then changed his line and said it happened last year. Names? Places? He had none.

"What will happen if Indian people in a referendum vote turn down [a settlement] and say we won't take money for birthrights?"

He was clearly agitated and said, "Then they're going to have the same thing happening to them next year." This was said in the tone of a promise. He then stood up and ended the interview.

After lunch, Walt and I came back to the capitol and Governor Thompson was giving a press conference on a timber export deal he has made for the state. Walt was carrying a "Not for Sale" sign. The sign actually came from a Milwaukee neighborhood struggle against realtors trying to scare neighbors into selling their homes cheap by putting up a lot of "For Sale" signs. The press there raised the issue that things were out of control up north . . . [and] the National Guard needed to be called out. The governor said: "Everything is fine. Law enforcement is doing its job. They have a tough job, they're facing problems from *both sides*" (emphasis added).

This was such a blatant lie. I couldn't stand and speak to it [I was so shook]. I hadn't felt that way for years, not since I was six months pregnant. Walt got up and said, "Governor, could you explain that statement?"

"Walter, Walter, I don't have time to talk about this now. This conference is on another matter."

Walt turned to me and said, "He called me Walter. I never met the man and he calls me Walter." We spent Monday and Tuesday there [in Madison]. We went to the university and spoke before law and history classes. We got on radio [e.g., WORT]. . . .

I didn't go home. I headed back up north. What I did then was remove myself from my documenting witnessing job to interview law enforcement (Tuesday through Saturday nights): Can you give me examples of trouble, harassment from spearfishers or from Witness observers? I spoke with forty officers. Thirty-eight said: absolutely none. Two said, no comment. Most said it was just the opposite: it's the protesters, but our hands are tied. . . . We're following a game plan. [For example] at Squirrel Lake, I was told [by law enforcement] that the game plan comes directly from the governor's office."[10]

By Any Means Necessary

Wednesday night, May 3, blew in another storm of protesters at Upper St. Croix Lake, located about thirty miles south of Superior, Wisconsin. High school students fired ball bearings and rocks at Red Cliff spearers from the shoreline. European-Americans Patrick Coughlin, a welder by trade, and Bruce Currie had tested pipe bombs a few weeks earlier at a northern Wisconsin gravel pit. They were drinking together this Wednesday night, when they heard that Upper St. Croix was going to be speared. They drove there, first to the Palmer boat landing and threw a pipe bomb into a ditch a ways from the landing, making a loud crack in the night. They then drove to the Hendry boat landing where the students and main body of protesters were. Walking into the woods near the landing to plant the second pipe bomb, Coughlin was spotted by police and arrested.[11]

Exasperated with the failure of all political and moral appeals to get the state to do its law enforcement job, the Lac du Flambeau tribal government played its one power card. They threatened to take 100 percent of the safe harvest (still only 35 percent of the walleyes, but it would close those lakes to anglers) on the spearing lakes where law enforcement was not adequate. "My people are suffering," said chair Mike Allen. "We are under incredible physical and verbal attack."

Governor Thompson responded by going into federal court to stop not the protests, but Chippewa spearing. On Thursday, May 4, the state of Wisconsin petitioned the Federal District Court to halt spearfishing at midnight on Friday and limit Chippewa spearing to 60 percent of the safe harvest. At a press conference at the state capitol, Governor Thompson said, "Today in northern Wisconsin, the public safety is at risk. Very clearly, the state lacks the capacity to provide an adequate level of on-water enforcement and protection." The governor then said he would rather halt spearfishing than call out the National Guard as peacekeepers. James Klauser, the governor's top aide, said that if Judge Crabb ruled against the state, the governor "would do everything within his constitutional authority to stop spearfishing."

Judge Barbara Crabb ruled on that Thursday that the Chippewa could take their court-affirmed quota on approved lakes in northern Wisconsin. "On what basis do you believe the Lac du Flambeau should give up a right that this court has recognized, the Seventh Circuit Court has recognized?" she asked. On Friday, Judge Crabb refused the state's request to end spearing at midnight, saying, "If this court holds that violent and lawless protests can determine the rights of the residents of this state, what message will that send? Will that not encourage others to seek to resolve disputes by physical intimidation?"

Judge Crabb criticized the state for trying to stop the Chippewa from doing what they were legally entitled to do:

It [the state] is seeking an injunction against the tribes solely because persons opposed to the lawful activities are engaging in illegal and wrongful acts against the tribal members. . . . We know from our recent past that racial tensions and controversies over the exercise of rights can lead to bloodshed.

But can we let the fear of bloodshed destroy our state and our country? What kind of country would we have if the brave people [the Southern civil rights movement] had not faced down the prejudiced, the violent and the lawless in the 1960s? What kind will we be if we do not do the same today?[12]

Crabb reminded Thompson, and the protesters, that treaty rights were not unequal fishing rights, but rather contractual rights agreed by the U.S. government and the Chippewa nation. In court, Thompson justified his position by saying, "I decided there was no walleye worth getting hurt over, getting drowned, getting killed [over]."

That same Friday afternoon, Crandon High School in northern Wisconsin closed after a bomb threat was made against the school and another threat was made against the principal, Jeffrey Jacobson. The day before, parents of fifty of the Chippewa students (20 percent of the school enrollment is Chippewa) had pulled their kids out of school because of a derogatory, anti-treaty T-shirt being worn by some of the European-American students. In Milwaukee on Friday night, two hundred people attended a vigil for peace at the WDNR regional office, sponsored by the Witness for Non-Violence, with African-American legislators, Native American community leaders, and European-American ministers and activists speaking.

The Witness scrambled to keep up with the nightly chaos, documenting as much as we could, and simultaneously keeping track of the daytime state political intrigue. We worked hard to get more people to stay for the week-night witnessing and rallied as many people as possible to come north for the expected turmoil of the coming, final weekend. As frightening as the boat landings were, the more terrifying prospect was the chance that we might not reach any audience or authority that would stop the nightly madness that was also the state's pretext for ending off-reservation harvesting.

At the boat landings on Trout Lake that night, according to the *Milwaukee Sentinel*, "at least three people were injured and more than 100 protesters were arrested . . . as police moved to quell a massive anti-spearing demonstration. . . . Officers swung riots sticks and several protesters fell to the ground as a wave of demonstrators broke through police lines and pandemonium broke loose."[13] Dennis Sloniker, owner of the Squirrel Lake Resort near Woodruff, said before his arrest there, "After the judge's announcement today, these people are more determined than ever."[14] Dean Crist said on Saturday that protesters would again try to storm the landings used by spearers, as had been done on Friday night. Thus the stage was set for what would be the season finale that night at Butternut Lake.

AIM Joins the Pro-Treaty Forces for the Season Finale: An Eyewitness Report from Walt Bresette

As the anti-spearing protests escalated at the landings during our 1989 Chippewa spearing season, we wanted an international forum to help us gain further support, and also to embarrass state officials who were contributing to the violence by supporting the political goals of the anti-Indian backlash. While many individuals thought an American Indian Movement (AIM) presence was needed, others, including myself, thought it would be even more effective if AIM came under the auspices of the International Indian Treaty Council (IITC), a United Nations-recognized nongovernmental organization. We asked IITC representatives in Minneapolis for a press statement saying that IITC would send monitors to the boat landings and report the situation of the Chippewa of northern Wisconsin to the United Nations. Instead, we heard AIM was sending members to the boat landings, with no mention of the role of the IITC. Thereafter, except through other international channels developed within the Witness network, no direct mention was made of the U.N. connection. I felt we had lost a great opportunity to elevate the issue to the status it deserved.

Our first encounter with AIM support of Chippewa spearing came at the boiling point of the 1989 season. The night of Trout Lake 1989 spearing, James Yellowbank (of Chicago's Indian Treaty Rights Committee) and I were at the LdF Witness office listening on the CB radio to events at that lake. The protests sounded awful. Then we received word via CB that AIM was on the way and the sheriffs were waiting for them. James and I had to make a decision. By the time the fifteen-to-thirty-car contingent arrived at LdF from Minneapolis, it would be dark and we didn't know what would go down with police and protesters if AIM continued as supposedly planned to Trout Lake. Rumors abounded that AIM was coming with guns. When they arrived, we'd decided: we gave them a gracious welcome at LdF and tried to get as many people as possible to give speeches. Towards the end of these, we said, "Well, thank you very much for coming. Get a good night's rest, because we're going to need you tomorrow."

The next day, things were tense on the LdF Reservation. "AIM is coming, AIM is coming. What's going to happen?" The refrain was a rising crescendo. Some in the tribal government wanted to toss AIM out. Yellowbank and I were trying to keep them in. Tribal chair Mike Allen and spearing coordinator Tom Maulson were trying to juggle all the community politics. Over at the community center, people were gathering for ceremonies and a rally. Things were chaotic, nothing was coming together.

Then I overheard the story that AIM had called the rally, trying to steal the thunder for our work. I was pissed they had so easily fallen back into the old mode that I'd witnessed in 1979 at Bad River. I went up to Vernon Bellecourt and told him that we had people from Madison and Milwaukee and Chicago come to the boat landings for us. "They risked their lives for us, they've done everything, and you people were nowhere to be seen. And now you guys come in here, jump in front of this big parade and, if you in any way imply that it's your show, I'm going to hold a press conference and denounce you."

Vernon said, "No, Walt, that's not what we're doing. We're letting the world know what's happening here."

Negotiating roles in the solidarity movement, especially with respect for Native leaders of past struggles, was difficult. Sometimes Indian people defend themselves by using the threat of AIM coming in, like the traditional mom of the past who said to her child, "Behave, or *Windigo* (a sort of Chippewa boogie man) will get you": Behave, or AIM will come in. But the wrong reaction by AIM to police or protesters in Wisconsin could have jeopardized the work already done here. Trout Lake the night before had looked like a setup for AIM and any trouble that might have happened there would have been blamed on Chippewa treaty rights. While Vernon had been upset that AIM didn't go to the landing at Trout Lake, AIM observed the nonviolent discipline that Tom Maulson and *Wa-Swa-Gon* had requested of them.

AIM helped calm things down within the overall solidarity movement— telling their own members to stay home if they couldn't come unarmed, and calming down Native elements more militant than they were. AIM also paved the way for a critical cultural aspect, so crucial to struggles of the 1960s and now today, by bringing the Indian drum to Lac du Flambeau and protecting it at the landings, especially that Saturday night.

The Battle for Butternut Hill

Over two thousand Native American and allied supporters rallied at the Lac du Flambeau Reservation Saturday afternoon. The entire day consisted of rallies, speakers, coming together. James Yellowbank spoke and asked the spearers to stand, to a rousing ovation and appreciation from the crowd. An emotional Tom Maulson described the kind of hatred spearers and families had to go through and thanked supporters for their efforts. After the speaking, two thousand people, Indian and non-Indian, joined together in a huge feast.

As Walt Bresette would later tell a national Greens conference:

One night, on a little lake called Butternut, 1500 people came and stood with us, and they kept coming and coming. Nick Hockings was the sixth car from a 300-car caravan—miles long of people going to Butternut Lake. And the contras were out there and we was listenin' to them on the CB's. And they said as they were reporting to the other terrorists who were elsewhere around the lake, "Oh my God, the whole *Ojibwe* Nation is on the move." And they were right. That night, that time, that moment, that cause, that issue made everyone *Ojibwe.*[15]

A crowd of five hundred protesters stepped back to allow the support contingent, led by the American Indian Movement (AIM) drum, through to a position near the shore and landing. The crowd was on the hill behind and above them, allowing protesters to throw objects as well as their usual verbal abuse down on Chippewa families, witnesses, and supporters. Police kept protesters off the landing but did little to stop the hilltop harassment. Gradually, a large group of supporters began to move and shoulder their way back up the hill (Walleye Hill, as one Native American vet said, a Porkchop Hill without guns). A while later, supporters were in the majority on the hilltop and the harassment stopped. The nonviolent battle for Butternut Hill had been won.

The following day, the Lac du Flambeau tribal government announced that it was ending the season's spearfishing. "It is a gesture of good will that neither the state officials nor the people of northern Wisconsin deserve," said LdF chair, Mike Allen, Sr., "but that we are freely offering them anyway." The anti-treaty protest declared another season's victory for themselves, as a canoe painted with a sign, "Winner by TKO: STA–Wis." joined a party of a hundred protesters at the Arbor Vitae Town Hall Sunday evening. But that Sunday afternoon in Madison, five hundred people had rallied in support of Chippewa treaty rights, hearing speakers from the Rainbow Coalition, Indigenous Law Students Association, Jobs with Peace, and spearing families and Native American supporters.

Mending: After the Season Was Over

The gatherings of Indian and non-Indian people that early May weekend in Wisconsin were the beginnings of the healing from the trauma of spearfishing protests. Sarah Backus said that May 6 at LdF and then at Butternut Lake was a wonderful, and necessary, symbolic statement of victorious nonviolence and the protection of birthrights.

Supporters and Chippewa families were reunited many times during the rest of 1989. GLIFWC chair Jim Schlender initiated a Chippewa Walk for Justice that began at the Lac du Flambeau Reservation June 20, with *Wa-Swa-Gon* organizing it and supporters joining along the way to another weekend rally in Madison. A small number of witnesses returned north for the brief gill-netting season (also a treaty-guaranteed right). July 4, 1989, brought supporters from around Wisconsin, from Chicago and the Twin Cities, and even from the Dakotas, to LdF for a rally and pow-wow and a Fourth of July parade through the neighboring city of Minocqua, where the *Wa-Swa-Gon* supporter contingent was met by ice throwing and verbal hostility from some local protesters but mostly curiosity from the large tourist crowd. On Labor Day weekend in Ladysmith, Wisconsin, the Protect the Earth Festival united the local residents fighting the proposed Kennecott mine there with Chippewa activists and treaty supporters. Spearfishers and families traveled to Milwaukee for the Indian Summer weekend and pow-wow and Walt Bresette gave a Columbus Day address at the University of Wisconsin–Milwaukee that was broadcast on public radio.

The emotional fallout and, for some, the transformation that resulted from this year of trauma was described by Sarah Backus this way:

> Some people stopped drinking, other people started. Some people's [primary] relationship broke up. Some new ones started. . . . There was a whole new understanding and a real awakening of cultural pride and curiosity. It became more important to Indian families. [Local] people were coming into the LdF Witness office that last week of spearing and saying, "We don't spearfish, we don't know who you are, but thank you for coming. Here's some food for you."
>
> Many people became more angry because of what happened. Many Indian women have told me how important it has been to write it down, to talk about it and keep talking about it. They were verbally assaulted, pushed and shoved and sexually grabbed at the landings. [No arrests were made for this "free speech" exercise, as protest leaders referred to the nightly harassments.] That anger is still there from this. And one of the good things is that we've continued to network and go up to the reservations and we at least provide a look at another way for European people to conduct themselves, to carry *ourselves*.
>
> I don't know that I'll ever really recover in a sense. I certainly won't go back to being who I was. We continue to meet, to actively work . . . toward peace with justice, for Indian people and ourselves. We are struggling for our people to be something honorable, something to be proud of. That's very important for my great-grandchildren in my European family.[16]

Steve Semmelmeyer resigned as president of the Minocqua Chamber of Commerce after the 1989 spearfishing season, saying that it was the protests, not spearfishing, that would hurt northern Wisconsin. "If tourism is down," he said, "they [the protesters] have only themselves to blame."[17] In July of 1989, Lac du Flambeau gill-netters returned to some off-reservation lakes. In gill-netting, the net, balanced with weights and floats, is lowered unfurled to a specific depth and then unrolled by a slow-moving boat and marked by buoys. Larger fish swim into the stationary net and are caught by the gills. Dorothy Thoms took out a netting permit and went out on Lake Minocqua with younger netters and was bumped by a protester boat and verbally harassed. On July 2, Tom Maulson and Sarah Backus were attacked, with rocks and ball bearings fired from protesters in high-powered boats, while checking gill nets on Big Arbor Vitae Lake. (See chapter 6 for a fuller report on this incident.) However, boat landing protests were small because resort and business owners were too busy taking care of a record number of tourists in northern Wisconsin that summer.[18]

Conditions for Peace? Evaluating 1989

1989 was the year treaty rights were to be won or lost at the landings. The scenario of massive political pressure from the state combined with the violence of the boat landings could have spelled the quick end of meaningful treaty rights. Some tribal governments were ready to accept any conditions of peace so their people would not have to face that kind of terrorism again. Wisconsin's congressional delegation had been convinced that the only hope was for the Chippewa to decrease or stop exercising their off-reservation rights. The Wisconsin state legislature was cajoled into passing a resolution asking the federal government to step in and solve the "treaty problem." State Senator Walter Chilsen (Rep.–Wausau) even went so far as to say he wanted the federal government to order Chippewa tribal leaders to the negotiating table. He argued, "I think the federal government would have more negotiating power, even if it's only the aura of the *great white father*" (emphasis added).[19] And the lack of enforcement at the landings was designed to permanently scare off spearers and to convince the press and public that popular (white, majority) opinion could not be eased without stopping off-reservation spearing altogether.

Some religious groups lobbied on behalf of peace and the treaties, most notably, Honor Our Neighbors Origins and Rights (HONOR), as did tribal governments,[20] but the major presence of European-American and other non-Indian supporters in 1989, up north and in the press, were the witnesses who had seen firsthand what was happening at the landings. Witnesses and numerous members of the press broke the taboo on the vile words and violence of the protests. These observers called rocks and pipe bombs what they were. Witnesses documented police behavior and helped tribes and religious allies pressure for accountable law enforcement. Lies on behalf of abrogation were effectively countered: the Witness added a supportive voice to tribal governments and their mainstream allies, condemning politicians who threatened to cut government funds if the Chippewa did not give up their other legitimate rights. We pointed out, in as many conversations and forums as possible, that the Chippewa taking 3 percent of the walleye harvest in the state was not "raping a resource," nor was it ruining the northern Wisconsin tourism season, which was a successful one in the summer of 1989.[21] Harvesting rights were, and still remain, constitutionally protected property rights and represent a different tradition of harvest, but aren't unequal rights. The deceit that treaties were racism against whites and that the protests were designed to help the Chippewa by ending reservation and treaty status and assimilating them into the twentieth century, were uncovered and shown, to most, to be a foolish sham by anti-Indian bigots.

In a letter of thanks to spearfishing and gill netting witnesses, *Wa-Swa-Gon* secretary Anita Koser said:

> During our past (1989) spearfishing season we sent out a cry for help and the Witness for Non-Violence responded immediately. Several people had been prepared to come at a literal moment's notice.
>
> It is our firm belief that the Witnesses' presence at the boat landings and their accompanying us to and from those landings via car caravans averted serious physical violence and possibly even death from being inflicted upon our spearers, their families, and our supporters . . .
>
> The Witness women have reached out to Chippewa women with empathy, giving us much needed moral support. (The anti-treaty people are especially vile and virulent to Chippewa women, who are shocked and sickened by degrading, sexually explicit threats and remarks made to them.)
>
> The Witnesses have helped our people to remain peaceful, courageous, dignified, and steadfast in the face of adversity. They have reinforced our resolve to not react to violence and confrontation with like actions.
>
> When our spirits were at the lowest, they showed us that not all non-Indians hate us and want to harm us. We need their peaceful support.[22]

Above all, witnesses broke the previous dynamic of a whole state, all white people, against the *Anishinabe*. It was no longer everyone against a few spearers. It was a state divided over the treatment of Indians and larger political agendas. The drama of what happened at the landings became a story told over and over again throughout Wisconsin and the Midwest. The many stories focused not only on the parallels to the southern civil rights movement but on the long and continuous struggle of Native Americans to teach how culture and preserving the land go together, and what political honor means among neighbors.

Notes

1. Quincy Dadisman, "Group lists plans to disrupt spearing," *Milwaukee Sentinel,* February 21, 1989.

2. David R. Obey, Congress of the United States, House of Representatives, letter to Lake Superior Chippewas Tribal Chairmen, April 18, 1989.

3. In her March 3 ruling, Federal Judge Crabb set the safe take from any lake at 35 percent of the total allowable catch, or about 12 percent of the total fish population. A quota of 60 percent of the safe catch would mean 7.35 percent of a given fish species in a lake. See "Chippewa slash spearing quotas in exchange for promise of safety," *Milwaukee Sentinel,* April 20, 1989.

4. Tom and Laura Maulson, Maggie Johnson, Dorothy Thoms, Art and Anita Koser, Freddie Maulson, Scott Smith, Bobby Chapman, Gibby Chapman, Nick and Charlotte Hockings, and Goldie Larson were the founders of *Wa-Swa-Gon*.

5. Frank Morris, "Northwoods tourism industry hopes for best," *Wausau Daily Herald*, April 23, 1989.

6. Maurice Wozniak, "Jeers, scuffle mar spearing by Flambeau," *Milwaukee Journal*, April 26, 1989.

7. *Witness for Non-Violence 1989 Report*, p. 19A. This report was given to Wisconsin's Equal Rights Commission on September 19, 1989, and also given then to Attorney General Hanaway, but no action issued from either office.

8. Witness statement of Monica Lauer, *Witness for Non-Violence 1989 Report*, pp. 1–2.

9. Maurice Wozniak, "Spearers brave snow, rocks, and protesters," *Milwaukee Journal*, April 30, 1989. The *Milwaukee Sentinel* (April 29, 1989) quoted a source saying the protesters also had military mines they might use on lakes that were being speared.

10. Sarah Backus, interview with Rick Whaley, January 19, 1991, Milwaukee, at her home.

11. Mary Jo Kewley, "Pipebomber: 'I'm not an Indian hater,'" *Wausau Daily Herald*, April 30, 1990. Coughlin was convicted and sentenced to a year in federal prison for possession of two pipe bombs; Currie was convicted for aiding Coughlin in constructing and carrying pipe bombs and sentenced to nine months.

12. Steve Schultze, "Judge likens furor to '60s rights battle," *Milwaukee Journal*, May 6, 1989.

13. Rick Romell (from reports by Lee Bergquist, James B. Nelson, Quincy Dadisman, and Terry Kuper), "95 spearing foes arrested," *Milwaukee Sentinel*, May 6, 1989.

14. Ron Seely, "Spearing tensions mount," *Wisconsin State Journal*, May 6, 1989.

15. Walt Bressete, "We are all Mohawks," keynote address at national Green Gathering, September 14, 1990.

16. Sarah Backus, interview with Rick Whaley, January 19, 1991, Milwaukee.

17. James Nelson, *Milwaukee Sentinel*, May 8, 1989.

18. See *Wausau Record Herald* front-page headline, "Profits preclude protests," July 3, 1989. Al Soik, president of STA–W, said, "This is our biggest weekend of the whole year and people that would like to be out there are too busy working in restaurants, hotels and other businesses. Some of our staunchest supporters can't make it."

19. Bill Gordon, "State urges visiting BIA official to aid talks on treaty rights," *Milwaukee Journal*, June 1, 1989.

20. The Oneida tribal government took out a full-page ad in state newspapers in support of the Chippewa. See, for example, *Milwaukee Journal*, Sunday, May 7, 1989.

21. "Tourism has grown every year since the *Voigt* decision and the 1989 season was up three percent over the 1988 season." Rennard Strickland, Stephen J. Herzberg, and Steven R. Owens, "Keeping Our Word: Indian Treaty Rights and Public Responsibilities" (The Strickland Report), prepared for U.S. Senator Daniel

Inoyue, April 16, 1990. In addition to pointing out the successful tourist season, the pro-treaty movement and the press, in general, also gave note to Jack Grey's 1981 study of northern Wisconsin resorts and tourism trends which showed that changes in vacationing patterns by families and the condition of older resorts were the main probable causes of the decline in fishing resort occupancies (see Chapter 2, Rural Gentrification section).

22. Anita Koser, *Wa-Swa-Gon* secretary, "Letter of Support," July 1989.

The Spearfishers: Walleye Warriors

Lac du Flambeau spearfishers Tom Maulson (front), Ed Chosa (middle) and Treat Chosa (standing). Photo by Paul Calhoun.

Photograph on this page:
     Spearer Chuckie Wolf waiting inside sherrif's snow fence to go out on North Twin Lake, 1990. Photo by Dale Kakkak.

Photographs on facing page, clockwise from bottom:
     Nick Hockings, a *Wa-Swa-Gon* leader, getting ready for a night of spearfishing on an off-reservation lake. Impact Visuals, photo by Andrew Lichtenstein.
     Gibby Chapman (left) and Robert Martin (right), Lac du Flambeau and *Wa-Swa-Gon* members, sharpen the tines of a spear. GLIFWC photo by Amoose.
     Spearer Yolanda St. Germaine with a ten-pound walleye. Photo by Chris Nelson.

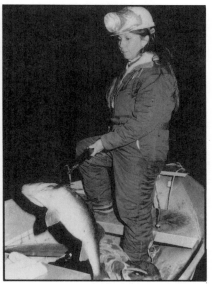

Photographs on facing page, clockwise from bottom right :

Ed Bearheart, a spearfisher from the St. Croix tribe, has also served as tribal council representative to the *Voigt* Task Force, 1987–1991. He was also a vice chair and witness coordinator. Photo by Barb Katt.

Dorothy Thoms (seated) and her daughter Anita Koser were key advisors and members of the Milwaukee Witness for Non-Violence and among the founders of *Wa-Swa-Gon* in 1988–1989. Photo by Casey Lake.

Gloria Merrill, human services facilitator for St. Croix tribe and St. Croix witness coordinator, 1989–1992, pictured with her granddaughter, Amber. Photo by Barb Katt.

Fred Ackley, Mole Lake tribal judge and spearfisher, also chairs the Mole Lake Mining Impact Committee. Photo by Ellen Smith.

Gaiashkibos, a spearfisher and tribal chair from Lac Courte Oreilles, is shown standing beside his wife Rita Barber celebrating his election as president of the National Congress of American Indians in 1991. GLIFWC photo by Amoose.

Photograph on this page:

Wa-Swa-Gon's Tom Maulson (left) with Bad River spearers, Joe Dan Rose (center) and Matt O'Claire (right), at Lake Minocqua spearing, Spring 1990. GLIFWC photo by Amoose.

The Protesters

Photographs on facing page, from top to bottom:

Spearer Reuben Zortman (silhouette left) watches protester boats try to block spearfishers' access to Plum Lake, April 25, 1990. Howie Caputo (front of boat at left) and Dean Crist (middle boat waving one hand) were both defendants in Lac du Flambeau/*Wa-Swa-Gon*'s lawsuit to gain a permanent injunction against STA–W for interfering with the walleye harvest. Photo by Charlotte Hockings.

Walt Bresette, Chippewa orator, cofounder of the Witness for Non-Violence, and advocate for the Greens and the Indigenous Environmental Network, superimposed on the Native American flag, symbol of spearing rights and displayed at many boat landing events by Indian supporters. Photo by Dale Kakkak.

Photograph on this page:

This masked protester at Balsam Lake, 1990, was recorded by a member of the Witness as shouting "Get a job and get off welfare" and "Did you buy that boat with our tax money?" Photo by Dale Kakkak.

STOP
MAULSON'S
MEATHEADS

TRIBAL JUDGE?
OR
TRIBAL SMUDGE
SLUDGE!

BALD EAGLE
Bar & Grill
FOOD DRINKS

SAVE A WALLEYE
SEND RAMBO
TO
FLAMBEAU!

ABORGATE
DON'T
NEGOTIATE

The Supporters

Photographs on facing page, clockwise from bottom:
    Big Eau Plaine, 1992, anti-treaty protest. Photo by Dale Kakkak.
    Protester sign. GLIFWC photo.
    Dean Crist (seated left) at one of his many court appearances with his lawyer, Fred Hatch (seated right). Photo by Amoose.
    Junction of county roads B and CC. No photo credit available.

Photograph on this page:
    T & L Mini-Mart at Lac du Flambeau was the staging area for the spearers and witnesses getting ready to leave each evening of off-reservation spearing. Pictured here is a drum gathering which often preceded the departure for the lake. GLIFWC photo by Amoose.

Photographs on facing page, clockwise from middle right:

Young Chippewa examines the catch, 1991. GLIFWC photo.

March on Ashland City Hall, 1987, to protest anti-treaty resolution; Red Cliff and Bad River members and supporters. GLIFWC photo by Amoose.

The 1988 boat landing witnesses included: (back row left to right) Bob Kasper, Blake Gentry, Sherrole Benton, and Aimee Dunn; (front row left to right) Sierra Powers, Linda Cree, and Rick Whaley. Photo by Rob Kanter.

Spearfishers and treaty supporters strategize during a day-long meeting at the Mineapolis American Indian Center, 1990. Everyone is concerned about possible violence at the boat landings. GLIFWC photo by Amoose.

Photograph on this page:

Despite a bomb threat, treaty supporters rallied in solidarity with spearfishers, May 6, 1989, at Lac du Flambeau, before going out to Butternut Lake for the closing night of LdF spearing. GLIFWC photo by Amoose.

Photograph on following page:

The drum-centered spearers and witnesses at boat landings during the roughest years of protest. Chippewa drummers at Lake Minocqua, 1990, Brandon Koser (center). Photo by Paul Calhoun.

MISKIWIMINI GISISS
(Moon of the Raspberries)

6

I come here for Dr. King
Who gave the people a precious thing.
He found a light in the darkest hour
And the strength for speaking truth to
power. *

—Jackson Browne

The River Opens to the Righteous
The Civil Rights Legacy and White
Backlash Today

Rick Whaley

THE FACT THAT NO Chippewa blood has been shed in the boat landing confrontations is one of the great legacies of the African-American civil rights movement, for the consciousness of what happened then and the base of political allies to fight injustice still remains. Because of public sensibilities about what happened in the Deep South and current laws against racial violence, a line of deadly force remains that anti-treaty protesters would not cross. Federal Judge Barbara Crabb would draw clear parallels between Black voting and desegregation rights and the Chippewa's harvesting rights, both of which had to be accomplished in the face of backlash protest. The support of progressive constituencies—liberal churches, the American Civil Liberties Union (ACLU), some journalists and a few editors, and foundations with money to give proved critical to the 1980s alliance for Native rights in

129

Wisconsin. While sovereignty rights of Native nations in the United States have a different constitutional basis than civil rights, the fact that the exercise of Native treaty rights was met by racist threats and violent disruptions made the protection of Chippewa spearers a civil rights issue as well. And, like the southern civil rights cause, the movement for constitutionally protected rights and an end to racial harassment brought forth, in the Native community, a renaissance of culture and history, and, among allies from many races, hundreds of nonviolent witnesses willing to risk themselves at northern boat landings.

The 1954 *Brown vs. Board of Education* Supreme Court ruling opened up school desegregation in the South. Similarly, Chippewa off-reservation harvesting rights were set forth in a favorable federal court ruling by Judge Doyle in 1987. The treaty rights case affirmed constitutional rights the Chippewa had always held but had been denied by dominant culture and state law for many decades. In October 1983, after the *Voigt* decision was affirmed by U.S. Supreme Court, then-Governor Tony Earl issued a proclamation calling for cooperation and government to government relations between Wisconsin and the tribes. However, the state of Wisconsin, especially the WDNR, continued to work hard against the exercise of treaty harvesting rights. As with the landmark school integration ruling, there was a critical period of time immediately after the treaty rights ruling during which the government— both state and federal—could have stepped in with accurate information to assuage European-American fears and with a program of policy cooperation and reconciliation.

From the 1987 headlines—"Three Judge Panel Gives Chippewa Unlimited Hunting and Fishing Rights"—to continued coverage of STA–W deceits as if they were fact, state newspapers, especially in northern Wisconsin, fanned the flames of misinformation and protest.[1] In the South following the 1954 Supreme Court decision, the atmosphere was moderately calm until 1956 when the Dixiecrat Manifesto signed by one hundred southern congressmen gave the green light to racial demagoguery and protests of all kinds.[2] President Eisenhower said in 1956 that he supported the laws of the land on school desegregation, but didn't say how he would enforce them. In the interim (1954–1956), one of Eisenhower's top aide's circulated behind the southern scenes a program for the South to resist and nullify the Court's decision. In Wisconsin, the state promised to appeal Judge Doyle's 1987 ruling and Judge Crabb's subsequent amplifications of the case.

The treaty protests in northern Wisconsin have been reminiscent of the protests in the Deep South that blocked school desegregation in Little Rock, voter registration in Mississippi, and the Freedom Riders in Birmingham, Albany, and McComb. Even the off-stage intimidation is similar, including death threats and bounties on Chippewa leaders. Rock throwing and large-scale confrontations against Chippewa spearing were common in 1989 and 1990.[3] A 1990 boat landing saw protesters rock the van of spearer Mike Chosa and sexually threaten the children inside. Boat landing protests with the most vitriolic of slurs against Native Americans (e.g., "red niggers" and "Indian women use fish instead of men") is the same as the shower of hate sprayed on the nine African-American students desegregating Little Rock's Central High and on the multi-racial contingent of Freedom Riders in Georgia and Alabama. State officials in the Wisconsin of late 1980s, like the shrewd Dixiecrats of the former era, condemned the mob violence (not wishing to scare off tourists), but continued to support (and use) the white backlash agenda of ending off-reservation harvesting. The ultimate protection the Chippewa had from the murderous conclusion to all the threats was the legacy—legal gains, political, religious, and media connections, and public consciousness—of the civil rights movement, a shield African-Americans had fashioned with their own blood three decades earlier.

Nightriders: An Eyewitness Report from Sarah Backus

In the summer of 1989, *Wa-Swa-Gon* requested witnesses for the brief gill-netting season. Despite the very few protesters at boat landings, an on-lake attack occurred that was as terrifying as any spearfishing lake protest. On a summer Sunday night, July 2, gill-netter Tom Maulson and witness Sarah Backus went out to check gill nets on Big Arbor Vitae Lake in Vilas County. There were twenty-five to thirty other observers/supporters at the boat landing that night, some Chippewa families and wardens from the Great Lakes Indian Fish and Wildlife Commission (GLIFWC). Only a handful of anti-treaty protesters, including Dean Crist, had made an appearance and apparently departed by the time Tom and Sarah went out to check the nets. It was very quiet out on the water—what seemed to be the most peaceful night of the *Ojibwe* fishing season.

Sarah Backus's complaint, filed with Vilas County Sheriff's Department, read in part:

The net buoys appeared safely anchored in their proper place so we started back to the boat landing. Within a minute or so of leaving the buoy area, we came alongside a pontoon boat with 6–7 men aboard. We fell into a lively but overall civilized question-and-answer dialogue that went on for about a half hour during which time our boats rested side by side.

Tom then observed two boats at the net buoys and called out "Move away from there. Leave the nets alone." He repeated this again and then said to me, "We're going to have to go over there." We headed off directly toward the buoys.

The boats had moved away by the time we reached the buoy but we were immediately surrounded by four motor boats and, within another minute, by two more of the same. This was the beginning of an assault that lasted for thirty to forty minutes. The boats, which Tom estimated at between 70 and 100 horsepower, continued circling us at high speed, causing tremendous wakes and quake. The occupants were screaming at us, hooting and hollering, "Die tonight!" "We got you now, Maulson," and vulgarities. A GLIFWC boat with two wardens, Leroy Cardinal and Larry Mann, were in the circle with us. They came alongside and clasped our boats together in an attempt to secure some balance to both boats. The water was tumultuous. We were taking on water as we attempted to stay calm and identify any of the numbers on the boats. This was nearly impossible as they had bright lights upon us at all times. Warden Mann called in a threat-to-life message to shore for WDNR and sheriffs, saying, "Get some help or we're going to lose one of our boats." At this point the attacking boats were closer, the yelling more frenzied and I felt a definite threat to my physical safety and/or life.

Approximately five minutes after the call for help, the circle seemed to widen somewhat. Tom said, "We're not going to be able to get the nets in tonight. We have to secure the buoys as best we can and get the hell off the lake!" We waited another minute or two for the safest apparent opening.

Our boats [Tom's and GLIFWC's] then separated. Tom approached the nearest buoy but we were surrounded again by the same boats, this time at even closer range [than] before we arrived at the buoy. Then, a repeat of the high speed attempt to swamp or capsize us. The same hooting and hollering with the additional statements: "You won't leave the water, tonight," "We're going to kill you, Maulson," "You're going to burn."

Tom's boat, a 25-horsepower, 20-year-old Shell Lake tri-haul, was pitching and shaking so badly now that all of our attention was focused on attempting to stay balanced and hoping that some help would arrive. At no time up to now did we shout or yell anything at our assailants. We did call to each other to "just hold on." Then one of the boats broke formation, followed directly by another boat, both coming at the same high speed directly at our boat. We didn't say anything to each other. I believed simply that they were going to ram us.

It was at that moment that I was struck by a wrist rocket on my lower left back just above my kidney. The pain was extreme, causing me to yell out and pitching me forward in my seat. Other rocks and stones were also hitting the boat, some falling into our boat. Tom was yelling at me, asking if I was okay? Was it a wrist rocket? (We didn't know until the following day for sure that it was a wrist rocket, as the bruised area on my back developed into the resemblance of a bull's-eye perfectly round inner circle with extended circles. We also discovered the fired ball bearings in the bottom of Tom's boat the next morning.)

The boats that appeared to be coming at us were just missing us. I don't know which boat the shot was fired from. Everything was going on so fast now and the lights were still brightly shining on us. I was leaned over in the boat that Tom was now motoring as fast as possible through their line. They chased us, cutting in front at angles when they could. Tom kept up a weaving action and somehow put twenty to thirty feet between us and them, then doused the lights so they couldn't see us. Tom got us back in to the boat landing. Five to ten minutes later the WDNR warden arrived, going out immediately in a boat. Apparently the sheriffs were simultaneously putting in at another landing. GLIFWC wardens got boat numbers on four of the assailant boats . . .

WDNR warden Scovel refused to hear my account or take a statement, saying I needed to report to the sheriff. Sgt. Mike Schuster [sheriff] first said I should talk to the WDNR. Then he [Schuster] took my statement and drove me to the hospital.

No arrests or citations were issued that night to the best of my knowledge. The men from the pontoon boat later said they weren't responsible to help us even if they did know we were in serious trouble because they themselves were not attacking us. "We're just observers out there." "Yea, we're just the advisors," followed by much laughter.[4]

Sarah was taken to the Howard Young Medical Center in Woodruff where the doctor told her she was lucky. If the shot had hit her a few inches lower, she would have lost a kidney. One citation was given out that night to a protester boat filled with rocks and ball bearings—for having no boat light on. Chippewa netters and witnesses felt that the men on the pontoon boat had been there to vouch for the "accident," had anything happened to Tom or Sarah. In our Deep North, the perpetrators' version of the story was accepted by sheriffs and district attorneys over the evidence of victims. One of the greatest obstacles to adequate law enforcement in northern Wisconsin remains, to this day, the unwillingness of local district attorneys to charge or prosecute anti-Chippewa actions to the full extent of the law, echoing again the old Deep South alliance of nightriders, law enforcement, and local district attorneys.

The Rise of the New Right:
The Rhetoric of "Equal Rights vs. Special Rights"

The New Right was the backlash product of the civil rights era and learned well the lessons from that movement, coopting its equal rights theme and adapting their strategies for the new issues and conditions of today. Their analysis (though not public) of why those opposed to the civil rights movement lost might go this way: the Klan protests and other tactics alienated even the southern press, sent clergy scurrying away (even some fundamentalists like Billy Graham), and did little effective coalition-building with white business people and professionals beyond the "old boys" (Jim Crow) network. Since the 1960s, racist backlash has continued to be central to the emergence and continuing

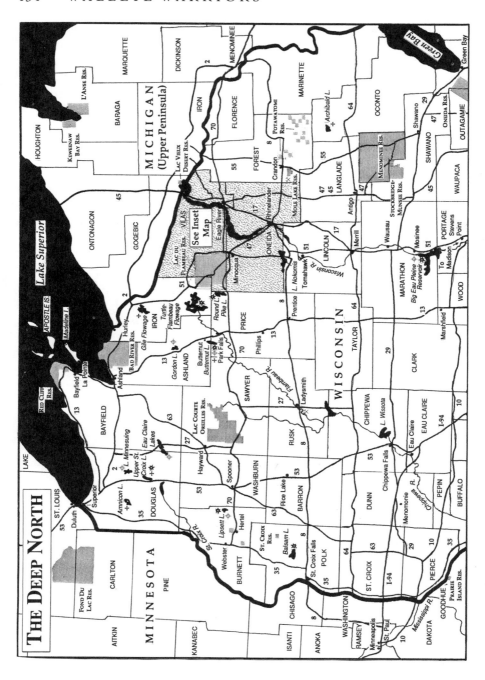

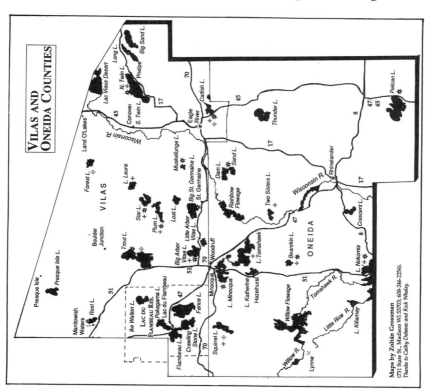

VILAS AND ONEIDA COUNTIES

Maps by Zoltán Grossman
(731 State St., Madison WI 53703; 608-246-2256).
Thanks to Cathy Debevec and Rick Whaley.

Highlights of Anti-Indian Harassment, 1988-92

✳ Large-scale rallies, confrontations, arrests, or on-water harassment

✚ Throwing of objects (rocks, bottles, cans, ball bearings, pipe bombs, etc.)

⊕ Gunshots on water

ASHLAND COUNTY
Butternut Lake: Crucible protests, 1987-88; 600 protesters and 1000 witnesses/ AIM, Guard helicopter, 1989; Gunshots, 1990
Gordon Lake: Gunshots, 1990

BAYFIELD COUNTY
Lower Eau Claire Lake: Gunshots fired at Judge A. Gokee, 1989; Gunshots, 1990

BURNETT COUNTY
Lipsett Lake: Gunshots, 1990; Father and son driven off lake, 1992

DOUGLAS COUNTY
Amnicon Lake: Rock-throwing, 1991
Minnesuing Lake: Gunshots, 1991
Upper St. Croix Lake: Pipe bomb arrest, 1989

IRON COUNTY
Gile Flowage: Full beer cans thrown at spearers, 1990
Turtle-Flambeau Flowage: Witnesses link arms to protect Chippewa drum and families, 1990

MARATHON COUNTY
Big Eau Pleine Reservoir: Drunk crowd surrounds AIM drum, witnesses assaulted, gunshots, 1990; Opening night crowds 1991-92

OCONTO COUNTY
Archibald Lake: Rock-throwing, 1991

ONEIDA COUNTY
Bearskin Lake: Rock-throwing by large crowds, 1988-89
Lake Minocqua: K. Hemming leads blockade, elders assaulted, 1988; T. Maulson coordinates spearing under death threat, 1989; Wakes nearly swamp gillnetting boat with D. Thorns, 1989
Lake Nokomis: Rocks thrown at boat, 1990; Crist incites with verbal abuse, police test ceremonial sage, 1991; Chair thrown at boat, 1992
Pelican Lake: Bomb threat, 1990
Sand Lake: Protesters on bridge, 1990; Chippewa family and African-American witness assaulted, 1991
Squirrel Lake: Rock-throwing, 1990-92; Gunshots 1991
Lake Tomahawk: Rock-throwing, 1991
Two Sisters Lake: Rocks thrown at boats, 1990

POLK COUNTY
Balsam Lake: PARR-AIM confrontation, 1990

PRICE COUNTY
Round Lake: Police arrest two for carrying Indian flag, 1990

VILAS COUNTY
Big Arbor Vitae Lake: Landing blockade,1989; Wrist rocket attack on gillnetter T. Maulson and witness S. Backus, 1989; Protesters surround drum, throw rocks at F. Maulson and witnesses, 1990
Big St. Germaine Lake: Crist leads mass arrests, 1990
Catfish Lake: Rocks thrown at spearers, 1989-91; Gunshots, 1990-91; Large wakes, 1991
Forest Lake: Gunshots, 1991
Lake Laura: Death threat against N. Hockings, rock-throwing, 1991
North Twin Lake: Rocks, bottles, ball bearings fired at spearers, protesters rush witnesses and families, 1989; Rock-throwing, 1990
Plum Lake: Rock-throwing, 1989-91; Wakes injure D. Hockings, 1990
Star Lake: Blockade, rock-throwing, and rooftop confrontation, 1990
Trout Lake: Mass arrests after STA protesters rush police line, 1990; Gunshot, 1991

appeal of the new single-issue groups the New Right has pulled together, often under a new "equal rights" banner: anti-affirmative action, anti-busing; anti-liberal textbooks and anti-multicultural college courses and disciplines; anti-crime, now called the war on drugs (where people of color communities often feel they are the target not the beneficiary); and, most recently, the national abrogation of treaties effort to get at Native American land and resources.[5]

The sports fishermen's backlash to the federal court ruling recognizing Chippewa off-reservation harvesting rights provided an ideal issue for New Right organizing in Wisconsin. PARR claimed a membership of 5000 in 1990. In 1988, they had estimated 9000 members. STA–W claimed a membership of 3000 in 1989.[6] These figures represented, if they had any resemblance to truth, their mailing lists, which they probably built through securing the mailing lists of various fishing and hunting magazines. Whether this backlash protest was initiated by the powerful conservative economic players here remains unclear. What is clear, however, is that Democratic and Republican politicians capitalized on the economic fears and social resentments evident in northern Wisconsin. More significantly, the political value of negating Native rights and influence over resource management and economic development was recognized right away and carefully cultivated by Republican politicians with ties to energy corporations with mineral holdings in the ceded territory.

The central psychology of this national white populist/New Right organizing has been the attitude that big government protects the rich *and* the poor, and neglects the Middle American.[7] "The working man's [sic] brew," Treaty Beer, was Dean Crist's effort to raise money and consciousness for his campaign against spearing and the treaties.[8] The New Right manipulates middle- and working-class men's feeling that they have been paying, with their taxes, for this special treatment accorded minorities and women by the legislation and court rulings of the 1960s and 1970s. Hence, the hammering away at Chippewa harvesting as unfair, "special" hunting and fishing rights. PARR Executive Director Larry Greschner said:

> What happened at the boat landings in northern Wisconsin on a couple of instances this past spring [1988] was not, for the most part, racism. It was, plain and simple, frustration on the part of concerned people who are not being listened to by their elected officials at both the state and federal level, people who feel nobody is looking out for their rights, which were very obviously denied at those boat landings.
>
> We don't believe that just because one dares assert that the majority has rights, also, and that these rights ought not to be superceded by court-ordered, not treaty rights, of a minority, that person is a racist. Aren't human beings really to be considered equal in American society?[9]

The behind-the-scenes influence of New Right advisors or congressional mentors can be seen in strategies developed by boat landing protesters. When the

1989 protests became racially ugly *and* were publicized as such, the protesters put away their "Save a walleye, Spear a squaw" signs and "timber nigger" chants, and pulled out for the TV cameras little American flags and their "equal rights" chant. The influence of the anti-abortion movement, so central to New Right success, can also be seen in the "Stop the Slaughter [of spawning walleye]" slogan, the "Save the Unborn Fish" sign at an anti-treaty rally in Madison in 1989, and the civil disobedience efforts to sit down in front of Chippewa trailers and boats trying to launch. Yet, despite the PR pleas, after 1989, of Crist and PARR's Larry Peterson, asking their members not to be racist, it was STA–W fabrications and PARR's reinterpretation of history and court rulings that continued to put protesters, including racists, at the landings each spring.[10]

In 1980s Wisconsin, the first major political stake was the state government's desire to control resource management. Despite the avowed hatred of PARR and STA–W for the WDNR (after all, it is WDNR wardens who arrest sport fishers and hunters for exceeding bag or size limits), the protesters' agenda of halting off-reservation harvesting fit well with WDNR desires to eliminate any co-management of resources with the Chippewa. Governor Thompson and Attorney General Hanaway even argued that any co-management plans were not permissible under Wisconsin's constitution.

The second major political stake was the desire to mine—which was threatened by the potential power of treaty rights to stop mining interests. As early as 1976, Exxon had attempted to mine for copper and zinc at a site near and under the Mole Lake (Sokaogon) Reservation. By 1986, a combination of environmentalist and Native American efforts to save the Sokaogon wild rice beds, along with an international decline in copper prices, saved this area for the time being. As the political intrigue of the 1989 spearing season unfolded, the treaty rights movement learned that multinational corporations had major lease holdings throughout northern Wisconsin and that exploratory drilling was already taking place. Department of administration head James Klauser repeatedly denied that efforts to end off-reservation spearing had anything to do with the possibility that treaty rights could be invoked to stop mining as a potential hazard to the health of the Chippewa's harvestable resources. (For more on this issue see chapter 8).[11]

White Wounds

As in many other places, the message of ending special rights for minorities and saving the economy fell on receptive ears. This was not because most European-Americans think who-gets-what-trophy-fish-by-what-method is really worth a one-sided race war. It was because the economic suffering of European-Americans in northern counties is as real and nearly as harsh as it is for Native Americans. Sociology professor David Damrell noted these points at the 1989 Weaving the Web Conference: the average income in Vilas County is $8,426/year; in Oneida County, $8,758/year; and in Iron County, $6,490/

year.[12] (Native American unemployment in Wisconsin is 46 percent; of those employed, 76 percent earn less than $7,000/year.) Two thirds of those people living in the northern tier of the United States are poor, by U.S. Congressional standards ($12,000/year or less for a family of four) especially since the U.S. economy shifted from an industrial base to service sector jobs in the early 1980s. This shift created a working class that cannot get out of poverty. In northern Wisconsin, there are now a few new jobs, a few old, well-paid union jobs, and a standard of living that is declining for all.

As Damrell noted, people share the same economic fate, but European-Americans are socially isolated with the attitude: "I'm poor, but at least I'm not Indian." "I think what we're seeing there is people who are losing the social privileges that used to come from being white that are no longer there because their standard of living is dropping too." Damrell added:

> At the end of the civil war in the South when the whites lost their privileges . . . what rose up? The Klan. We may be seeing a similar phenomenon. . . . These people [PARR and STA–W] are not the Klan, yet. But they had the same mentality: to contain Native Americans, to not let them exercise their sovereignty because they will lose their white privilege which is all they have.[13]

Numerous signs indicated that the resentments and building backlash in Wisconsin were of interest to Far Right organizers. A notice put up in an Eagle River bowling alley in 1989 was signed A.N., believed to be Aryan Nations. The notice called for gunshots to intimidate spearers and urged snipers to fire at boats in the caravans to the landings. (This was one key reason why witnesses caravaned to the boat landings with spearers and their vehicles.) Milwaukee Skinheads from the White Patriots League were in attendance at the anti-treaty rally in Madison in 1989. The Populist Party USA, which in 1988 had nominated David Duke as its presidential candidate, held a meeting in DePere, Wisconsin, in 1990. PARR and STA–W members were among the main invited constituents. Dean Crist was widely quoted in the press as saying he liked what David Duke had to say. "It's as if he's been reading STA literature," Crist said.

Even the emotional wounds of the Vietnam War were mixed in with the frustrations and bias at the boat landings: On April 29, 1989, at Rest Lake, I listened to one drunken protester wander through our witness crowd mumbling, "The Chippewa are a conquered nation, just like the Vietnamese." Laid-off millworkers, fishing guides, and low-income cottage owners who need fish aplenty for their own tables, and resort owners worried about hard times, joined the anti-Chippewa crowd at spring landings. The political wounds European-Americans felt were blamed, not on the economic powers that ruled their lives, but on their neighbors who suffered worse, thereby adding the salt of social hate to the wounds of economic hardship.

African-American Roots: A Speech by Walt Bresette

Unlike those protests leaders who see Dr. King as a co-optable populist with no analysis of racism, many see Martin Luther King, Jr., as a living legacy. At our pre-spearing Witness public meeting in Milwaukee in March 1989, Walt Bresette gave a keynote speech along with African-American Lutheran minister Kenneth Wheeler. Walt recollected:

I was in the army when Martin Luther King was assassinated, stationed near [Washington] D.C. They put us off-limits but I snuck out before they closed the gates the next day because I wanted to watch the Capitol burn.

I don't even know why, I didn't know why I was so upset. I didn't know why the tears 'cause I didn't know this man from no one. [I] heard a few speeches by him. I was a kid.

I remember I went across the Key Bridge in D.C. at eight, nine o'clock in the morning. Things were like they always were. I was driving around and pretty soon people started walking a little faster. About ten o'clock, people were running and the sirens were going. At eleven o'clock, it was just total chaos . . . the city was beginning to burn. And I just drove around and watched it. I watched Washington, D.C. burn.

About twelve o'clock noon, I had no idea where I was. I pull into this driveway and this Black man jumped on the hood of my car. He looked at me. I looked at him. I said, "I'm on your side."

He said, "Well, then, get the hell out of here." So I did. I turned around and eventually found my way back to the Key Bridge and drove across and looked back and there was D.C. burning.

I don't know if I felt good but [it] felt necessary to somehow bear witness to that tragedy. And I don't even know why. . . .

Martin Luther King had at least three fundamental faiths I think we'd all do well to consider. I think he believed firmly, absolutely, in Jesus. He had a spiritual faith. Whether we're agnostic, non-Christian, whatever our beliefs are, you got to turn to somebody like him and say, why was he able to do the things he did? I think because of that faith. . . . It's through that faith, whatever it might be, and you really got to believe. You can't let the Reverend pray for you. You have to pray for yourself . . . from the heart and from what you know in your mind. This [meeting room] is kind of like a [crowded] sweat lodge . . . we've got to lean on each others' shoulders.

I think the second faith that he had was the firm belief in love and non-violence as a fundamental truth of change. And there's got to be something to that, too. He couldn't have done what he did, moved even a little Chippewa from northern Wisconsin who he wasn't even thinkin' about, to the kind of fundamental change in my life, without some power. And I think that fundamental faith in love and nonviolence is something we should all consider.

Not just on the posters. Not just to do more fundraising and get more people involved. . . . You . . . me . . . you got to feel it, you got to believe it!

And I know he had a third belief, an absolute faith in the U.S. Constitution. I know that. He believed that no matter what needed to be done, that entrenched in that Constitution was the ability to display the truth of [those] rights that were being hidden, that were being pushed down. This issue is tied to that belief, too. You know, we may be a flea on the ass of an elephant, as Chippewa people, as semi-sovereign, domestic people. But as long as that elephant goes along, we're going with it in that political sense. As long as that Constitution is there and it says it protects our rights, and if those rights are allowed to be lost, or taken, or intimidated out of being exercised, then that elephant is one step closer to disaster. Which means you're one step closer to disaster.[14]

Civil Rights Allies

[Dr. King] knew that oratory could aspire only to enlightenment, and that enlightenment was not enough. Power was needed. Toward that end King devised a number of plans. While trying to build his own organization, he labored also to register several million new Negro voters, enlist the organs of mass communication, harness the influence of the organized clergy, gain the endorsement of the highest white leaders, and mobilize a "non-violent army" of witnesses.

—Taylor Branch, *Parting of the Waters* (1988)

The civil rights movement brought allies into its ever-broadening movement in the 1950s and 1960s. As the winds shifted to carry in new issues and constituencies in the 1980s, old allies remained able and willing to respond. Grassroots and antiracist organizers, northern Wisconsin farmers and home-makers, students, unions and churches with a history of involvement in civil rights, lawyers and financial supporters, and even a few brave politicians saw the parallels between the Wisconsin Chippewa issue and the southern African-American movement and these allies found roles in the solidarity work here.

The Milwaukee Witness and the Madison Treaty Rights Support Groups did outreach in their cities' respective African-American communities. In January 1989, the Witness invited longtime civil rights activist Dr. James Jackson of Muskegon, Michigan, to come to Milwaukee to discuss his Witness for Peace trip to Nicaragua, followed by a Witness training the next day. Each spring, Milwaukee's *Community Journal* published articles on treaty rights and what was happening in northern Wisconsin, including supportive columns by State Representative Marcia Coggs. State Representative Gwen Moore and Jobs with Peace activist Ann Wilson always made time for treaty rights support in their busy schedules. Madison brought African-American students to witness at boat landings. It also secured the support of Steve Braunginn, from the state Rainbow Coalition, and of the University of Wisconsin's Indigenous Law Students Association, which included Native American, African-American, and Puerto Rican law students.

In the Twin Cities, treaty support sprouted from the decades-old alliance of African-Americans and Native Americans. In 1989, Sam Grant of the Committee Against Racism, Police Brutality and Community Violence began linking up activists in the African-American community with AIM activists in a series of informal discussions, then meetings on Chippewa treaty rights. Sam was also active with the North American Bioregional Congress in 1986 and 1988, and served on their steering committee until 1990. In Sam's perspective, violence against people of color, whether it happened in city streets or rural woods, was an issue that needed an immediate response. This black/red alliance was built on a similar commitment to neighborhood organizing in their respective communities: the Soul Patrol in the African-American community in the 1960s paralleled the AIM Patrol from the 1960s on (begun as a witness against police brutality, expanding again in 1987 in response to the serial murders of three Native American women), and continued with the Guardian Angels and the Committee Against Racism in the African-American community of the 1980s. By the late 1980s, both communities were working on the issues of gangs and crack houses and then began working together in response to clashes between Native American and African-American youth in the Phillips neighborhood in Minneapolis. Twin Cities supporters came to the landings in 1989, and in 1990, Patty Sheppo (originally from Lac du Flambeau) formed the Twin Cities Witness for Non-Violence and hundreds of supporters were trained.

In July of 1989, Sam Grant and Chris Nisan of the Africana Student Cultural Center (University of Minnesota) and the Committee Against Racism journeyed to Lac du Flambeau for the July 4 rally, parade, and pow-wow. Speaking to the rally, Chris quoted Frederick Douglass:

Those who profess to value progress yet deprecate agitation are people who want the crops without ploughing up the ground. They want the rain without the thunder and lightning. They want the might of the ocean but don't want to hear the roar of its many waters. Where there is no struggle, there is no progress.

Chris continued and then paused, reaching for the clincher, he said to much applause, "The regular niggers is here to help the timber niggers."

The anti-treaty movement has used two misleading and contradictory analogies to apartheid: 1) that treaty harvesting rights (and Native gambling rights) represent a form of apartheid against whites; and 2) that reservations are a form of apartheid against Indians and should be abolished to free Native Americans from high unemployment, alcoholism, and poverty on the reservation. Yet of course the motive for abolishing U.S. reservations has nothing to do with correcting the injustices that created reservations here or *bantustans* in South Africa. The anti-treaty motive is to "free up" reservation land and resources and end Native rights and government programs, and no one has bought their argument but the anti-Indian press and hardliners. When Bishop Desmond Tutu toured the United States in May 1988 and stopped in Wisconsin, he counseled, "Insure that your native Indians in this state can say that there are people who want to see justice done for them." At the same press conference, Bishop William Wantland, Episcopal Diocese of Eau Claire, said, "Some of the attitudes that led to apartheid are the same base attitudes that led to the racism and racial prejudice against Indians here. There are a lot of parallels that one can draw between the way Indian people are treated in this country and the way Blacks are treated in South Africa."[15]

In late 1989, United Auto Workers (UAW) organizer Phil Haney sought to invite Walt Bresette to the Martin Luther King, Jr., Birthday Celebration and Dinner sponsored by the Kenosha-Racine UAW Civil Rights Committee, scheduled for January 1990. The committee decided to invite Bresette to join the African-American speakers on the panel, but PARR sympathizers within Kenosha's Local 72 were furious. Lula Smith, an African-American woman and then chair of Local 72, said, "Civil rights isn't [just] a Black issue. I felt human issues, civil rights issues were involved—the names and rocks [thrown at boat landings] were violations. It was very important that he [Walt Bresette] address us from a civil rights [perspective]."[16] On Saturday, January 13, 1990, just a block away from the rubble of what was once the Kenosha AMC/Chrysler plant, Walt joined African-American activists—Chicago attorney Thomas Todd, Nathan Head of the UAW's International Civil Rights Department, and Marshall Tharpe, president of the Kenosha-Racine UAW Civil Rights Committee—on the speakers panel celebrating the legacies of Dr. King and the southern civil rights movement.

Efforts to bridge Wisconsin's struggle with the national Rainbow Coalition were continually frustrating. This Rainbow and Jesse Jackson's runs for the Democratic presidential nomination in 1984 and 1988 emerged at the same time as the major events in Chippewa treaty rights: the 1983 *Voigt* decision followed by off-reservation spearing, and the emergence of racial protests at the landings in 1987 and 1988. While the Rainbow Coalition's position on respecting treaties with Native nations was solid, Walt Bresette (who was a Jackson supporter in Wisconsin in 1984) could not get through to the coalition and secure public condemnation for what was happening at the boat landings. When Walt was asked to appear on the dais with Jackson at an 1988 Wisconsin primary rally, he threatened to picket the event because of the lack of public support for Chippewa treaties. This challenge gained him a quick audience with Jesse in the summer of 1988. While not unsympathetic to the cause, Jackson was exhausted from being on the campaign trail and "saw me as just another mosquito to be dealt with," said Bresette.[17] No much-sought public statement or appearance at the boat landings by any one from the Rainbow Coalition leadership was forthcoming.

While major civil rights organizations' support remained elusive, key African-American activists and legislators remained outspoken in their solidarity. European-American allies resurfaced—church leaders and lawyers who were part of past Native and African-American struggles. Foundations, inspired by the sixties struggles, were willing to give grant money. And, finally, northern state legislators, notably Rep. Frank Boyle of Superior, became willing to step past threats to their lives and political careers and publicly support Chippewa treaties.

Deep South, Deep North: Similarities and Differences

The protesters' rocks that are fired past spearers and land in the water each spring in northern Wisconsin create concentric waves that spread out in patterns similar to the Deep South backlash of the 1950s and 1960s. But the thirty-year difference in time and the long history of white and Indian relations, unique in its own way, have brought different dynamics to the surface. The main difference between the Deep South then and the Deep North today is that African-Americans were a near-majority in some of the four Deep South states. Once their right to vote was protected and exercised, they became a major influence in southern politics. In Wisconsin, Native Americans are less than 1 percent of the state's total population (of almost 5 million), and in the ceded territory, about 4,000 *Ojibwe* are again less than 1 percent of the population there. This has amplified the need for allies fiftyfold.

A nonviolent strategy and an appeal to the churches for support (whether they came to the landings or not) has been essential to successfully defend the treaties. The fact that no ministers publicly supported what went on at the landings, and the public statements in support of treaties, have been helpful. Reverend Tim Kehl of Madison has been an outspoken supporter of treaties and the Witness concept. The work of Honor Our Neighbors Origins and Rights (HONOR), a membership group of church activists begun out of the Lutheran Human Relations Association, has been a critical lobbying force to counter the scare tactics of the Wisconsin Counties Association (WCA) against treaties. HONOR has also been the main organizer of the boycott against treaty beer. Clergy in northern Wisconsin have met privately to talk about what the treaty dispute is doing to their congregations and what they can begin to do about it. Still, the rarity of northern Wisconsin clergy's presence at the boat landings and public challenge to the racism of their own congregation members left Chippewa activists frustrated. The Witness continued to search for the frontline witnessing role clergy had once played in the South.

In the Deep South, the liberal press shaped the nation's images of the civil rights struggles and often aided the civil rights cause. Far from exerting monolithic hegemony or even very much influence these days, the liberal press has been the wavering ally of nonviolence and the exercise of treaty rights. Despite the detailed coverage by many reporters (e.g., Kathy Olson of the *St. Paul News Dispatch* or freelancer Scott Kerr) who were quite shocked by what was happening at boat landings, newspaper editorials throughout the 1980s ranged from abrogationist in northern Wisconsin to *Milwaukee Journal* editorials that spoke against violence but favored an end to off-reservation harvesting (through government regulation, court ruling, or buyout). The Witness worked hard to change editorial opinion, repeatedly writing letters to editors and occasionally meeting with editorial boards. We tried to deepen media coverage of protest leaders and the economic underpinnings of the dispute.

Various reporters told the Witness that their news stories of landing incidents were edited or pulled by higher-ups not sympathetic to Native treaty rights. In another effective censoring tactic, media would reassign reporters off of treaty coverage after they'd gained some knowledge of the issues (and some sympathy for what the Chippewa were put through each spring). For example, in a grievance filed with the Lake Superior newspaper guild in February of 1990, reporter Susan Stannich said the *Duluth News Tribune* pulled her off of spearfishing and treaty court case coverage despite her six years of experience and contacts with the Native American community. While the paper said she was biased in favor of Indians, Stannich charged the paper's editors with ignorance about Indian people and issues and a bias toward government and corporate officials allied against the treaties. Even when rotation of reporters is less political, it is a loss to the truth to have new reporters taking Dean Crist at his word with little sense of his long record of interfering with Chippewa treaty rights.[18]

The southern civil rights movement brought forth the leadership of African-American women and helped spawn the feminist movement that followed.[19] Outreach to women's groups in the Chippewa treaty rights movement brought statements of support from NOW and from Ellen Bravo of 9 to 5, in 1989, but organizational participation in the Witness didn't break through until 1990, with the involvement of Women of All Red Nation (WARN), in Minneapolis and Chicago and Women Against Military Madness (WAMM) out of the Twin Cities. Nonetheless, women have been key to Witness leadership from the beginning.[20]

A second critical difference between the Deep North and the Deep South is that thirty years later, "racism" is now a dirty word. Protest groups and protesters in Wisconsin went to great lengths to prove they were not racist or white supremacist—something the Klan had no fear of claiming. The two teenage Chippewa women nearly hit by Dean Crist's pickup truck on the road near Butternut Lake in 1988 could hardly be expected to believe Crist's claim to the nonviolent, civil disobedience legacy of Dr. King. But it was a claim Crist felt it useful to make. Such inconsistency didn't appear to bother most people in northern Wisconsin.

Most striking however in this national abrogation of Native rights was the open recruitment of nontribal persons claiming to be Indians into anti-treaty groups. These anti-Indian rights members with some Native heritage believed in the full assimilation of Indian people into the "American mainstream" and fully supported the agenda of dismantling treaties and the reservation system. While few in number within the protest groups, these so-called Native Americans (e.g., Chuck Valliere in PARR) were put up front and became effective in "proving" to some that the agenda of PARR and STA–W was not racist because they were not white-only organizations. Standing next to European-American PARR members at the landings, dressed in blaze-orange hunting jackets, and next to STA–W members in their camouflage (another color of the culture of killing), again in the name of equal rights, didn't bother these protesters who had partial Indian heritage. The fact that most Native Americans, including tribal governments, condemned these abrogationists who claimed Indian blood, and the fact that not a single African-American supported PARR and STA–W, did not sink in with protest leaders who still claimed a civil rights legacy of nondiscrimination.

Coming to northern Wisconsin after working for the Bureau of Indian Affairs, Fred Hatch was the attorney for STA–W throughout the late 1980s. Hatch is a longtime acquaintance and admirer of James Klauser (Governor Thompson's chief advisor and his Secretary of Administration). "Sitting Bull and all the great chiefs are dead and gone, and their time is dead and gone," Hatch believed. He felt the treaties were similarly outdated. Hatch dismissed the media's coverage of violence at the boat landings: "All, or much, of what's been written on this is pure journalistic crap." Klauser has defended his visits to STA–W as part of the state's efforts "to meet with all parties" to cool the situation. STA–W and the state of Wisconsin have always shared the political priority of appealing Judge Crabb's "stupid" (as Hatch says) decisions through the higher federal courts. While some African-Americans in the South did not at first support the goals and methods of the civil rights movement, none ever joined the opposition. Not so in Wisconsin in the eighties. Fred Hatch is of Chippewa descent.[21]

This involvement of people whose ethnic heritage is under attack was more than a matter of class differences within the Native American community, more than a ex-BIA lawyer making a living working for treaty abrogation groups, more than Native American large-scale land owners afraid of what tribal/nation claims mean to their land holdings (e.g., Billy Big Spring, a Montana Blackfeet rancher, and member of All Citizens Equal). It was more than the family and personal decision of which heritage or how much of any traditional culture to claim while living in and raising a family in today's society, a balance every person and ethnic group decides in America. It had more to do with whether or not to acknowledge any *cultural* identity and loyalty in a country that has tried to wipe out a race with smallpox blankets and beat out what culture remained at boarding schools.

In an odd concession, PARR and STA–W will occasionally concede that Chippewa "full bloods" might have some treaty rights, but the "half breeds" don't and they're the ones causing the trouble. If Chippewa spearers don't meet protesters' version of what a real Indian is, so their argument ran, treaties shouldn't apply to them. What this ignores (among other things) is the right of Native American nations, any nation for that matter, to establish the conditions for membership, i.e., citizenship.[22]

Claiming the equal rights legacy of the southern civil rights movement continues to be a stock in trade of this (predominantly) white populist cause in Wisconsin. The strangest example of social backlash wedded to equal rights rhetoric was articulated by anti-treaty advocate Joe Handrick. In a 1987 article in *PARR Issue,* Handrick argued:

> BECAUSE OF Indian spearing, more and more people are acquiring racist attitudes. . . . Racism is the result of spearing, not the cause for protests against [it]. . . . The good people of northern Wisconsin will no longer accept being branded as racists simply because we share Martin Luther King's dream. A dream that how many fish a person can catch will be judged not by the color of his skin but by the strength of his fishing line.[23]

For such thinking, Governor Thompson appointed Handrick to Wisconsin's Equal Rights Council in 1988.

But the sport fisherman's equal rights analogy fails on all counts. The protesters are not trying to *gain* rights in Wisconsin, i.e., the equal right to spearfish or equality in subsistence hunting rights. (In fact, European-Americans can spearfish in Wisconsin, e.g., sturgeon can be speared in designated seasons. This is not a treaty property right, but a fishing right, regulated by the DNR, and anyone can apply for a license.) Anti-treaty protesters are trying to *take away* rights. The rights they are trying to take away, through mob violence, are property rights, not "special" hunting and fishing rights set up by the WDNR or federal courts. These property harvesting rights were not given by the treaties. They were rights the Chippewa always had and retained when they signed the treaties. They are rights of contract and rights of heir that all Americans have an equal right to have protected.[24] And by the same token, no one has an equal right to someone else's property or inheritance.

The other disguise within the equal rights argument is the notion that all Americans came from the same place, politically as well as geographically. Implied here is the idea that the Bill of Rights and other benefits of U.S. citizenship were the same gift to all people at the same time in our history. For male European-Americans, it was a real benefit and political landmark, far more progressive than the oppressive monarchies (and famines) of Europe. Native Americans gained little from the Constitution (they counted as nothing unless they paid taxes), which provided the governmental base from which the economic expansion/conquest of the continent was to proceed. The notion of all citizens as equal seeks to obliterate this history and its legal, not to mention moral, obligations.

Native Americans lost nearly everything: land, culture, rights, 20 to 30 million lives, because of the establishment of the United States as a government (including its Bill of Rights). The U.S. (dual) citizenship given Native Americans in 1924 was not asked for by Indian people and many did not acknowledge or even know of it for a long time.[25] It is significant, however, to note that many of the major progressive U.S. social policy precedents have been established by Native American nations in their negotiations with the United States: the right to homestead protection against forced sales and taxes;

the right to free schools and vocational training; the right to free public health facilities; social security (food and clothing) in times of distress; and freedom from imprisonment for debt.[26] Rights in America have never been won equally. They have always been gained through movements and struggles, and respecting those struggles is the first step in learning and applying the gains of each.

The single most overriding dynamic of racism in which Wisconsin protesters (and government) participate is the following long and evil history: when whites get tired of living up to their end of the bargain, they break the treaties. In every treaty signed by the United States and Native nations, when treaties were in the way of land, resources, or rights that European-Americans wanted, treaties were broken. The excuses varied, but the pattern of violence, political maneuvering, race hatred and stereotypes, and assumed cultural superiority has institutionalized the inequality of Native Americans throughout U.S. history. Northern Wisconsin today is no different.

Touchstones

In the civil rights movement, every local struggle stood for a critical question before the nation. Not every one became a national issue, but in crucial times in national history, many of the local struggles break through to public consciousness and become focal points of national policy and national direction. For example, the murder of Emmett Till raised the issue of Jim Crow brutality and fears of interracial sex. The bus boycott and restaurant sit-ins posed the basic question: would post-World War II America be segregated like the southern bathrooms or integrated like baseball? School desegregation at Little Rock demonstrated the lie of "two nations, separate but equal."

Today, each ecological question has become as critical as the social justice ones still aching for solution. How will we live on the land? What kind of economic development is sustainable? What kind of planet and society will we leave our children? Why is the survival of rural culture important and why is it so tied to our society's technological choices and the crisis in big cities? The call to a consciousness of the Earth as sacred is as powerful as the early civil rights ideal of a *beloved community*. In Wisconsin as nationally, every local Native American land and rights struggle stands for this debate on our national direction.

The fish are poisoned with mercury in northern Wisconsin and with PCBs in southern Wisconsin. How much is clean lake water worth to us? In the Chippewa Fourth Fire prophecy, it was said that in the coming of the light-skinned race, those people would wear two faces: one the face of brotherhood, peace, and shared knowledge; and the other, the face of weapons, death, and greed ("the face of brotherhood and the face of death look very much alike"). "You shall know that the face they wear is the one of death if the rivers run with poison and the fish are unfit to eat."[27]

Cultural Renaissance

I dreamed I am an eagle
Flying high in the sky.
I hear the wind when it whispers,
I see the thunderbird's eye.
Beautiful Chippewa people,
The fire must never die.
—Bobby Bullet

Many times in history, the great gift of political movements is cultural rebirth for those made to search for their past and create a means of survival, expression and a future of integrity. Veterans of southern civil rights campaigns became leading writers (poet and novelist Alice Walker and theologian Vincent Harding, to name just two) and the themes of ancestors and roots, liberation spirituality, and cultural restoration taken from the sixties remain current today. The treaty rights movement in Wisconsin has brought forth a renewal of *Ojibwe* culture as well as stories and songs of struggle from their allies. Eddie Benton-Benai, an *Anishinabe* spiritual leader, has said that many in the younger generation of Indian people are finding their way back to the sweat lodges, spirit ceremonies, drum societies, *Midewiwin* lodges, pipe ceremonies, longhouse meetings, sun dances, and kivas that have survived to this day.[28] Before the spearing season begins, pieces of clothing from one's family are gathered in special bundles and placed in reservation lakes to honor the water and the coming of life-giving spring. A tobacco offering, thanking the creator and the fish to be taken, is made at off-reservation lakes on spearing nights (a ceremony that is often ridiculed by protesters). Some witnesses have been invited to sweat lodges and pipe ceremonies that often precede the trek out to the landings where the protests are expected to be intense.

In some tellings of the Seventh Fire prophecy, it is only the Native peoples returning to traditional ways and reasserting their rights who are the New People. In other tellings, the light-skinned race is included in the New People reemerging. Whatever the case, this prophecy drew people together with its hope of an Eighth Eternal Fire of peace, brotherhood, and sisterhood. The Seventh Fire Prophecy also, according to Benton-Banai, poses the choice between the road of blind technological development and the spiritual road that honors the earth.[29] As Walt Bresette has noted, the power of the prophecies is not so much their accuracy of prediction but the way they clarify choices that need to be made today.

Native and witness songs and stories like those of the Civil Rights movement also inspired supporters. The ballads of Chippewa singers Bobby Bullet and Frank Montano are sung in the treaty rights movement. Jackson Browne's praise song to Dr. King and Nelson Mandela is sung with a new verse for spearfishers:

> *We come here to praise the spearers*
> *Who bring the beauty of the earth nearer.*
> *Freedom for the right to be*
> *What the treaties guarantee.*[30]

At the boat landings, it is the Native American drum, brought by AIM and LdF drummers and other Native treaty supporters, that has played the role of songs like "We Shall Overcome" in the earlier era. On the worst nights at landings, the drum can have a calming presence. Its dramatic rhythm can reach in your center and overwhelm fear. It can re-focus energies and sometimes even drown out or slow down the shouters.

Spearfishers have said the drum sound is a binding cord to shore and family when they are far out on lonely, dangerous lakes. The drumming foretells a time when the spring spearfishing will be a season for gathering in celebration and hope. And the river opens to the righteous.

Notes

1. Among the outright fabrications in STA–W's 1989 pamphlet, "Wisconsin's Treaty Problems: What Are the Issues?" are: 1) In addition to the harvested walleyes, "the number of fish that were fatally injured during spearing and later died is estimated at an additional 75,000 walleyes and muskies." This has no basis whatsoever. Because spearing is such an efficient harvesting method and because of spearers' skill, few are wounded and die later. As with fish who die after escaping hook and line fishing, including catch and release, no statistics are kept; 2) "Tribal members are allowed to shoot hundreds of eagles every year. These eagles are shot solely for financial gain." Again, this statement has no basis in fact. Tribal members can apply for permission to obtain birds of prey for religious purposes, but not for financial gain; 3) Tribal members get from the federal government "a cost of living allowance of over $20,000/household/year . . . pay NO state income tax, NO state or federal sales tax . . . virtually no taxes at all." Again, this is false on all counts. Indians pay state and federal income taxes, and sales taxes for items bought off-reservation. Neither Indians nor non-Indians pay sales tax on the reservation.

Judge Crabb characterized these statements as rural version of "urban legends." "A distinguishing feature of an urban legend is that no one is ever able to produce an eye-witness to the actual event . . . Although defendant Crist was questioned at length about the sources of the statements in the [STA–W] brochure, he was uncertain about many of them and unable to identify any statement for which he had first hand knowledge . . ." *Lac du Flambeau Band and* Wa-Swa-Gon *Treaty Association J. STA—W, et al.,* January 6, 1992, p. 21, FN 7.

2. Harry Ashmore, quoted in Carey McWilliams, *Brothers Under the Skin* (Boston: Little, Brown, 1942; revised edition, new Introduction, 1964), p. v.

3. *Witness 1989 Report* to Wisconsin Equal Rights Commission, and *1990 Witness Report: Chippewa Spearing Season,* especially pp. 10–13.

4. *1989 Witness for Non-Violence Report,* Madison Treaty Rights Support Group, pp. 19B–19D.

5. Allen Hunter, "In the wings," *Radical America,* Summer 1981.

6. Dewey Pfister, "PARR members debate boat landing policies," *Wausau Daily Herald,* April 8, 1990 (PARR figures). Scott Kerr, "A case of racial conceit," *Shepherd Express,* November 9–16, 1989 (STA–W figure).

7. See Samuel T. Francis's essay, "Message from MARs: The Social Politics of the New Right," in *The New Right Papers,* edited by Robert Whitaker (New York: St. Martin's Press 1982). Middle American Radicals (MARs), the social movement whose values, resentments, aspirations, and fears the New Right represents, are most likely to be: of northern European or Italian descent; $3000–$13,000/year family income; twice as common in the South as North; high school but not college educated; more Catholics and Jews than Protestants (except for evangelical Christians); among Protestants, more Mormons and Baptists; thirty to sixty years old; more skilled or semi-skilled than managerial or professional.

8. A boycott was threatened in each state STA–W attempted to find a producer of Treaty Beer: in Ohio, Washington State, Louisiana, and Wisconsin. HONOR has led this effort against what the governor of Washington called "hate in a can."

9. *PARR Issue* (newspaper), winter 1988.

10. See footnote 1 in this chapter. Also in 1989, before the worst protests on record, Crist told a radio reporter from WUWM (Milwaukee) that there would be no trouble from STA–W that spring, but a federal agent had told him (Crist) that he was expecting trouble from downstate supporters and radical students. *PARR* has reinterpreted the 1924 Citizenship Act to mean that Native Americans lost all treaty and land rights when they became U.S. citizens. The 1850 Presidential Removal Order (which was supposed to move the Chippewa west if there was trouble, but there was none) is also interpreted as negating the treaties. PARR has also reinterpreted the various "misguided" federal court rulings by Doyle and Crabb which "gave" the Chippewa off-reservation rights. Obviously, no court of law has substantiated PARR claims and few historians give them any credence.

11. Treaty rights could also be invoked to challenge acid rain pollution, paper mill sludge ponds and water pollution, the siting of garbage, toxic, or nuclear waste, or diversions of water from the Great Lakes, if any of these could be shown to negatively impact the harvestable resources of the Chippewa. (See chapter 8.)

12. David Damrell at the March 1989 Weaving the Web Conference, sponsored by Citizens for Treaty Rights. Held at the Lakeland Center of Nicolet College.

13. Ibid.

14. Rick Whaley audio tape of Walt Bresette address at Witness for Non-Violence public meeting, Mobilization for Survival office, Milwaukee, March 18, 1989. WUWM radio also taped the event for later broadcast.

15. "Eau Claire bishop hopes Tutu's words on Indians are heard," *Milwaukee Journal,* May 6, 1988.

16. Lula Smith characterized the split within the union as a misunderstanding based on the Local 72 Executive Board's position not to get involved in treaty rights because it was an already (legally) decided issue, i.e., the treaties were in effect, whereas the Civil Rights Committee saw the treatment of the Chippewa at the landings as a civil rights issue. One story from within the union at the time tells of Lula's principled stand, even if it possibly meant risking her position on the Executive Board, on behalf of Walt if he were bumped from the panel. The misunderstanding was patched up in time for the King Day event. Shop chairman and now Local 72's president, Rudy Kuzel backed Lula, and said later, "If King was here, he'd be up there [on the panel] with Walt, not with the jerks from PARR."

17. "What this meeting taught me," says Walt Bresette, "was that I was not a good politician. I witnessed the power of the African-American community unto itself . . . and was very envious of it." In 1989, Walt and James Yellowbank, through their work with the Japanese Civic League in Chicago, gained an audience at an Operation Push Bread Basket meeting where they were well received. Still, no nod of approval from on high came. Finally in 1990, away from the pressures of high-voter-turnout issues, Jesse Jackson, the TV journalist, did a special program on Wisconsin that was sympathetic to Chippewa treaties.

18. In his pickup truck, Crist clipped a mirror off a spearer's van, after he "had earlier just missed hitting two teenage Chippewa girls" (*Milwaukee Sentinel,* April 19, 1988). He has been forcibly removed from meetings between the Chippewa and state of Wisconsin for disruptive behavior. In 1989, he was arrested for creating hazardous wakes, thereby endangering spearfishers. WDNR wardens had to chase him around the lake and finally jumped him in his boat near shore. Crist was acquitted of resisting wardens. In a 1992 injunction against Crist, Federal Judge Barbara Crabb said "Defendant Crist decided where Stop Treaty Abuse would protest. It was his stated policy to crowd the boat landings with people and vehicles to make it more difficult for spearers to launch boats, to use artificial decoys to interfere with spearing, to get as many boaters as possible driving back and forth on the lakes making waves to make it difficult for spearers to stand in their boats and to see the fish. . . . Defendant Crist made wakes on lakes where Lac du Flambeau members were spearing on almost every evening that there was spearing in 1989 and 1990. He did so intentionally, in an effort to impede spearing." Judge Barbara Crabb, *Lac du Flambeau Band and* Wa-Swa-Gon *Treaty Association v. Stop Treaty Abuse–Wisconsin, Inc., et al.,* January 6, 1992, p. 11–12.

19. See Sara Evans, *Personal Politics: The Roots of Women's Liberation in the Civil Rights Movement and the New Left* (New York: Knopf, 1979).

20. For example, Linda Cree of Citizens for Treaty Rights, Sierra Powers and Sarah Backus in the Witness for Non-Violence, and, particularly, Native American women in their communities: Patty Sheppo in Minneapolis, Dorothy Thoms and Anita Koser in Lac du Flambeau, Gloria Merrill in St. Croix, the Benton-Benai family at Lac Courte Oreilles and the Twin Cities, and many more.

21. Information in this paragraph is indebted to Scott Kerr, "Hatching an attack on treaties," *Shepherd Express*, December 1989.

22. The issue of blood quantum runs the other way as well. For example, tribes have raised concerns that people claiming to be Indian are getting college scholarships set aside for Indian students. For many Native nations (and for the U.S. federal government), a certain percentage of Indian heritage is required to become enrolled in their particular tribe. Each Native nation has the sovereign right to decide this and other criteria for enrollment (tribal citizenship). However, this situation is hard to generalize because a person could be culturally (and partly, racially) Indian, but not automatically an enrolled tribal member. Also, some indigenous groups are not recognized by the federal government and therefore not officially acknowledged as Indian or as tribal government entities.

23. Joe Handrick, "We are not racists," *PARR Issue,* June 1987.

24. The closest Crist and STA–W came to acknowledging these property rights is the 1989 letter STA–W sent out claiming (in their twisted logic) that the courts had given the Chippewa rights to other people's off-reservation property (i.e., homes, land, etc.): People should come to the landing to protect not only "their" fish but their homes.

25. This appears to have been motivated by a positive premise—recognition of Native American soldiers' service in World War I—and by a negative premise—the desire on the part of the United States to assimilate Native Americans and possibly lay the legal basis for settling (ending) Native American land claims.

26. Felix Cohen, "Americanizing the White Man," *The American Scholar*, vol. 21 (1952). It is also worth noting how much Native Americans, particularly the Iroquois Confederacy, gave the Constitution in the way of basic democratic ideals: the concept of states within a state which we call federalism; referendum; recall; the right of women to vote (which took European-Americans another 130 years to affirm); and the notion that a leader is a servant of the people, not their master. See also Bruce E. Johansen, *Forgotten Founders: How the American Indians Helped Shape Democracy* (Boston: Harvard Common Press, 1987). PARR and the national anti-treaty movement has also made a point of ridiculing and denying this Native American contribution to U.S. democracy and the writing of the Constitution.

27. Edward Benton-Banai, *The Mishomis Book: The Voice of the Ojibway* (St. Paul: Red School House, 643 Virginia St., St. Paul, MN 55103, 1988), pp. 89–90. This wonderful book is the story of the *Anishinabe,* their history, spirituality, ceremonies, teachings, and prophecies.

28. Ibid., pp. 111–112.

29. Ibid., p. 93.

30. Witness John Okolowicz's spearfisher verse of Jackson Browne's song, "When the Stone Begins to Turn." (Jackson Browne performed with Native American recording artists John Trudell and Floyd Westerman in a 1991 treaty rights benefit concert in Madison, Wisconsin, as part of a national show of support for Chippewa treaties). The chapter title and closing line are from the song "I am a Patriot" written by Steven van Zandt, used by permission.

PART IV

The Culmination of Years of Battles: 1990

7

I had a dream. I was at a parking lot in the woods and an eagle was flying high above us. Suddenly a helicopter appeared and began chasing the eagle around and around. Then they both flew out of sight. Someone said, "I'm afraid for the eagle." "Don't worry," I said. "I've seen eagles outfly helicopters many times."

—Linda Cree

MININ GISISS
(The Blueberry Moon)

Small Miracles and Heavy Hitters
The Third Year of Spearing and Witnessing, 1990

Rick Whaley

VICTORIES ARE OFTEN FOLLOWED by attempts to defeat or punish those who have stood fast for their rights and for justice. In the July following Flambeau's successful 1989 spearing, news broke that the state of Wisconsin would offer the Lac du Flambeau Chippewa $42 million in exchange for no longer exercising their off-reservation treaty rights.

This dramatic, highstakes attempt to buy out Lac du Flambeau treaty rights in the autumn of 1989 set the stage for what 1990 would bring to Flambeau. Under the terms of the proposed agreement between the LdF tribal council and the state of Wisconsin, announced in the summer of 1989, the tribe would give up: 1) all off-reservation spearfishing and netting, except for 2,500 fish taken for ceremonial uses; 2) all gathering rights, except firewood and wild rice, including timber rights; and 3) all sale of fish, deer, or crops, except wild rice and furs. In exchange for not exercising these treaty rights for ten years (which is why the state called it a "lease," not a buyout), Lac du Flambeau was offered $42 million. This money was to be in the form of an annual payment divided up among 2300 tribal members ($2,173 in the first year, $1,739 the second, and $1,304 each subsequent year[1]) over a ten-year period. Also included was $2.5 million to retire a tribal debt incurred when it had purchased Simpson Electric in 1985, $200,000 for educational programs at LdF, and $1 million for the construction of a new elementary school there. The state of Wisconsin justified this move as the only way to relieve the tensions in northern Wisconsin and buy time for the state's appeal of Judge Doyle's *Voigt* decision.

Opposition to the buyout from *Wa-Swa-Gon* Treaty Association was swift. Members pointed out that the tribe was entitled to educational and economic development funding already. Why should they give up legitimate rights in exchange for other rights they were owed? The lease agreement said that the LdF would give up their sovereign status only for the purposes of any potential legal disputes over the terms of the agreement. What was really going on here and what precedent might be set in partially giving up sovereignty? The agreement implied that LdF would make sure other Chippewa bands would not spear lakes in the LdF region. While Flambeau may have lacked the legal authority to keep other Chippewa from spearing anywhere in the ceded territory, the settlement was designed to knock out the biggest spearing team and pit reservation against reservation.

The response of protest groups against the buyout was just as vociferous, but for different reasons, of course. Why should the state buy out rights it and the protesters where trying to abrogate or reverse in court? Would a settlement with just LdF stop any or all off-reservation harvesting? Why should taxpayers give the Indians any more? When asked where the money would come from to buy out LdF, James Klauser said it would come out of the state's surplus revenue, with no tax increase required.

Why not use that kind of money for economic development instead of a buyout? asked treaty supporters at a press conference in Milwaukee, on October 1, 1989. Create a plan that would give loans to small resort and restaurant businesses up north so they could give better benefits to their local employees. Create a plan that would develop a more sustainable logging economy so unemployed loggers wouldn't be at the landings each spring yelling at the Chippewa. Walt Bresette spoke, accusing the tribal government of suing the state for peace, of capitulating to terrorists. If the agreement went through, Bresette argued, then Flambeau should demand a fish processing plant as part of the agreement and handle the commercial fish market from other reservations' spearing.

Wisconsin Greens at the press conference pointed out how Exxon had offered money to the boat owners in Valdez to *not* take media out into Prince William Sound to see the oil spill. Kennecott Corporation had circumvented the local anti-mining moratorium and promised $100,000 in taxes each for five years to the town of Grant, the city of Ladysmith, and Rusk County. When the committee from these local governments approved the local agreement for mining, Kennecott picked up their $60,000 in negotiating legal costs, $20,000 to each municipality.[2] What was happening with money and

democracy in America? Just as environmental regulations and environmental activists were in the way, Chippewa treaties could be in the way of serious economic agendas (mineral exploration, in particular).[3]

State representatives Gwen Moore and Frank Boyle both spoke publicly against the LdF buyout and warned that the Wisconsin state legislature would not approve such an agreement. Lac Courte Oreilles tribal chair, Gaiashkibos, said he had no interest in any kind of settlement like LdF's for LCO, and Bresette warned that Red Cliff spearers would come to the LdF area in 1990 and invite Flambeau spearers to harvest with them. "Violence County" Sheriff James Williquette answered that the buyout was only a band-aid solution and that the whole problem was caused by a small group (of spearers) at LdF bent on forcing the state to pay an even *larger* (emphasis added) cash settlement. "We're not anti-Indian," said the not-quite-objective professional Williquette. "We're anti-spearing."

Most of Wisconsin, including witnesses and treaty supporters, fully expected the LdF settlement to be approved, and wondered what, if any, role we would have come next spring. Wednesday, October 25, 1989, was a tense day on the "res." Citing death threats against him, tribal chair Mike Allen and Vilas County Sheriff Williquette imposed strict security on the referendum voting. *Wa-Swa-Gon* set up their drum across the street from the tribal center and the traditional drumming continued all day. Media from around the state flocked to Lac du Flambeau as the governor promised to move quickly to get the legislature to approve the settlement. The 10 P.M. TV news was live from Lac du Flambeau: in a stunning vote, tribal members had defeated the referendum, 439–366.

The defeat of the $42 million buyout was the single most important event in the Wisconsin treaty rights struggle since the Tribble brothers walked the line, with spears in hand, on Chief Lake in 1974. LdF members had felt their culture and pride were at stake along with their treaty rights, the gift of their forebearers. The memory of Governor Thompson openly siding with boat landing terrorists, and his subsequent moves in court against Chippewa spearing, were fresh in the minds of Flambeau families. The tribal government had worked against their interests and plan by not being forthcoming with critical information on what the agreement really was about. For example, why were only four-page summaries of the agreement available, and only one week before the vote? Did giving up sovereignty mean giving up jurisdiction over resources and rights? Did it mean treaties couldn't be used to protect resources from mining? Was there a missing timber rights section? *Wa-Swa-Gon* lawyer Lew Gurwitz said if they gave up their rights for these ten years, they'd probably never get them back. The solidarity of the spearers' families and friends, centuries old and forged anew at modern boat landings, had carried over into a vote that set the state of Wisconsin on its ear.

Grassroots Support Blossoms

After the 1989 spearfishing season, Steve Semmelmeyer had resigned his post as president of the Minocqua Chamber of Commerce after having his car tires deflated and receiving a death threat on the phone. This threat against Steve was well known in treaty rights circles. On February 11, 1990, Steve Semmelmeyer and Thomas Notter were killed in a troubling early morning fire at Steve's house on Blue Lake near Minocqua. Steve had died two days before eleven northern chambers of commerce issued a public statement of support for the tribes.

On Tuesday, February 13, 1990, eleven chambers of commerce formally issued a statement that recognized "the legal rights of the Chippewa and their prerogative to exercise these rights without interference or threat of violence."[4] The chambers blamed the protesters' interference in spearing with threatening the economic and social balance of northern Wisconsin. This support however had not been won through moral suasion for the Chippewa's just cause. Lac du Flambeau tribal government agreed to lessen the harvest of walleye in those areas where the chambers signed on: rights given up for peace, but a public relations coup and a politically necessary step to isolate the hard-core protest. (*Wa-Swa-Gon* opposed all trade-offs of legitimate rights for peace with terrorists, in this case and in all other negotiations around lower fish harvests.)

STA–W attorney Fred Hatch responded defiantly, saying that some chambers would be forced to dissolve if they tried to push such a resolution. Driving the wedge deeper between himself and his former allies, Hatch accused the chambers of being a vehicle for Tom Maulson.[5] Whether intimidated by protesters, keeping their own silence, or colluding with protest groups, chambers up until this time, except for LdF's, had been no allies of Indian people in northern Wisconsin.

That same day, the push for peace was extended when representatives of eleven tribal councils met with religious leaders in Wausau. The conference was called by the Ecumenical Advisory Committee of the Wisconsin Indian Resource Council and sanctioned by the Wisconsin Conference of Churches. A statement issued by the religious leaders present affirmed Chippewa treaties, called for peace in northern Wisconsin, and said ministers would come to the landings in spring if that would help. The offer to come to the landings was an important gesture, although the Witness is not aware of any of these ministers coming to witness spearing until the 1991 season.

But the pull of powerful anti-treaty players was also strong. In February Walt Bresette and Chippewa artist and elder Esther Nahgahnub were on their way to federal court in Minneapolis, charged with selling dream catchers that contained migratory bird feathers. In a case that would become known in the Indian community as Feathergate, U.S. Fish and Wildlife agent David Duncan of the U.S. Department of the Interior had arrested Bresette at his shopping mall store in Duluth in December of 1989. Not only was this arrest seen by supporters as retaliation for Bresette's role in treaty causes, but it promised to tie him up in court during the 1990 spearing season. Walt pointed out the irony of a new mall development going in just down the road on what had been wetlands. Agent Duncan and the U.S. Department of the Interior apparently had no concern for what *this* development would do to migratory birds.

In 1990, major political players, most of whom had not been to boat landings, openly entered the fray over Chippewa treaty rights. State and local governments, chambers of commerce, churches, editorial writers, federal government, and court officials all knew that political balances, not to mention the tourist season, would be upset if any Native American were killed over off-reservation spearing. Their efforts to disguise or temper the racism of the anti-treaty protests and to obscure the real political questions—resource co-management, timber rights, the environmental protection afforded by the treaties—defined for the Witness and treaty supporters our education and lobbying work for the year.

In addition, law enforcement officials, notably Al Shanks, coordinator of the State Division of Emergency Government, had only praise for 1989 law enforcement at the boat landings and were resistant to any pressure for detailed assurances about safety for 1990 spearing. In response the Witness prepared "Detailed Demands for Safety" in February 1990 for the consideration of tribal governments and spearing groups. Aimed at pressuring Governor Thompson and Al Shanks, it listed the following:

- safe and separate places at boat landings for Chippewa families and supporters away from protesters;
- safety on the lakes—banning protester boats or making sure WDNR boats protected spearing boats, including arrest and follow-up prosecution on violent protesters;
- security of Chippewa vehicles at landings;
- safe passage along roadways where families and supporters had to park and walk in to landings;
- security of rest room facilities or wooded areas safe from protesters' stalking/harassment;
- continued ban on alcohol consumption at landings and arrest of people driving drunk;
- clarity of who is in command of law enforcement agencies at landing; and
- monitoring of CB radio bands to intercept protester disruptions or off-landing terrorist activity.

This work gave the Witness and Midwest Treaty Network another clear lobbying role and made it an eminent necessity to reach many, many more supporters.

The *Ogichidaa* Tradition: The Witness Prepares for the 1990 Season

The Witness began to prepare for a welcome 1990 spearfishing season. The hope was tempered by the seriousness of Sheriff Williquette's prediction of "an all-out war" at the boat landings come spring. Where would we get the political and spiritual resources we needed to prepare ourselves and many more witnesses for what lay before us in northern Wisconsin? George Amour, long-time *Anishinabe* educator and activist in Milwaukee, spoke at Marquette University along with Walt Bresette in January of 1990. George had been at Wounded Knee as part of the solidarity effort in 1973 and been involved in many protests, boycotts, and occasional physical fights in defense of Native rights.

George said it had been hard to go to Butternut Lake in 1989 and be part of the nonviolent battle for "Walleye Hill" there. But he gathered strength for the nonviolent way by recalling the words given him twenty years ago when he became part of the struggle. These words, known as "I Am Young Indianhood," are part of the creed of an old *Ojibwe* society being re-established called *Ogichidaa* (meaning servant of the people or hero) that Indian men and women are joining today:

I am young Indianhood, stalwart, unafraid. Ahead of me lies life, challenging and thrilling. I want to throw myself to it, to live gloriously and fully, even as that bronze young warrior of old.

My ancestor lived lustily and bravely, and so would I. Even as he fought to the end to protect his people, so would I. Even as his red blood boiled in [his] veins when he saw his people suffer from injustice, so does my blood boil when my people suffer unjustly.

I would that I could fight bravely and die gladly for Indianhood. It would be glorious. But, comes the voice of our beloved ancient one. "My son, in a quieter way lies a greater glory. He who fights because he is young and loves battle is too noisy and enjoys fighting too much to be a true hero. He who works steadily and patiently, ever glorifying his cause and forgetting himself, relying more on wisdom than on willful love of battle, is the greater hero."

I, young Indian, have found the words sunk into my mind. I did not want them there, for it is greater delight to glory in blind fighting than to work wisely and patiently toward a goal. But, I know in my heart that our ancient one is right. His words are true. And knowing the truth, my self-esteem will not allow me to live falsely.

And so, it is to thee, Great Spirit God, life giver, Earth-maker, that I pray for steadfastness and patience and wisdom that I may help lead my people along the long, slow, steep path to happiness.

This *Ogichidaa* prayer became part of Witness trainings along with Gandhi's and Martin Luther King, Jr.'s, philosophies of nonviolence.

Witness trainings for the 1990 season began in December 1989. Training for trainers took place in Madison, Minneapolis, and Chicago.[6] By the start of spearfishing in 1990, well over a thousand people, over a three-state area, had taken the Witness training.

In early April, Sarah Backus spoke at a mainstream forum in Minocqua, the heart of protest country. After the discussion, two people came up to her and said they agreed with her remarks that mining and resource protection were the real issues. They had protested last year, but this year they were not going back to the landings. Like Tom Maulson's boat landing conversation in 1989 with two young protesters who ended up leaving, saying they had no business bothering Indian people, these small miracles began to appear at the Witness trainings and public forums.

International grassroots support added to the growing U.S. Midwest solidarity. Through the organizing work and European connections of Zoltán Grossman and the Madison Treaty Rights Support Group, demonstrations and vigils in support of the Chippewa took place on April 6 and 7 at U.S. embassies and consulates in Austria, Britain, Norway, and Canada, with letters of support arriving from Australia, Ireland, and the Soviet Union. School children in Parma, Italy, sent thirty drawings about spearfishing and the protests in northern Wisconsin to show support for LdF spearers.

Clutch Hitters

Long-hoped-for invitations from tribal governments came to the Witness from the St. Croix Tribal Council (January 26, 1990), from the Red Cliff Tribal Council (March 5, 1990), and informally from the Bad River tribe through spearers on the tribal council. This confirmation made the Witness appeal to mainstream allies easier and lent Native American credibility to our press statements. In April, Honor Our Neighbors Origins and Rights (HONOR) issued a statement to ensure that there were no public differences between the Witness and religious non-Witness supporters that could be exploited by unsympathetic press or treaty opponents. It said:

> The treaty support groups, whether they be local, regional, or national, Indian or non-Indian, recognize that there is much to be done to advocate for treaty rights. While groups may differ in their approach, each brings special gifts to the struggle for justice. This accord signals to all that here is a unity in purpose and mutual respect.

On October 21, 1989, lawyers first met with spearfishers at a Witness home in Milwaukee to review the LdF buyout proposal, less than a week before the vote. In attendance were Walt Kelly, past president of the Wisconsin American Civil Liberties Union, lawyer/activist Jackie Boynton, and Lew Gurwitz of Boston who had worked in many Native American struggles including Wounded Knee and Big Mountain. Lew agreed to represent *Wa-Swa-Gon* in their dealings with their tribal council and Walt Kelly set in motion a legal support team that would work with the spearers and witnesses to gather evidence in 1990 on protest activity and police inaction.[7] As part of the Witness trainings in 1990, lawyers advised we be very specific in the kind of information we document—record information immediately and not collectively (only individual testimony will stand up in court); document the exact time, location, and descriptions of protesters and what they do. Include the actions of police officers and their names or badge numbers, and racial remarks and signs if they seem part of harassing or violent activities (this might establish racial motivation and pattern to disruptions). Witness training materials also continued to draw on the experience of past religious witnesses and Native American struggles (including Clergy and Laity Concerned/Big Mountain Witness) to deepen our understanding and discipline.

On April 13, Good Friday, Reverend Jeff Wartgow, United Church of Christ minister in Eagle River, Wisconsin, preached a sermon comparing the harassment of spearers to the humiliations Christ suffered on his way to the cross.

Fires of Prejudice

Grassroots treaty opposition forces continued to light the fires of prejudice throughout the ceded territory. Jay Tobin, a witness in 1989 and Vietnam vet, recalled an incident that happened in mid-February 1990. Larry Peterson, founder of PARR, spoke at a church in Osseo, Wisconsin. According to Tobin, Peterson began his talk with disparaging remarks about Native Americans, like, "Some of my best friends are Indians, but they are all drunks. Some of my best friends are Indians, but I know they abuse their children . . ." Tobin walked up to the stage and asked Peterson what he would do to stop the violence at boat landings. Nothing, said Peterson. Tobin then handed him a white (Klan-like) sheet and said, "Here's the sheet so people know who and what you are." Parishioners in the audience were shocked by Tobin's behavior, but only a few expressed dismay afterwards at Peterson's remarks.[8]

Anti-Indian feeling continued to swell. A Minocqua-area radio station announced the possibility that the heavy satellite-TV trucks of the downstate media might not be allowed to go on the soggy, unpaved boat landing roads during the upcoming spearing season—though these restrictions didn't seem to apply to heavy logging trucks during this kind of weather. In Wausau, Walt Bresette's nephew, a high school student at Wausau West, was bullied and threatened by a crowd of his fellow students. Gaining no support or remedial action from school authorities there, the young man's parents pulled him out and sent him up to Red Cliff to finish his high school education. A sixteen-year-old LdF softball pitcher, Monica Allen, was harassed during an area softball game that April—called spearchucker and timber nigger. She would join the spearers this spearing season. Lakeland High School officials, however, secured an apology from the teenage protesters to Allen and LdF.

When Lac du Flambeau spearers raised the possibility of an intertribal celebration/pow-wow to open spearing at Big Eau Pleine Reservoir near Wausau, state newspapers ranted and raved in editorials against Chippewa provocations. One published a front-page map on how to get to Big Eau Pleine.[9] When asked what his response would be to this kind of pow-wow, Larry Peterson said, "I don't care if I was God himself, I wouldn't be able to stop something from happening." The spearing season was almost upon us.

"I see a shack full of weapons waiting to be used," the shaman/witness advisor tells me. "You need a prayer to the four directions and a power pouch with a rock, a feather, a match, and a white shell. Pray that no one goes to the arsenal in the woods. . . . If you are ever in danger, move towards the light."

In early April, *Wa-Swa-Gon* member Goldie Larson and Eddie Benton-Banai were traveling back with members of their respective families in a car and a van late one night. They stopped in Crandon, Wisconsin, for help because a radiator was overheating. Police gave them water. As the two vehicles passed over into Oneida County and neared Rhinelander, they were stopped by five police cars. Guns were drawn and pointed at the children. The children were made to get out and stand, without coats, across the highway, despite the rain mixed with snow that was falling. Police held guns on the adults in the car and searched the van on the pretext that it had been stolen. Police found nothing. Benton-Banai asked if they had been stopped because they were Indian. Police acknowledged that they had received a report of "a van full of Indians" coming their way. Police conducted a twenty to twenty-five minute search before identifying which officer was in charge. They refused, when asked, to apologize to the children, saying only that a colossal mistake had been made. No police investigation of this episode was made and no local press chose to comment on this insensitive treatment of Chippewa families. What could this portend about the role of law enforcement at the landings in the weeks just ahead?

Two Rallies

On April 14, STA–W held a rally in Minocqua, while treaty supporters rallied at the Bear River Pow-Wow Grounds on the Lac du Flambeau Reservation. Crist asked supporters to protest without "racism, violence, or confrontation," but said they had no choice but to protest in order to stop the slaughter of tens of thousands of spawning walleye. The LdF rally that same day was the coming together of two journeys that had begun the weekend before. From Pipestone, Minnesota, came the Pipestone Peace Run lead by Native Americans from this eastern Dakota/western Chippewa region. From Stevens Point in central Wisconsin, heading north through Minocqua, came Tom Noonan on a solo, spiritual walk for peace. All arrived safely.

The two rallies presented a contrast of themes and appeals and accusations:

53 percent of the calls to the Vilas County Police come from LdF . . . [but] it's not the Indians' fault. The government made them that way. . . the incest, the alcoholism out there [at LdF]. . . . Get rid of the reservations and make them just like us. —Don Penfield, STA–W

We are reminded that people suffering in the countries of their origins fled that land to come here to seek their freedom and to seek their sanctuary. And it was our people who welcomed them here to this sacred land and gave them their freedom. And almost immediately most of them reversed their roles . . . and became the oppressors of the natural peoples of this land. —Vernon Bellecourt, AIM

We are a nation where all men [sic] are created equal. Special rights are contrary to everything we've been taught. . . . These ridiculous court cases . . . gave blood-diluted Chippewa superior rights over U.S. citizens and Wisconsin residents. . . . Before the *Voigt* case, we lived as neighbors. —Al Soik, STA–W

It's good to see so many colors here. Back in Oklahoma, we have the Seminole nation, really a confederacy of fourteen bands and four dialects. Two bands of the Seminole council today are Black people. . . . We gave sanctuary and citizenship to [runaway] slaves. . . . We had a Rainbow Coalition a long time before [Jesse] Jackson thought of it. —Mike Haney, Seminole nation

Beware of co-management. . . . Even Judge Crabb can see the danger in allowing unstable governments to manage our fragile environment. . . . All subsistence hunting and fishing is a fantasy. —Chuck Ahlborn, STA–W

Treaties are our last environmental defense of the northwoods. Hundreds of thousands of acres have been quietly leased to Exxon and [to] the worst polluters. . . . The Legislature has quietly terminated citizen opposition to mining. —Sierra Powers, Witness for Non-Violence

Crist called the Witnesses treehuggers and quasi-environmentalists, and announced this day as the first official day of STA–W protests against environmental terrorism, resource blackmail, and political intimidation. The season would tell who the instigators of trouble would be and which analysis of history would hold water. The powers that be would come to a reluctant understanding of the strength of the treaties and the resolve of Chippewa spearfishers.

Spearing and Strategy: The Season Begins

I plan my good-byes. To combat the cold and the fear, I pack my navy-surplus snowpants, my amulet, and bail money. I wish for the safety of my family in the city while I am gone, and write my mother a letter. She is the one who has taught me to respect justice and to love words, as I also gain from my Chippewa friends the meaning of a country honoring its "word" and hints that words reach powers beyond just accuracy and insight. I tell my son, if anything happens to me, remember two things: Take care of our family and read Wendell Berry when you get older.

STA–W's main strategy this spring 1990 was to: 1) blow whistles and sound sirens as close as possible to spearers and supporters in order to counteract the Native American drumming; 2) threaten mass civil disobedience arrests; and 3) step up the on-lake harassment of spearers. Despite attempts to get legal observers and media to go out regularly with spearing boats, the Witness had no effective on-lake presence during this season. Our main hope for on-lake safety rested with the recently passed Hunter Harassment Bill, which promised to arrest and fine protesters who came too close (in the view of WDNR wardens) and interfered with spearfishing.[10]

The 1990 Witness was hosted by the Midwest Treaty Network, in conjunction with the reservation spearing groups at St. Croix, Bad River, Red Cliff, and Lac du Flambeau. The Witness increased our level of coordination by opening three Witness offices, one at Bad River, one at St. Croix, and one in Lac du Flambeau at Tom and Laura Maulson's T & L Mini-Mart. We secured volunteer Witness coordinators for the two weeks of spearing.

Governor Thompson borrowed our estimated number of a thousand witnesses trained when he stated publicly how angry he was that *AIM*(!) was bringing a thousand supporters to the landings—"You have hot heads and militants on both sides," he asserted. The Witness regularly clarified our nonviolent observer stance to the media and sent an open letter to law enforcement officials in the state. The major strategic problem for the Witness became whether and how to intercede nonviolently at the landings given the failure of law enforcement to act preventatively.

Star Lake, Saturday, April 21, was the worst boat landing incident of 1990. On hundred or so witnesses arrived at 7:30 P.M., about half an hour after the main body of four hundred-plus protesters. Sheriff Williquette and the Vilas County sheriffs had set up snow fences and Stop Treaty Abuse–Wisconsin was poised for action. The police and protesters were on the north side of the boat landing. When the witnesses arrived they went to the south side of the landing where they found themselves in an unprotected, unlit space on a hill behind police fences and the outhouse. The Native drum was set up by the fence with three layers of witnesses and supporters around it. The media was given a small, fenced-in area down near shore so they could get an up-close view of Crist or Soik working the crowd from an off-shore boat, bullhorn in hand ("The Nazis seemed to think they were the superior race. What we have here is the 'red race,'" ad nauseam.) Reporters would have to walk through the crowd at their own risk, as would Chippewa trying to get to the lake to offer tobacco.

Death whispers in the trees. "I have a list of fifty [Native Americans] killed in South Dakota," says Joe Geshick of the 1970s movement there, "because they let themselves get caught alone. We must stay together at the landings."

What should the Witness do? Stay in the woods where we could not document anything and be easy targets? Try and make our way, en masse, through the protest crowd? At Balsam Lake, April 18, for St. Croix spearing, an AIM contingent had tried to march through a PARR crowd to get to a safe place at the shore. In the ensuing pushing and press of the crowd backward, two protesters went over the snow fence, injuring one. Two AIM members were arrested, though charges were later dismissed. Should we try and mingle with protesters, with or without our armbands on?

Documenters were sent undercover into the crowd. This worked for awhile until protesters recognized Sarah Backus, who had insisted on not waiting in the woods away from protests. "I was surrounded by six to seven individuals, four men and two women," she said, "then more joined. The whistles that they were blowing surrounded my head with two placed directly in my ears and blown. I was shoved and pushed from several directions and punched two times in the back." She made her way to the police lines and after much effort finally got the attention of local sheriffs. Could you identity those harassing you, an officer asked, while the whistles and pushing continued. Going over the fence didn't look promising—would she be any safer under police arrest? If protesters followed her over the fence, would witnesses be blamed for starting the riot? She was forced to make her way back through similar harassment out of the protesters' side of the landing.

Witness coordinators and *Wa-Swa-Gon* lawyers requested a visible police presence on the south side of the landing. A while later, protesters began to make their way along the fence line over to the supporters' side of the landing. Protesters' comments overheard by witnesses included: "She's lesbian and she's going to get raped" (it was not known who this was directed at) and "Nobody would pick a fight with a nigger on TV" (in reference to an African-American journalist present). Four teenage protesters climbed up on top of the outhouse and began waving the American flag. The protest crowd cheered wildly. Not to be outdone, four AIM members climbed atop the outdoor facilities and began waving the Indian flag (the stars and stripes with an Indian superimposed on them). The STA–W crowd was in a frenzy—"Push them off, push them off," they called to their teen adventurers. Sheriff Williquette quickly handed Dean Crist a megaphone and asked him to get his people down. Crist, who had earlier ignored the suggestion to pull his people back out, complied and the young protesters came down. "Noose, noose, noose," the protest mob hollered at the AIM-sters. *Wa-Swa-Gon* soon talked the AIM liberators into coming down also. That night, Native supporters used humor to fight back en masse, throwing protester slogans back at them.

Out on Star Lake that evening, three boats of spearers were stoned as they passed through the narrows near the landing, and protest boats followed spearers out onto the lake, making high wakes to try and swamp them. "Anyone got a grenade?!" shouted one protester at a docking spearing boat. Commenting on the whole evening, Williquette reiterated his favorite theme, "We're not here to enforce treaty rights. We're here to keep the peace."

Witnesses linked arms around the Native American drum that night at Star Lake as they had the night before at Turtle-Flambeau Flowage, where protesters' whistle-blowing and crowd pressure had been intense. This arm-linking strategy helped keep protesters away from some direct confrontations with Chippewa families and far enough away so they could not cut the drum (this had been rumored all season), and eased fears that protesters might isolate

Witnesses near the cliffs overlooking some spearing lakes. But this strategy raised questions within the spearing groups and Midwest Treaty Network. Were we restricting protesters' freedom of movement? Were we creating a confrontation with such obvious collective action? Or, were we enacting the proactive strategies we'd talked about that could prevent violence? Front-page photos in newspapers in Milwaukee and Wausau showing witnesses linking arms at Turtle-Flambeau provided the most dramatic evidence of Witness efforts in 1990. While witnesses would stand around the drum for many more evenings to come, armlinking was not used after this.

Throughout the season (and after), state officials and much of the media (especially television) tried to downplay the level of violence and racial harassment. The state of Wisconsin did not want things to get out of hand right before the tourist season, nor did Governor Thompson want to jeopardize his reelection bid that autumn. At the same time, the state was still playing the protesters as one of their cards in efforts to get federal congressional involvement in Wisconsin's treaty dispute. These efforts to gain peace by declaring it failed to mask what was, except for the lower number of protesters arrested, a worse, more frightening season than 1989.

Surrounding Lac du Flambeau spearing, usually in Vilas or Oneida counties, the season's worst violence occurred. The Witness documented many incidents in addition to Star Lake. Rocks were thrown at spearers (Big Arbor Vitae, April 19, and Plum Lake, April 24). Gunshots rang out on Catfish Lake (April 25), Gordon Lake (April 28), and Forest Lake (April 29). In other attempts to intimidate spearers, a bomb threat was phoned into a Wausau TV station (for Pelican Lake and other lakes to be speared, April 12), and threats of plastic explosives were heard at Big Eau Pleine (April 17). A dark-colored van tried to run down witnesses on the roadway out of Big Arbor Vitae (April 19) and four vehicles tried to run a St. Croix spearing family's car off the road near Half Moon Lake in Polk County (April 20). Lug nuts were loosened on spearer Brandon Thom's car at Gordon Lake (May 1), and only discovered later as he was driving the highway home. As part of this nasty boiling pot, members of the media were also threatened on numerous nights (Big Arbor Vitae, April 19, Star Lake, April 21).

On North Twin Lake, Tuesday, April 24, rock throwing was so intense that Tom Maulson had to pull the spearing boats in off the lake and negotiate with the WDNR to arrest rock throwers and drivers of the boats trying to swamp spearers or leapfrog them (i.e., run one's boat immediately in front of spearing boat, throw out a fishing line and tell spearers to go around). Amidst this turmoil, spearer Robert Martin fell into the lake trying to spear a muskie. The protest crowd nearby cheered until Martin emerged, standing in shoulder-deep water, with a record muskie on the end of his spear.

On this North Twin night, as on many other nights of 1990 spearing, WDNR wardens were slow to enforce the hunter harassment law. On some evenings (e.g., Plum Lake, April 24), they would repeatedly warn protesters who were easily within twenty yards of boats and hindering spearing, before making arrests. And on nights they did make arrests, the cases would end up in county courts in northern Wisconsin where judges are not sympathetic to the Chippewa. Walt Kelly and the *Wa-Swa-Gon* legal team's efforts to get these cases heard in Madison, or get federal marshals to the landings, were not successful.

At the Witness office, mid-season, another veteran of the 1970s Native struggles tells me of the time when AIM men were chained to jail cells in South Dakota and beaten: if Indian people are treated this badly again, the perpetrators will die. An older man, drunk and ducking reservation cops, comes to the office. I give him coffee and the Native supporter talks to him. The next day word comes that my mother has died unexpectedly. Was one in the family due to be taken this spring? I walk into the Flambeau woods. It is drenched in every shade of moist green from a spring storm and I try to call my mother back. If I couldn't be with her when she died, this is the place I would like to be, doing what I'm doing.

Crist and the Governor

In the 1850s, Chief Buffalo canoed Lake Superior on his way (then by steamer, sailboat, and train) to Washington, D.C., to speak face to face with the U.S. president in order to *maintain* fair dealings for his *Anishinabe* people. Governor Tommy Thompson would probably have paddled the same route, in his efforts to *undo* treaties, if it would have done him any good. The governor had been promising his anti-treaty friends in PARR and STA–W that federal involvement was just around the political corner. During LdF's second week of spearing, the governor placed a direct call to Dean Crist and asked him to hold off on STA–W plans for mass arrests as he (the governor) was on his way to Washington, D.C., to try and secure a congressional delegation to visit the boat landings.[11] The jet-age governor had chosen Senator Daniel Inouye (Dem.–Hawaii), chair of the Senate Select Committee on Indian Affairs, to be the front for federal intervention in Wisconsin's treaty dispute.

Welcomed in early February 1990 to Wisconsin with the *Milwaukee Journal* headline "Inouye a dream come true for treaty-weary governor," Senator Inouye had a mixed history on Native American issues. As a Japanese-American familiar with the World War II internment of Japanese-Americans, Inouye was said to be sympathetic to Native American causes. Yet, in his own state of Hawaii, the senator sided with developers and the U.S. military against the interests of indigenous Native Hawaiians. In the salmon and treaty dispute in Washington state in the 1970s, Inouye was helpful in resolving the issue in favor of the Native nations there. The Big Mountain solidarity effort, however, found Inouye no ally of the Dine (Navajo) struggle to resist forced relocation. How Inouye would act in Wisconsin was a worrisome unknown.

However, Inouye's involvement brought, on the surface, two very positive developments to the Chippewa, both of which caused chagrin to Thompson and the protest movement. First, Inouye affirmed the tribal sovereignty of the Chippewa and said any negotiations could only be done with the initiative or approval of tribal governments. Second, Inouye had earlier commissioned Rennard Strickland and Stephen Herzberg, two experts in American Indian law, to study the treaty dispute. On April 23, in the middle of the LdF spearing season, the Strickland Report was made public.

The Strickland Report laid clear blame on the governor and the Wisconsin WDNR for their inaction and their heightening of the problems in northern Wisconsin. Economic stagnation, state inaction, and the racist exploitation (by PARR and STA who "use common organizing hate-group techniques") were the three components of the northwoods dispute. The WDNR, the report said, had manipulated fish statistics and announced the lower bag limits for anglers in an effort to shift the blame to Chippewa spearing. The governor had failed to specifically denounce the racism at the boat landings and failed in his obligations to uphold constitutional rights. The report recommended the state stop its many efforts to deny the exercise of rights, stop meeting with protest groups, and look to cooperation rather than confrontation to solve the issue.

Plans for a visit by Wisconsin's congressional delegation fell through while Inouye secured federal money for a study of the fish population in northern Wisconsin. On April 25, Crist was arrested on Catfish Lake for harassing spearers and refusing to obey a game warden. Two nights later, Crist led fifty protesters across police lines to be arrested at Big St. Germain Lake. This time,

Vilas County Judge James Mohr said protesters could spend Friday night in jail or sign a $500 signatory bond and agree to stay one hundred yards away from spearers. An outraged Crist threatened to stay in jail and go on a hunger strike, but the threat never materialized.

The governor had grown tired of the show. The media had grown tired of the no-show. On Saturday night, April 28, treaty supporters, dancing around the Native drum, easily outnumbered protesters at Big Arbor Vitae Lake. When anti-treaty protesters tried to make trouble, AIM leader Clyde Bellecourt responded, "Cowabunga, dudes. Come join us [dancing]." The protest movement's last chance for confrontation in 1990 slipped away.

Power Hitters

On May 6, 1990, the state of Wisconsin apologized for the 1832 Bad Axe Massacre of hundreds of Sauk and Fox men, women, and children who had been with Black Hawk. On the same day, James Klauser said that there were peace signs in the northwoods, but the good feelings did not decrease the need for a swift solution to the *treaty problem* (emphasis added). Higher powers than he were at work on it. On May 9, Judge Barbara Crabb ruled in *LCO VII* that the Chippewa had a right to 50 percent of the off-reservation resources (reversing the previous ruling of 100 percent and lessening future walleye harvests) and that the WDNR had management sovereignty over all of Wisconsin's resources, thereby ruling out Chippewa co-management. Many observers felt that the 50-50 ruling and the treaties themselves implied co-management of the resources of northern Wisconsin. Most environmentalists and Greens would have welcomed co-management, given the Chippewa's far better positions on the issues of water quality, nuclear waste dumps, mining, beaver control, and a host of other issues. In October 1990, in *LCO VIII*, Judge Crabb further clarified the *Voigt* decision by saying the Chippewa did not have the right to claim back damages for the 130 years the WDNR had prevented them from harvesting off-reservation. While she made clear that the state had deprived them of their rights, she followed higher-court precedents that disallowed state governments being sued by Native nations for deprivation of rights.

Governor Thompson would come up empty-handed, in terms of stopping off-reservation spearing, from Senator Inouye's involvement in Wisconsin. Inouye, like Judge Crabb, acted to protect off-reservation harvesting rights and demanded respect for Chippewa sovereignty and lives. Judge Crabb, however, gave the state of Wisconsin the other major legal victories it had been seeking.[12] Between the 1990 and 1991 spearing seasons, all but the safety rulings issuing from Judge Crabb's court were favorable to the major power interests in Wisconsin. The state saved $200 million in back damages. The WDNR retained resource management hegemony, and Judge Crabb was reconsidering Chippewa timber rights. Though Thompson and his former protester friends lost the federal support they expected, the governor was sitting comfortably with a pat hand on resource management, no back damages, and reconsidered timber rights.

Native Americans picketed the January 1990 Salt Lake City conference called by the Wisconsin Counties Association (WCA) in conjunction with the nonpublic National Coalition of Federal Indian Policy (NCFIP) (formerly S/SPAWN).[13] Native American county supervisors, including Menominee supervisors from Wisconsin, were barred from this conference that sought to get Congress to look at the treaties. Though it was roundly condemned by various states, Wisconsin state legislators, and county associations, Mark Rogacki, executive director of WCA, nonetheless defended the conference and called criticisms "inflammatory."

When the NCFIP met in Washington, D.C., in May, Keith Ferries, also president of WCA, denied that these groups were seeking to abrogate Indian treaty rights. The main dispute, he said, was over timber rights. What did timber have to do with all the fuss in northern Wisconsin?[14] In the 1800s, European-American timber companies decimated the ancient pine forests of Wisconsin. In the 1900s, Wisconsin taxpayers had to help pay for the reforestation of northern Wisconsin. Despite the far better record of timber conservation practiced by Wisconsin's Native nations, and despite the possible employment of non-Indians loggers also, the WCA vehemently opposed Chippewa timber rights.[15] They had filed a brief in Judge Crabb's court early on in the timber phase of treaty litigation. Money was of course a key issue—county governments receive significant income from the sale of timber on county-owned land to major timber/paper companies—Weyerhauser, Nekoosa, and Consolidated Paper.

In September, WCA held its state convention in Milwaukee and witnesses and supporters crashed their evening cocktail party at Milwaukee's public museum. Witnesses talked to county supervisors and handed out a leaflet questioning WCA's connection to a racist, anti-treaty organization in Washington state and the WCA's anti-Indian agenda. Inspired by Walt Bresette's "We are all Mohawks" speech (from the national Greens Conference the week before), two witnesses risked arrest and stayed at the party, refusing to leave until a food service worker, dressed as an Indian selling buffalo meat, de-costumed.

We in the treaty rights movement were sharply divided on the question of whether to proceed into electoral endorsements and voter turnout based on our small but statewide activist core. The pro-treaty and anti-mining constituency had forced one major player, gubernatorial candidate Tom Loftus, to come around on two key positions on treaty rights and to publicly endorse a moratorium on mining in Wisconsin. But many activists, Chippewa and Greens, questioned how we could support a man who, in the past, was no friend when Native American lives and rights were on the line, and who still supported spearing restrictions in a negotiated settlement that included co-management.[16]

Our own divisions paled by comparison to Loftus's inability to reach the constituencies that had been built around treaties, racial justice, and stopping the mines. (See chapter 8 on the mining threat). After running a passionless campaign, Loftus was trounced in the general election. Adding to this year of small miracles (e.g., Treaty Beer had been pulled from shelves in Washington state and WDNR wardens in Wisconsin were taking cultural sensitivity courses), James Doyle, son of the late Judge James Doyle, upset Hanaway in the race for attorney general. While the pro-treaty movement may have helped define some of the issues in this race, it was Hanaway's political ineptitude and the women's rights vote that put him out of office.[17] The liberal Doyle, who had once worked on the Navajo reservation in the U.S. Southwest, would be nonetheless hamstrung. As the state's chief lawyer he had little direct role in boat landing law enforcement and was in charge of the state's appeal of the Doyle (Sr.)-Crabb treaty rulings.

Successes of the Witness

The 1990 Witness trained 1000 to 1500 witnesses in the philosophy of non-violence, in the strategy and discipline of nonviolence for the boat landings, and in the cultural, economic, and environmental issues of northern Wisconsin. Often inspired by the earth-centered philosophy and spiritual centeredness of this *Anishinabe* struggle, these hundreds of people were ready to risk themselves so past injustices would not be repeated.

Significantly, most of those trained this year as witnesses came from northern Wisconsin and Minnesota, from the heart and borders of ceded territories. Charlotte Hockings remembered crosses burning against Indian families when she was a young girl growing up in northern Minnesota.[18] For her, the Witness was a way to prevent the flames of misdirected anger and economic fear from burning again. For many farmers, Vietnam vets, church activists, unionists, and environmentalists who witnessed, it was a way to prevent someone from getting killed while we opened the door of dialogue with protesters about the real issues of common ground in the northwoods.

Yolanda St. Germaine, a LdF tribal member living in Madison, returned to spear with her brother Harold and to assert her rights and culture. On Catfish Lake (April 27), they were attacked with rocks and boat waves and verbally harangued from shore. "Let us have your squaw bitch. Let us take turns on your squaw. . . . We'll trade her for breakfast for you, fat boy." After this terrifying night, they had to decide whether to go out again. "My mom said it depends on whether you came for fish (then we could spear on the Res) or whether we came to prove a point," Yolanda recounted. She and her brother went to Twin Lakes the next night to spear. Pity, Yolanda said later, was the main emotion she felt towards these protesters.

The Witness extended its credibility with media, that uneasy ally of peace-making, by providing press releases and interviews throughout the spearing season. Although we were often referred to as the nonviolent observers present at landings, much of the media did not see or choose to portray the same depth of intimidation and hatred we saw on many nights. Some reporters were exceptions to this (e.g., Mary Jo Kewley of the *Wausau Daily Herald*), but most state media editorials continued to call for some settlement.

On November 12, the Witness released its 1990 Report to the press and state representative Frank Boyle's American Indian Studies Committee. It documented ninety-four acts of racism, eighty-eight racist incidents, ninety-seven cases of inadequate law enforcement (mostly in Vilas, Oneida, and Iron counties where LdF speared). It also made recommendations for better law enforcement, and state and federal monitoring of that enforcement. Al Shanks of the state's Division of Emergency Government dismissed the report as "rubbish" and the stories vanished except for those who'd been there and for the lawyers working on a case for 1991.

For the spearing of St. Croix, Red Cliff, and Bad River, witnesses (called treehuggers and Green slime) usually outnumbered protesters throughout the season. Except for the first nights of St. Croix spearing, most boat landings were uneventful. The *Polk County Ledger*, a weekly newspaper in northwest Wisconsin, praised the work of the Witness in that area in a May 3 editorial:

> There is no doubt that the presence of the witnesses was a major factor in the peaceful situations at the landings. Their numbers no doubt quieted some who would have protested in a more disruptive manner. Their quiet, peaceful presence showed protesters and TV cameras alike that support for Indian treaty rights exists in the county . . . Close to 500 Polk County residents were trained in witnessing. Those numbers show the outpouring of emotion that many feel because of the conflict.

In 1990, the Witness and treaty support network had entered, however reluctantly, the political arena away from the boat landings and helped shape the debate on race, economic, and environmental issues. But we were nowhere near influential enough to counter the weight of Senator Inouye's involvement, the federal court rulings, Tommy Thompson's campaign clout or even the Wisconsin Counties Association. Nor could we uncover any evidence on what happened to former chamber of commerce president, Steve Semmelmeyer. It was buried in the bureaucracy as deep as the dirt that authorities filled his basement with a week after the fire. Whether accident or arson, the deaths of Semmelmeyer and Notter had sent shock waves through the treaty movement that were felt throughout the year.[19]

The treaty network had enthusiastically joined the Lac Courte Oreilles and Rusk County Citizens Action in their lobbying, research, and direct action efforts against the Kennecott/Rio Tinto Zinc proposed mine at Ladysmith. Plans were being laid for a direct-action Flambeau Summer 1991 modeled after the Redwood Summer 1990 in California. At the LCO Protect the Earth Festival, Labor Day 1990, Roger Moody of People Against Rio Tinto Zinc and Subsidiaries (PARTiZANS) expanded the arena of indigenous people's and environmentalists' struggles against the world's largest metal mining company by sharing the work of PARTiZANS in support of indigenous struggles in Australia, the Philippines, Panama, and Brazil.[20] Winona LaDuke, director of the Land Rights Organization, challenged people: If these mineral and energy corporations do not get the minerals they want in Wisconsin or the hydro-energy they want from James Bay, Canada, they will still be going after it somewhere else on indigenous peoples' land.

For spearfishers on the lakes, 1990 was no better than 1989, with gunshots still ringing out, spearers and passengers injured, and harvesting disrupted. There were few county prosecutions of on-lake protest harassers and the hunter harassment law was challenged in court and struck down as unconstitutional by a Vilas County judge. Trying to refocus the public debate, Walt Bresette raised the question of why people still had to risk their lives and spear under police guard, and why spearers and anglers were still harvesting poisoned fish.

We were building a movement of many trained witnesses, of many Green, anti-racist, and religious allies, and of some political influence. Were we helping to build something that could actually win for Native Americans their treaty rights?

Notes

George Amour's January 14, 1990, remarks and *Ogichidaa* prayer quoted in this chapter with permission.

1. This money was not to count as income or in any way be used to reduce benefits from other government programs. To the surprise of the three Chippewa reservations in Minnesota, they had lost eligibility for welfare and other benefits because of the settlement income under the terms of their buyout-of-harvesting-rights agreement there, in 1988. The Fon du Lac reservation later dropped out of what was called the Tri-Band Agreement in Minnesota.

2. Ron Seely, "Northern officials give state poor grades," *Wisconsin State Journal*, March 24, 1991. The *Eco News* story of Exxon offering Prince William Sound boat owners money to "stand by" and not talk to reporters after the oil spill comes from "Hush Money," *Green Net* (Madison), vol. 2, no. 6 (Summer 1989), p. 5. Exxon reportedly also hired the sole reporter in Valdez into their public relations division, and offered $32,000 to the Alaska Public Radio Network for coverage of the oil spill (this was redrawn when news of the offer leaked).

3. In Germany, the government prosecutes antinuclear activists under the anti-terrorist, national security laws. While this avenue has not yet been pursued against U.S. environmental activists, the 1990 bombing of activists Judi Bari and Darryl Cherney in California signals the beginnings of an assault (condoned by lack of government action) by those with interests similar to those dismantling state and federal environmental protection laws/regulations, and those interested in dismantling Native American treaties.

4. The eleven chambers of commerce were: Minocqua, Lac du Flambeau, Arbor Vitae-Woodruff, Eagle River, Boulder Junction, Rhinelander, Manitowish Waters, Mercer, Presque Isle, Winchester, and Sayner.

5. Donald Bluhm, "11 Business Groups Back Treaty Rights," *Milwaukee Journal,* February 13, 1990, cites Hatch's prediction that the chambers would be forced to dissolve if they supported this resolution, and Hatch's statement that the chambers were a vehicle for Maulson and a radical group of spearers.

6. The Witness trainings for the 1990 season began in December 1989 with a training at the Breadline Restaurant in Eau Claire, Wisconsin. Trainings for trainers took place in Madison in December 1989, and then in February 1990 in Minneapolis (set up by Sherrole Benton), in Chicago through the Indian Treaty Rights Committee, and in Madison again. Following these, witness trainings blossomed throughout this three state region, including Chicago (training led by Elisa Farmilant), Duluth-Superior, Luck and Eau Claire (in northwest Wisconsin), and small communities in southeast and central Wisconsin. Pat Sheppo and Diane Anderson hosted weekly trainings in the Twin Cities from March through April 1990, with additional support from Joe and Ellen Geshick, Women Against Military Madness (WAMM), student groups, and others.

7. In February 1990, the ACLU of Wisconsin Foundation announced its campaign of support for Chippewa treaties, including education, advocacy, and litigation. By 1991, Gretchen Miller of the ACLU-WI had raised $40,000–$50,000 in grants (from C.S. Fund, Deer Creek Foundation, J. Roderick MacArthur Foundation, and the Wisconsin Trust Account Foundation) for a lawsuit against violent protests at landings and lakes during spearing. The ACLU enlisted the support of Irv Charne of the law firm of Charne, Clancy and Taitelman which provided the lead lawyer, Brian Pierson, and legal services worth in excess of $150,000 for this case, that was finally heard in federal court in 1991.

8. Jay Tobin interview with Rick Whaley, July 5(?), 1991, at LdF, and phone interview with researcher Dyoni Thompkins, August 10, 1991.

9. See George Stanley and Terry Koper, "Spearing pow-wow could attract 600," *Milwaukee Sentinel,* March 14, 1990; and Editorial, "Pow-wow won't help," *Milwaukee Sentinel,* March 20, 1990.

10. The bill, A.B. 656, was originally introduced to prevent animal rights activists from interfering with deer hunting in Wisconsin, though animal defenders had caused no major disruption of the hunting season here. This issue divides Greens in Wisconsin, but treaty supporters, by and large, welcomed the bill as a best hope for ending on-lake harassment of the Chippewa. The possibility that this law could be used to protect spearers threatened to delay the bill, but, in the end, probably helped lead to its passage, as lawmakers continued to worry about violence having a negative

impact on the summer tourist season. Crist and STA–W threatened to test the law during spearing and in the courts. Forgetting his base in the outdoors lobby, Crist alienated many hunters with his opposition to the hunter harassment bill.

11. Steve Schultze and Maurice Wozniak, "Thompson irked by Crist's new call," *Milwaukee Journal*, April 27, 1990. This story reports that Crist promises to delay his mass arrests strategy if the governor can bring back federal officials to observe the boat landings, i.e., how upset people are at spearfishing.

12. Journalist Scott Kerr uncovered a phone call from Patricia Zell of Senator Inouye's office to Judge Crabb in late 1989, ostensibly made to set up a meeting on "neutral" turf when Inouye came to Wisconsin. Through her clerk of court, Crabb notified tribal lawyers of the call, but Zell and Crabb's office said nothing of legal substance was discussed in this phone conversation that preceded Inouye's trip to Wisconsin. Tribal leaders then refused to meet with Inouye on his trip to Wisconsin because of his office's *ex parte* contact with Crabb.

13. In June 1990, the Washington state anti-Indian group S/SPAWN (see chapter 2) officially changed its name to the National Coalition on Federal Indian Policy. NCIFP became the front for S/SPAWN's efforts to move county governments against Native treaties on a national level.

14. PARR leader Larry Peterson told Zoltán Grossman that his employer, Park Falls Paper Company, had sold him paper at an employee discount. Peterson was also given time off of work during the spearing season.

15. The old-growth timber outline of the Menominee Reservation in Wisconsin can be seen from satellites.

16. The compromise solution within the Green network in Wisconsin was to send out a three-part mailing: one piece from anti-mining and treaty rights individuals endorsing a vote for Loftus-Doyle; one endorsing the Labor Farm Attorney General candidate, excellent on treaty and mining and women's issues; and a Wisconsin Greens report card on Loftus: Mining, a "B," and Treaty Rights, a "D."

17. While both Thompson and Hanaway opposed abortion, all the major policy initiatives against it were left to the attorney general. Hanaway opposed treaties but publicly compared the anti-treaty protests to Klan protests during the civil rights movement. Thompson distanced himself from Crist, but never condemned the anti-treaty sentiment in Wisconsin. Thompson also received a significant vote from Milwaukee's African-American community for his support of their school choice program.

18. Linda Cree also remembered hearing stories that the Klan was in northern Michigan's Upper Peninsula during the 1930s depression, and heard about cross burnings in the Upper Peninsula when she was growing up in the 1950s.

19. In June 1991, Leonard Belstner, head of the State Arson Division, Department of Criminal Investigation (Attorney General's office), said the cause of the fire was undetermined because there was so much damage. No traces of accelerants or other evidence to suggest arson or foul play were found, he said. He would not comment on reports of traces of cocaine being found in the remains of Semmelmeyer and his companion, or on the cause of the ball of smoke during the fire. Local fire investigators speculated that a newly installed gas fireplace had exploded, and that the reason the

front door was open was that one victim had gone back inside to get something or someone (both bodies were found inside on the floor near windows). Richard Tews, a private investigator specializing in arson, reviewed this case for the authors. He felt that the state had done an excellent job in its investigation of the fire site and possible causes and that the details and evidence matched the probability of accidental fire.

20. The Protect the Earth pow-wow and festival was inspired by the tradition of defense of land and culture emanating from such LCO actions as the July 1971 demonstration and three day occupation of a dam site of Northern States Power Company in Sawyer County. Led by a group of one hundred LCO members and twenty-five AIM members, this unified action had the support of LCO's tribal government. They protested against the renewal of Northern States' 50-year lease because the company had not fulfilled the original lease terms to move Chippewa graves and homes when the dam was built in 1921. By 1924, Northern States Power had flooded 14,5000 acres of federal land (now the Chippewa Flowage), including 6,000 acres of the LCO reservation, and destroyed three major LCO wild rice beds. The company has yet to resolve the situation to LCO's satisfaction. See Nancy O. Lurie, *Wisconsin Indians* (Madison: State Historical Society of Wisconsin, 1987), pp. 55–56.

8

If the Chippewa spearfish without any environmental restraints, northern Wisconsin will end up looking like Appalachia.

—Fred Hatch,
anti-treaty rights attorney

MANOMINIKE GISISS
(The Wildrice Moon)

Interwoven Issues
Indian Treaty Rights and the Mining Threat

Rick Whaley

NORTHERN WISCONSIN IS THE birthplace of rivers and visions. This is the land the *Anishinabe* came to, the land where food grows on water. Some 11,348 lakes dot ceded territory and six major rivers have their headwaters here. The rivers of northern Wisconsin are pulled to larger waters—the Bois Brule and Bad River to Lake Superior; the Brule and Menominee Rivers to Lake Michigan; the St. Croix, Flambeau, Chippewa, and Wisconsin Rivers to the mighty Mississippi. The rivers tie together human communities along the way. The Wisconsin River, making its wildly crooked path from far north to southwest Wisconsin, is yoked along the way for electricity, farm irrigation, and paper mill cooling and discharge. Witnesses from Chicago, Milwaukee, and Madison travel highways that cross the Wisconsin River five times on the way to Lac du Flambeau. The rivers knit together ecological communities as well. In the wilderness headwaters of ceded territory, deer and eagle still go to the river to drink and mountain lion and wolf are rumored to be returning. Bear, otter, and heron fish the rivers. Cattails and jewelweed grow along the forest shores before the rivers break out into bogs (natural and cranberry) and then wind through farmland.

Sustenance for the human body and spirit can still be found on the rivers. Canoeists on the Brule, the Flambeau, or the Wolf River can find serenity on the expansive river passages or test themselves on the many class I to III rapids. Some of the best trout fishing in America is on the rivers of northern Wisconsin. Lac Courte Oreilles Chippewa still gather sacred medicines from the Chippewa and Flambeau waterways.

Sulfide Brines: A Brief History of Mining in Northern Wisconsin

Grander than these rivers was the ocean that covered northern Wisconsin 1.8 billion years ago, and mightier were the volcanoes that split the ocean floor and spit forth brines rich in sulfur, iron, and copper from the earth's core. When these minerals mixed with the cool sea water, particles of iron sulfide and copper sulfide were formed. As the centuries wore on, these deposits made the sulfur-rich ore that is now so desirable. This band of Middle Precambrian metavolcanic rock runs across northern Wisconsin from Ladysmith east and north, roughly around and under Highway 8, to the Wisconsin-Michigan river border.

Throughout the 1970s and early 1980s, approximately forty multinational mining companies leased over 400,000 acres of land in northern Wisconsin. During this period, Third World countries started to exercise greater control over their nonrenewable resources (e.g., Allende elected in Chile in 1970). The corporate giants recognized that mineral resources as well as their political influence was diminishing in these countries. The acquisition of mineral rights and subsequent exploration on Wisconsin farmland and in state and national forests were part of the corporate effort to develop oil and mineral resources in the "politically stable" United States. Formerly called the Chippewa Lobe, the northern Wisconsin mineral belt is the southernmost extension of the Canadian Shield geological formation containing some of the largest concentrations of copper, nickel, and zinc in the United States, as well as deposits of vanadium, gold, lead, chromite, titanium, and radioactive uranium and thorium. More than two dozen companies drilled in the 1970s, testing core samples for the best prospects.

In 1970, Kennecott Copper Corporation announced the discovery of a six-million-ton copper deposit (1 percent copper in ore) worth between $14 and $223 million in Rusk County near Ladysmith, Wisconsin. The state government was caught unprepared, with no mining taxation code or regulatory framework for mining or its environmental consequences. In 1975, Phelps-Dodge, second largest copper producer in the United States, developed a proposal for the Lac du Flambeau Reservation actually asking the LdF tribal government for $250,000 to make them a partner in the exploratory drilling for copper on the reservation. LdF turned them down. Also in 1975, Exxon Coal and Minerals Company found a huge copper-zinc deposit near Crandon,

Wisconsin, and the Mole Lake reservation. Samples in this 73-million-ton ore body tested at 5 percent zinc and 1 percent copper. In the late 1970s, Kerr McGee optioned from Chicago Northwestern Railroad the mineral rights to 22 percent of the land on the Potawatomi Reservation in Forest County because Department of Energy (DOE) surveys had identified this area as a possible "uranium hotspot."

Along with their European-American neighbors, reservations were very cautious about the mineral companies' exploration. Undeterred, companies entered reservations for unauthorized and illegal testing. In 1980, Exxon agents were escorted off Lac Courte Oreilles with their water samples. Two years later, LCO tribal police caught Uranerz (a subsidiary of Urangesellschaft of Germany) geologists taking unauthorized rock samples in violation of an LCO ban on mineral exploration. Even the DOE had gotten into the act, hiring Bendix Corporation to explore (unauthorized) for uranium on the Red Cliff and Bad River Reservations. These "emissaries" of the mining companies were testing the waters (and rocks) in Indian county for the modern conversion to economic development.[1] The number of exploratory drilling projects declined in the 1980s, but the most serious prospects moved closer to realization.

Near the Willow River not far from the Lac du Flambeau Reservation is state-owned land where Noranda wants to mine 10 million tons of zinc and silver (samples: 28 percent zinc; 5.5 ounces of silver per ore ton). Noranda is seeking a permit for a fifteen-year project that includes two to three years of exploration, ten to twelve years of milling the ore on-site, and then one to two years of "reclaiming" the forest/wetlands around the project. Additional mining projects include gold being sought by NDU Resources in the Chequamegon National Forest near the Yellow River in Taylor county and by Noranda under a farm in Marathon County.[2] Union Carbide (of Bhopal infamy, the chemical gas disaster in India) owns the rights to a vanadium deposit between Round Lake and the Tiger Cat Flowage, a tributary of the Chippewa Flowage.

The New Mining District

Economic schemes are visions to some men. "Wisconsin has world-class mining potential," said James Klauser in June 1981—and he was in a position to know. Before entering state government in 1987, Klauser worked as a lobbyist for the Exxon Coal and Minerals Company, and simultaneously as an attorney and mining consultant for the Wisconsin Association of Manufacturers and Commerce, the state's most powerful and influential business lobby. Other former clients included Union Carbide, manufacturers of aldicarb (a now restricted pesticide), and FMC, also an agri-chemical manufacturer. Klauser noted that Wisconsin had the potential for six to ten major metallic operations in the next two decades.[3]

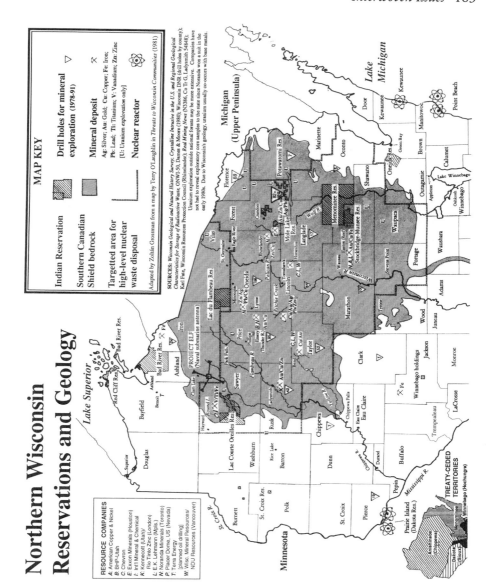

Northern Wisconsin
Reservations and Geology

However, Klauser's main focus in the early 1980s was the Exxon Crandon project. Exxon Coal and Minerals Company had rights to 70–80 million tons of ore containing zinc, copper, silver, and gold near Crandon. Exxon was one of the many major oil companies to start diversification into mineral investments especially after the 1973 Middle East War and oil embargo. The Crandon deposit was rated as one of top ten metallic sulfide deposits in North America. As a lobbyist, Klauser touted the mine as a fine example of what mining could do for Wisconsin: investments (Exxon originally projected a $900 million investment); jobs (1000 construction jobs and 2000 ripple-effect jobs throughout Wisconsin); total personal income ($13.4 billion); and $16 million a year in taxes to the state. Exxon planned to mine 3.5 million tons a year for twenty-five years.[4] The proposed mine found support in a local timber industry family who had leased land to Exxon and from some area business-people looking for a boom-time economy.

Opposition arose from local residents and many businesspeople, especially those downstream from the mine. People feared that the constant pumping of groundwater would dry up wells and springs and lower the lake where many had retirement homes or resorts. Economic fears centered on the financial burden to local tax payers that would result from the sudden influx of workers and demands on local services for Exxon. Above all, apprehension arose over what the waste and acid drainage from the mine would do to area waters. The proposed mine would be located at the headwaters of the Wolf River in Forest county and would discharge, over twenty years, 58 million tons of acid waste into tailing ponds near the river.

The Mole Lake (Sokaogon) Chippewa, the Menominee, and the Forest County Potawatomi Reservations joined residents, sport, and environmental groups in opposing the mine. Significantly, the ore deposit lay next to the Mole Lake Reservation on land the Sokaogon still claimed was due them from the 1854 treaty. The Sokaogon went to federal court in 1986 claiming this twelve square miles. In 1989, the Seventh U.S. Circuit Court of Appeals ruled against the land claim but said the Mole Lake Sokaogon could sue Exxon for any infringements of their off-reservation harvesting rights.[5]

Nestled in the southwest corner of Forest county, this reservation and its wild rice lakes provide the Sokaogon with an important food source, a cash crop, and earth bounty for their religious rituals. Exxon biologists expressed surprise that the Mole Lake Chippewa were so concerned about what impact mining would have on "those lake weeds"—a dye test had shown the rice beds would be in the line of the discharge. In 1975, Exxon had offered the Mole Lake tribal chair a check for $20,000 for rights to explore on their 1900-acre reservation, but the tribal council tore it up. In 1983, an Exxon report admitted that the "means of subsistence on the reservation" might be "rendered less than effective" once the mine got going.[6]

In the early 1980s, a strong local coalition of Native Americans and European-Americans fought Exxon in a series of strategies. The Wolf River Conservation Club demanded that the WDNR require Exxon to remove the acid-generating pyrites from the mine waste before it all went into tailing ponds. The Langlade county board (Forest county's neighbor) passed a resolution opposing Exxon's plan to store toxic mine waste at the headwaters of the Wolf and their plans to dump mine waste into the river. The Nashville town board refused to act on Exxon's permits in October of 1986, saying they would wait until after the WDNR master hearings. Exxon withdrew from the permitting process and blamed depressed world copper prices for their decision. They promised the site would be "developed in time."

Klauser's Ascendency

Republican Tommy Thompson was first elected governor in November 1986.[7] With his election victory, the man who had courted the PARR vote by saying spearing was wrong no matter what the federal court said, now brought anti-treaty politics from the fringes to the mainstream of Wisconsin politics. One of his first moves as Governor-elect was to appoint Exxon/Union Carbide/Wisconsin manufacturers' lobbyist James Klauser to the position of secretary of the Department of Administration (DOA). He was to be Thompson's top aide, "the second governor." Klauser moved quickly on behalf of mining development in Wisconsin, all the while downplaying his past work and saying any mining would be environmentally sound.

In January 1987, Klauser set up a meeting between Ray Ingram, an Exxon vice-president, and Governor Thompson, in order to see under what circumstances Exxon might reconsider applying for the Crandon-Mole Lake permit. While this project remained on hold, another, more feasible project was moving again that could be the starter for the mining district idea. Kennecott, originally thwarted by local opposition in 1976, had re-applied for the Ladysmith permit. According to political strategy documents later uncovered from Klauser's government files by a *Wisconsin State Journal* investigation, Kennecott would develop a sophisticated legislative strategy to "neutralize" the small vocal opposition at Ladysmith and override the county's "extremely onerous" mining moratorium.[8] They would also return with a scaled-down project to need less acreage for the pit, to ship ore out of state and not smelt it on-site, and to seek WDNR variances for the operation.

In May 1987, Thompson created the Governor's Ad Hoc Task Force on Mining. It helped pass into law, without public debate or legislative scrutiny, a statute that circumvented local mining moratoriums or bans, and instead, allowed mining companies to negotiate directly with business committees set up by local units of government. This divided residents within Ladysmith and

Rusk County, and the environmental bottom line for these communities became irrelevant if the local negotiating committees chose to deal with mineral companies.

Throughout Thompson's first term as governor, Kennecott continued to appraise the governor and Klauser of attempts to renew the Ladysmith permitting process. Klauser continued to stonewall the press about his influence on mining, saying the governor did not even ask him for advice. Klauser denied the January 1987 meeting between the Exxon vice-president and the governor ever took place, and said if it did, it was a coincidence.[9] Meanwhile, in 1988, representatives from Kennecott had sat down with a Rusk County negotiating committee to hammer out a local agreement for the Ladysmith mine. The new mining district was moving closer to rivers.

Fighting Kennecott: The Eye of the Fisherman

The state public hearing portion of the Kennecott Ladysmith permit finally took place in July 1990 at the high school in Ladysmith. Area residents (European- and Native American), Greens, environmentalists, and sportfishing groups showed up, two hundred strong, to oppose the permit. Kermit Benson of Muskies, Inc., said that the mine was too risky—the mine's treated water could hurt the fish and fishing in the Holcombe Flowage, downstream of the Flambeau River. Wisconsin Greens, who had participated in the canoe flotilla protest with Earth First! and Greenpeace two weeks earlier, also testified: What would be the *regional* impact of mines on the agriculture and tourist-dependent communities of northern Wisconsin? What would be the *cumulative* effect of mining waste on regional waters from the rest of the mines likely to follow?

Creative challenges were raised against mining on behalf of the Flambeau waters. At the Kennecott hearing on July 16, Cassandra Dixon gave dead fish to hearing examiner David Schwartz throughout the day, until Sheriff Rozak made her stop, citing sanitation conditions in the hearing room. He would not comment on sanitation in the river nearby. A funeral bouquet sent to Mr. Schwartz from the Midwest Treaty Network represented the death of the tourist industry in the Ladysmith area. Most of the concern for ground and river water centered on sulfuric acid and what it does. As Al Gedicks had pointed out:

> What's wrong [with] this type of mining, a mining which extracts minerals from sulfide deposits, [is] that when the minerals are taken out of the massive sulfide deposits, those sulfides are released into the environment. Those sulfides under the pressure of air and water become sulfuric acid which is, of course, very detrimental to air and water quality. But it also releases other heavy metals like copper, arsenic, cadmium, lead, and mercury which are toxic to fish at parts per

Mining in Wisconsin History

Before European contact Indigenous people make copper implements and ornaments. Lead is used in southwest Wisconsin and the *Anishinabe* mine copper in northern Wisconsin.

Late 1600s Nicolas Perrot passes on crude mining techniques to Native Americans and they start mining seriously and trading lead for goods from settlers.

1800s The Sauk and Fox dig lead and smelt ore over open fires, as a way to supplement their incomes from hunting and trading. (Paull and Paull, *Geology of Wisconsin and Upper Michigan*, p. 136.) The forced land cessions against the Sauk and Fox, particularly the 1804 treaty and the war against Black Hawk in 1831–1832, were for mineral and agricultural lands in southwest Wisconsin and northwestern Illinois.

1828 N. Morris and two partners strike lead near Mineral Point, Wisconsin. First Wisconsin mining boom begins. Winnebago driven from western Wisconsin homeland because of pressure for mineral resources.

1836 Col. Henry Dodge, miner and "hero" of the Black Hawk War, is inaugurated as Wisconsin's first territorial governor.

1837 "Timber Treaty": Chippewa cede to the United States a large section of north central Wisconsin.

1842 "The Copper Treaty" with the Chippewa cedes northernmost Wisconsin and Michigan's upper peninsula to the United States ("Federal commissioner Henry Dodge, governor of Wisconsin, . . . had never seen this area, but reports convinced him that it had plenty of pine timber and copper and was suitable for agriculture. Dodge feared bloodshed if aggressive whites were not allowed to purchase and exploit this attractive region." Danziger, *The Chippewas of Lake Superior*, p. 87.)

1848 Lead boom hits its peak. Bust cycle begins in southwest Wisconsin.

1840s and 1850s Copper mining boom on south shore of Kitchigami (Lake Superior).

1854 The La Pointe Treaty with the Chippewa. Last of lands taken. Reservations assigned. The United States secures coveted northern Minnesota mineral range.

1870s Zinc ore boom in southwest Wisconsin. Boom periods return during World War I–II.

1880s Iron ore boom in northern Wisconsin Gogebic Range.

1930s–1960s Wisconsin iron ore mining in decline. Last mine closes in 1965.

1970s Multinational mineral corporations drilling exploration for copper, zinc, silver, gold, and uranium.

1970 Kennecott announces copper ore find near Ladysmith.

1976 Exxon announces zinc and copper find near Crandon-Mole Lake.

1977 Legislature passes mining regulation and taxation laws. DNR rejects Kennecott application for Ladysmith mine.

1980s Political groundbreaking for the New Mining District.

1982 Natural Resources Board rejects nondegradation of groundwater standard; opts for federal maximum contaminant levels for drinking water.

1986 Exxon temporarily shelves Crandon mine project. Kennecott renews interest in Rusk Co./Ladysmith mine. Tommy Thompson elected governor and announces James Klauser will be top aide.

1987 Thompson creates mining task force to promote Kennecott mine.

1988 Local agreement amendment to state budget allows mining companies to bypass local regulations.

Main source: Wisconsin State Journal series by Ron Seely and Jeff Mayers, March 24–28, 1991.

billion and parts per million. So very small amounts of these heavy metals if they get into the water supply [and] food chain are going to destroy the fish population . . . wildlife . . . wild rice of lakes in northern Wisconsin.[10]

Kennecott's track record elsewhere is not good. Their Bingham Utah mine is the largest open pit mine in the world—3,000 feet deep, producing 77,000 tons of ore a day. Sulfur dioxide dust used to blow off the huge tailing piles made by the mine and sulfide acid from leaching copper has contaminated local wells and may be headed toward the Salt Lake Valley aquifer. The cyanide tailing pond at Kennecott's Alligator Ridge gold mine in Nevada killed 1400 migratory birds in 1988 and the company was fined $90,000.[11] In Ontario, Canada, the uranium mine of Rio Tinto Zinc (RTZ), Kennecott's parent company, killed every fish in the Serpent River and made the water radioactive and unfit for humans to drink. RTZ's actions and policies engendered racial clashes in 1969 and guerilla war in 1988 over their land grab against aboriginal people in Papua New Guinea.[12] Before independence in Namibia (1990), RTZ had used a South African army detachment complete with tanks to defend the world's most condemned (by government and U.N. resolutions) mine. The WDNR dismissed Kennecott's record of pollution and government fines in its other operations, saying it was not an appropriate part of the Wisconsin Environmental Impact Statement.

In attendance, too, at the Ladysmith high school auditorium hearing were Chippewa representatives from Lac Courte Oreilles, Mole Lake, Bad River, *Wa-Swa-Gon,* and the Great Lakes Indian Fish and Wildlife Commission—all opposed to the mine. Gaiashkibos, LCO tribal chair, said Kennecott had not proved the mining would not harm the resources in ceded territory. LCO demanded that Kennecott do monthly water-monitoring reports, cease operations if a change is reported in water quality, require an analysis of mining's impact on harvestable resources, and release core sample information to the public.

The WDNR's position was that treaty rights were beyond the scope of the environmental impact statement and that Kennecott did not have to prove water and resources would remain safe, only that they were in compliance with state law. The WDNR was ready to grant four variances from the law to make the mine possible: to approve a mine within 140 feet of a river instead of 300 feet as in state law (swimming pools in Wisconsin still can't be closer than 300 feet to a river); to allow construction of the mine in a floodplain, saying that protection was adequate; to allow waste piles within 1000 feet of a highway; and to allow the company to forego groundwater testing for turbidity (cloudiness), organic compounds, and radioactivity. Significantly, the WDNR also did not require Kennecott to say where the ore was headed and who would mill and use it. Thus if uranium were part of the package (which WDNR and Kennecott say is not possible from *this* ore body) it would leave the state unknown to the public.[13]

Mining company representatives and their political supporters had managed to rewrite Wisconsin's mining laws to make mining company compliance possible in ventures that still looked lucrative. Two examples of this were the mining tax law in 1974 (revised in 1977 to further entice mining) and the 1982 change in Wisconsin's nondegradation of groundwater standard to one that allows mining companies to contaminate drinking water up to the federal maximum contaminant levels. This legislative prowess was matched by the mining companies' effectiveness in their public relations and pressure campaigns. For example, Kennecott/RTZ (which called its Wisconsin operation The Flambeau Mining Company) hired a public relations firm that put out a newsletter, *The Flambeau News*, highlighting the benign activities of Kennecott. The company sponsored contests on how best to spend the money the mine would bring to the community, and sponsored a country soap radio show called "The Copper Cafe." This good neighbor approach also included a $60,000 donation to buy Ladysmith a new fire tanker and, later in 1990, $4000 to support a Desert Shield cookie campaign.[14] More to the point, however, Kennecott threatened, in 1987, to sue Ladysmith for deprivation of economic use of property if the local zoning ordinances or mining moratorium held up the local agreement. Kennecott also threatened to petition for the mine site to be annexed to Ladysmith (thereby cutting the town of Grant out of mining revenues) if the Grant dissidents didn't change their tune.[15] Local activists in the Rusk County Citizens Action Group promised to challenge the August 1988 local agreement that Kennecott had secured.

Reflecting on the Ladysmith hearing of July 1990, Gaiashkibos, also an LCO spearfisher, maintained that the issue went beyond food or economics. "All water is sacred. It is the gift of life . . . that's something the hearing examiner probably didn't even understand."[16]

Chippewa Treaties:
Potentially the Greatest Obstacle

The local mining bans and state environmental regulations were not the only impediments to mining that needed to be neutralized. Chippewa treaty rights stood as potentially the greatest obstacle to mining in northern Wisconsin. Could the treaties, signed in the 1800s and affirmed in the 1980s, be used to protect the integrity of off-reservation resources from pollution and damage from mining? This is exactly what began to happen during the Mole Lake struggle with Exxon when, in 1986, Mole Lake filed suit in federal court saying Exxon's fencing of land just off the reservation interfered with their court-affirmed rights to gather, fish, and trap there. And in 1989, LCO went on record against Kennecott's permit to mine in ceded territory near LCO waters.

Anti-treaty politicians and protest leaders have often criticized the pro-treaty movements for not producing evidence of mining company collusion with the anti-treaty protests. While there is no cancelled check, no "smoking gun" to link this business agenda to boat landing violence, a clear and direct programmatic political connection does exist.

Klauser and powerful state politicians have worked systematically to limit or negate the exercise of Chippewa treaty rights. Klauser and the governor steadfastly opposed the use of treaty rights as environmental arguments against economic development and opposed tribes as co-management partners in northern Wisconsin. Throughout Thompson's first term as governor (1986–1990), he and Klauser promised that they would appeal all of the *Voigt* litigation, even if it took decades and the hiring of independent (treaty-busting) law firms. The governor used boat landing violence, created by his anti-treaty friends, to justify his move in federal court in 1989 for an injunction against spearfishing. Judge Crabb turned him down, but from 1987 to spring of 1990, backlash violence was Thompson's main excuse for needing help to solve the treaty "problem" (see chapter 5).

Powerful politicians have attempted to punish or neutralize Chippewa treaty activists as they extended the meaning of treaties into environmental protection areas. Walt Bresette's firing from GLIFWC in the mid-1980s after openly challenging Congressman Obey and the government's attempt to site nuclear waste dumps in northern Wisconsin (see chapter 2) is only one, early example. Efforts by Governor Thompson and James Klauser to portray spearers as "militants" or "extremists on the other side" (in comparison to protesters) have sought to isolate treaty activists and narrow the range of debate on rights of sovereignty. Pressure from protest groups and state leaders led to the unusual case of federal involvement in blackmailing a racial minority to give up rights in exchange for future federal program funding (Congressman David Obey's famous letter of April 1989 to the tribal chairs—see chapter 5). To make this approach seem moderate and reasonable, Congressman James Sensenbrenner, heir to the Kimberly-Clark paper fortune, introduced legislation in Congress to abrogate the treaties.[17] (The measure went nowhere in Congress.) Late in 1989, the Wisconsin Legislature, with approval of the governor, passed a resolution asking the federal government to get involved in Wisconsin's treaty dispute.

Fred Hatch's old acquaintance with Jim Klauser proved valuable to the anti-treaty movement as well. Hatch, the attorney for STA–W in the late 1980s and for PARR in the early 1990s, facilitated numerous meetings with protest leaders on Klauser's trips north, especially preceding spearing and buyout times. Klauser maintained, "In a free and open society, representatives of government have to meet with all parties involved and not pick and choose." The fact that the boat landing protesters' agenda matched Klauser's political-economic program against treaties explains why he would pick and choose to meet with

THE MILWAUKEE JOURNAL

groups analogous to the KKK, as the Strickland Report called them, instead of meeting with spearfishing and witness groups.

Significantly, Klauser took the lead as the governor's main representative in the 1989 buyout negotiations with Lac du Flambeau. Klauser argued the deal as cheaper than the "do-nothing, black cloud alternative" (i.e., spearing with protests again) and then harangued the spearing "militants" when the proposal was defeated. The part of the proposed buyout that said LdF would give up off-reservation jurisdiction over resources implied LdF would not interfere with economic development in ceded territory and could have negated off-reservation timbering.

Rather than claim credit for doing what a lobbyist moving into government would logically do, Klauser continued to dismiss all pro-mining/anti-treaty links as a "conspiracy" created by "convoluted minds."[18] George Meyer of the WDNR, who had come around on points of fish facts and the need to protect treaty rights, saw the connection. He said:

If, in fact, any of these mines would be shown to adversely affect, to any significant amount, the fisheries or the wildlife in northern Wisconsin, I believe that the Chippewa would be able to sue the mining companies, or the state of Wisconsin if we had granted such a permit, for hurting their treaty rights because it wouldn't make sense for them to have hunting and fishing rights and then turn around and have those damaged by mines or any other industry in northern Wisconsin.[19]

Anishinabe Niijii (Friends of the *Ojibwe*) was formed on November 11, 1989, and brought together *Wa-Swa-Gon* and other spearing groups, a number of tribal governments including LCO, pro-treaty groups, and anti-mining organizations, with Gaiashkibos as chair. Its main purpose was to protect water and resources in light of the proposed mining plans in ceded territory. To the eye of the spearfisher, the threats of more pollution of waters in northern Wisconsin looked even more dangerous than the protesters. To the eye of the protester, still clouded by racism and false fish facts, stopping (or qualifying the conditions of) mining had nothing to do with protecting resources.[20] "If Exxon's behind us, they're way behind us," said Crist, "We're looking for the check. It's not there. But if Exxon comes in with a $2 million check to STA–Wisconsin, we'll be off and running. We'd love it. We'll make them an honorary member."[21]

Behind the stonewalling of his role in mining development, Klauser's work continued. He was an observer at the Utah gathering sponsored by the Wisconsin Counties Association (WCA) in early 1990 when Native American county supervisors were excluded.[22] WCA executive director Mark Rogacki welcomed Klauser's participation at the Utah conference as a reflection of the Thompson administration's shared perspective that federal involvement was needed to settle this intergovernmental dispute over fishing, timber rights, and dual jurisdictions.[23] At a February 1991 WCA meeting in Wisconsin, Robert Mulcahy, WCA general council, made it plainer: "Timber is not the only issue. . . . Mining is the real issue." Of public land in Wisconsin, 56 percent is in the county forest system, added a Wisconsin Counties Forestry Association representative, and "big profits" were to be made if county land were leased to mining companies.[24] Klauser continued to ally himself with the national agenda to abrogate or minimize treaty rights and to solve "intergovernmental disputes" outside the court system (where they were already resolved).

By the end of spearing in 1990, and especially in an election year, Governor Thompson publicly distanced himself from STA–W, although Klauser continued to meet with them. Boat landing violence had become more a hindrance than an ally for the mining cause. While the protest movement was waning, the mining companies were gaining in Ladysmith and at the state capitol—their noses still clean of racism and (direct) violence to people. Klauser continued to meet with European-American business leaders in northern Wisconsin, nominally to promote peace at the boat landings (but able also to discuss major economic development possibilities). Said *Wa-Swa-Gon* lawyer, Lew Gurwitz, "We believe Klauser has never stopped working for Exxon. . . . He left a $300,000 a year job for an $80,000 a year job. That's an awful lot of love for public service."

Native American land today is often the frontline sacrifice to the mineral and energy needs of the military, of industry, and even of urban consumers.[25] As *Forbes* magazine pointed out in November 1981, 5 percent of U.S. oil and natural gas, one third of the strippable sulfur coal, and one half of the uranium privately held in the United States is on Native American reservations. Not only has the heat been turned up on Wisconsin minerals on or near reservations, but possible oil reserves are being sought in Bayfield County (which could impact the Red Cliff and Bad River Reservations and the area tourist industry). Geologists also believe that natural gas and manganese might also be found in northern Wisconsin's Chippewa Lobe formation. Thus Native American people, and their land and rights, remain pivotal in these efforts across the United States to gain mineral and oil wealth, land for dumping, and even for hydroelectric power. If the Wisconsin boat landing protests were the bullets and the state aimed the gun, Walt Bresette asked, who pulled the trigger of mega-development plans that needed treaties negated? In addition to misinformation, intimidation, and a declining economy, resource colonization is the final and most powerful force acting against Native sovereignty and treaties.

Envisioning a Sustainable Economics

Visions, of course, are far more than economic schemes complete with an accompanying public relations campaign about jobs and environmental protection. A vision gives people hope for the future and does not trade one security for another (e.g., employment for health). A vision is inclusive, holding within itself a broad constituency and a variety of concerns. A sustainable vision addresses people's fears and their longings for a sense of community and roots, a sense of safety and trust of neighbors, and a love of place and traditions there. It does not substitute technological prowess, quick gain, or career advancement for those values. A vision works when people can place themselves and their community inside it.

A sustainable vision has an economy based on renewable resources, and on values that recognize that production and growth are grounded in the health of ecological and human communities. Like a healthy ecosystem, regional economics needs diversity, not all of its eggs in one boom or bust basket. Sustainable economics doesn't displace costs or problems like contamination or depletion onto other places downriver or onto future generations. Because visions expand the possibilities of what a better life could be, qualitative measures (of clean air and water, safe communities, rewarding and safe work, mental and spiritual well-being) become more important than quantitative measures (of income—except for the poorest who need more of jobs, or of the gross national product and great numbers on Wall Street). The balance of culture, ecology, and real economic health should be the goal for northern Wisconsin. A healthy river and groundwater makes for a healthy people and economy, and vice versa. That's a different vision than Kennecott promising to transport water to Rusk County citizens if mining contaminates their wells.

Walt Bresette has argued that mining has found some support in northern Wisconsin not because people support this technology or its consequences, but because they see few other job possibilities and no other economic vision for their communities. Our rural rights/treaty rights/environmental coalition in Wisconsin faced the question: we know what you're against, but what are you for? What is your program, especially on jobs? For starters, Bresette proposed that northern Wisconsin to be declared a toxic-free zone. This idea addresses the health of fish, forests, farmland harvest, rice, etc. as the real issue and lessens the fear of economic hardship that drives the hysteria around Chippewa resource depletion. Food from a toxic-free zone (including no Monsanto growth hormones in dairy cows) and fish (without mercury or PCBs) from America's water capitol would be a lasting source of wealth and a job producer for the state. Designating northern Wisconsin as an environmental and recreational zone could promote a tourism industry, in-scale and respectful of cultural and biotic diversity, and be another sustainable industry.

In 1990, Walt Bresette and James Yellowbank developed a unique and useful co-management plan for northern Wisconsin based on the constitutional integrity of treaties and what treaties could do for resource management and sustainable economic development.[26] Phase One of the plan conceives of ceded territory as this environmental zone. A thirty-year plan involving all governmental jurisdiction would carry out a $1 billion campaign to make lakes and rivers toxic-free, stabilizing the region ecologically. Phase Two—ceded territory as an economic zone—calls for tax credits for small business diversification and capital infusion so local businesses can compete with the franchises. This would include setting up a loan capitalization fund for banks in northern Wisconsin, redirecting State Investment Board money (some of it is now in South Africa) to ceded territory, and creation of a venture capital fund for new small businesses that would ask major timber corporations in Wisconsin's northwoods to contribute. Phase Three—ceded territory as an energy zone—would implement a three-decade program to eliminate the area's currently 90 percent dependence on outside energy fuels. The first decade would emphasize tax credits for energy conservation measures, and could save up to 40 percent of the area's energy needs. The second decade would emphasize the shift to alternative, renewable energy sources and save another 20 to 30 percent. In the third decade, the state and regional governments would require climate-specific energy technologies for any new industry or business locating in the zone.[27]

Because copper mining is so destructive, the solutions already at hand should be adopted to provide the electrical conductors and pipes our society needs.[28] Substitution of less damaging materials provides one easy answer that would prevent tearing up rural counties for new copper.[29] Of U.S. copper consumption, 60 percent is already supplied by recycling and a 1979 Office of Technology Assessment analysis concluded that reuse, repair, and remanufacturing of metal-containing products were the best methods of conserving America's metals.[30] Such concentrated metals *are* treasures, not to be discarded so more earth can be destroyed to make the new.

Work being done regionally by the Midwest Renewable Energy Association and nationally by the Worldwatch Institute points the way to a full-employment solar economy. Alternative or renewable energy provides the most hope for the creation of jobs and ecological well-being while meeting the energy necessities for home and business.[31] The move to a solar economy would create a renaissance in the traditional skilled and semi-skilled fields of insulation installers, carpenters, and sheet metal workers. New careers in ecologically sound professions would be created for wind prospectors, photovoltaic engineers, and solar architects. In addition to the restoration of skilled work and its employment ripple effect, a solar economy could restore balances within cultural, economic, and ecological systems. Local economies would flourish *because* the rivers were clean, the air breathable, life spans longer.

Emissions of carbon dioxide could almost be eliminated in a solar economy—the ozone layer saved, unnecessary cancers prevented. Eliminating acid rain (especially sulfur dioxide from electric utilities, smelters, and business and home heating) could mean mercury wouldn't be released in northern lakes and trees would not wither. Organic, in-scale farming with as much fertilizer and energy (wind power, horse power, methane) as possible produced on-farm, coupled with direct farmer-to-consumer markets and a fair land tax system, could reverse the trend of 12,000 farms lost in Wisconsin this last decade. New forestry practices would: a) protect wilderness with its genetic and biological diversity; b) continue to sustainably manage secondary forests and tree planta-tions; c) improve efficiency in forest product manufacturing (saving one out of every four trees now cut); and d) increase recycling.[32]

By implementing the already-at-hand technologies and policies in energy, minerals, agriculture, and forestry, the rivers of Wisconsin could be maintained and those most damaged restored, so fisheries, rice, and the water's restorative powers are preserved. The integrity of rural life—Native American and European-American—would be replenished. To those for whom profit still remains the bottom line, University of Montana Geology Professor Johnnie Moore put it most succinctly, "What is more cost effective—losing a river or going without a mine?"

On January 15, 1991, the headlines rang out the news that President Bush had sent U.S. bombers to liberate Kuwait (and its oil fields). Buried in the back pages was a small item that State of Wisconsin hearing examiner David Schwartz had approved Kennecott's permit to mine at Ladysmith.

Notes

For an in-depth understanding of this Wisconsin mining story—the grassroots opposition throughout the northwoods, the critical role treaty rights play, the impor-tance of the local citizens/environmentalist/Native coalition, and the political intrigue of Wisconsin with international mineral companies—the authors highly recommend Al Gedick's recently published book, *The New Resource Wars: Native and Environ-mental Struggles Against Multinational Corporations* (Boston: South End Press, 1993).

1. These examples are given in Al Gedick, "Multinational Corporations and the Internal Colonialism in the Advanced Capitalist Countries: The New Resource Wars," *Political Power and Social Theory: A Research Annual*, vol. 5 (1985): 190–191.

2. This project is called the Reef Project and would lie between the Eau Claire and Plover Rivers east of Wausau. Cyanide leaching remains the state-of-the art method for extracting gold from ore.

3. Jack Norman, "Will Klauser aid business?" *Milwaukee Journal*, November 20, 1986. State geologist Meredith Ostrom predicted there would be twenty mines by 1996 in the region stretching east from Tiger Cat Flowage to Marinette County and the

Upper Peninsula. Long time anti-mining activist Al Gedicks said this new mining district could eventually include multiple mines, concentrating plants, tailings piles, electrical generating plants, transmission lines, a smelter, and a high-level nuclear waste repository.

4. Ron Seely, "Mining has strong potential in Wisconsin," *Wisconsin State Journal,* January 31, 1982, gives Klauser's statistics on Exxon's proposed Crandon mine. The projected $16 million per year in state taxes is mentioned in "Smith defends mine-tax vote," *Milwaukee Journal,* October 29, 1981, as an estimate by state officials. This *MJ* article also quotes Klauser praising the Wisconsin state legislature's action in lowering the mining tax rate from 20 percent to 15 percent.

5. Governor Thompson's predecessor, the Democrat Tony Earl, a supporter of the Exxon mine, credited treaty rights, in part, for the defeat of the Crandon project. The import of treaties being used to stop mining was not lost in the Thompson administration's efforts to buy out the treaty rights of both the Sokaogon in early 1989 and the Lac du Flambeau later in 1989.

6. Al Gedicks, "Exxon Minerals in Wisconsin: New Patterns in Rural Environmental Conflict," *Wisconsin Sociologist,* vol. 25, no. 2/3 (Spring–Summer, 1988): 91–92.

7. He defeated Democrat Tony Earl, who would later go on to become a lawyer-lobbyist for Noranda.

8. Ron Seely, "Sophisticated lobbying neutralizes mining foes," *Wisconsin State Journal,* March 24, 1991.

9. 1990 interview with reporter Marla Donato. See Marla Donato, *Spearfishing Treaty Rights and Mining,* video, 36–37 (Highland Park, Illinois, Earth Network, 1991). Exxon also had previously complained of state mining regulations in the "People's Republic of Wisconsin" (see "Treasure or Trouble?" Bauman, *Milwaukee Journal* Insight Magazine, October 24, 1982).

10. Marla Donato, *Spearfishing Treaty Rights and Mining,* video, 36–37 (Highland Park, Illinois, Earth Network 1991).

11. Larry Mercando, head of Kennecott's Flambeau Mining Company operation at Ladysmith, described this corporate liability as being like someone falling in front of your house and suing you. Ron Seely and Jeff Mayers, "Mining company check uncovers violations," *Wisconsin State Journal,* March 27, 1991.

12. Cited in the work of Al Gedicks and in Roger Moody, *Plunder!* (Chippenham, United Kingdom: Rowe, Ltd., 1991), pp. 70–73. In Papua New Guinea, local residents shut down RTZ's Bougainville copper mine because of the massive local environmental degradation. Kennecott was first bought out by British Petroleum in 1987, then sold to RTZ in 1989.

13. Because the Wisconsin Geological and Natural History Survey would get ore samples, it is possible the WDNR could find out if uranium were present, but this information would not be public. Would the WDNR move on the issue if there were not public pressure?

14. Ron Seely, "Mining company donations: generosity or bribe?" *Wisconsin State Journal,* March 28, 1991. This was part of *WSJ*'s excellent five-part series, "Mining in Wisconsin: boom or bust?"

15. Seely, "Sophisticated lobbying."

16. Ron Seely, "Expert sees little ground-water threat," *Wisconsin State Journal,* March 26, 1991.

17. Steve Watrous, "Congressman Sensenbrenner: hawk defends his toilet paper in Central America," *Shepherd Express,* April 1986. Also significant is that Kimberly-Clark itself sank five exploratory drill holes in Forest County in 1978–1979.

18. Donato, *Spearfishing Treaty Rights and Mining.*

19. Donato, *Spearfishing Treaty Rights and Mining.*

20. Donato, *Spearfishing Treaty Rights and Mining.* Dean Crist said in his 1990 interview with Donato that the spearers take was 49,000 walleye and the anglers, 600,000 walleye. The actual 1989 figures are approximately 26,000 for spearers and 639,000 for anglers. Crist also said that with the new WDNR walleye size limit raised to fifteen inches, the angler take would probably go down and be the same as the spearing harvest. No such event occurred as percentages (4 percent Chippewa, 96 percent anglers) remained the same in 1990.

21. Donato, *Spearfishing Treaty Rights and Mining.*

22. Scott Kerr, "Indian leader calls treaty conference a betrayal," *Milwaukee Journal,* January 14, 1990, and Associated Press story, "Barring of Indians prompts protests at Utah conference," *Milwaukee Journal,* January 19, 1990.

23. The probability is high, said journalist Scott Kerr, that Klauser helped plan the meeting. Anti-treaty elements in WCA, led by its executive director, Mark Rogacki, affiliated with the National Coalition on Federal Indian Policy (NCFIP). NCFIP was created by S/SPAWN (the Washington state equivalent of PARR and STA–W), by Citizens Equal Rights Alliance (CERA) (with Dean Crist on their advisory board), and by WCA allies with funding from WCA dues. See Rudolph Ryser, "Anti-Indian Movement on the Tribal Frontier" (Kenmore, WA: Center for World Indigenous Studies, 1991, pp. 36–38), which lists 1988 CERA board and advisory board members. Fred Hatch represented STA–W at CERA board meetings in 1990. According to "WCA presses anti-treaty agenda," *HONOR Digest* (July, August 1990), Rogacki said in June 1990, "We'll never let the Indians cut our timber."

24. Sharon Metz, "WCA wants to promote mining on county lands," *HONOR Digest,* February/March 1991.

25. For energy/mineral companies, finding allies and gaining political security is becoming a subtle game in the United States. In August 1988, Exxon joined forces with the right-wing American Freedom Coalition and the anti-Indian CERA at the "Multi-Use Conference" in Reno, Nevada. This conference was called to undermine the efforts of environmentalists to rewrite the 1872 Mining Law which, to this day, allows mining companies almost free access to the $4 billion of hardrock minerals on federal land, without paying royalties to the United States or reclaiming the land. These mineral resource companies, on a national strategic level, have enlisted ranchers, loggers, and especially anti-Indian groups as their allies.

26. James Yellowbank with Walt Bresette, "Regional resource co-management: saving the land for the next seven generations," *Indian Treaty Rights Newsletter,* vol. 2, no. 1 (Winter 1991): 1–2. Walt Bresette expanded on this proposal in a workshop at the "Stop the Plunder of Native Lands Conference" on mining and treaty rights, November 1, 1992, Treehaven Conference Center, Tomahawk, Wisconsin. While co-

management is not formally recognized as a legal concept, these economic projections are still valid. A policy of cooperation does now exist between the Wisconsin DNR and the Chippewa tribes on matters of fish and game management.

27. Concurrently, state policy could guarantee: 1) close monitoring and regulation of paper mills in order to protect water quality; 2) the canceling of timber and pulp imports from rain forests thereby preserving jobs for Wisconsin loggers; and 3) the gradual prohibition of fossil fuel emissions and the development of ecologically safer and renewable energy resources. For example, wind mills, once common throughout the Midwest, could return as today's advanced wind machines and provide, in concert with solar, hydro, and biomass (wood and agricultural waste), much of Wisconsin's future energy needs. Bresette cites the work of the Rocky Mountain Institute (Amory and Hunter Lovins) for the projections on energy conservation savings.

28. John E. Young, *Worldwatch Report 109: Mining the Earth* (Washington, D.C.: Worldwatch Institute, July 1992), p. 42. Especially dangerous are the acid drainage from mined and concentrated ore and the sulfur dioxide emissions from smelting. Additionally, to produce 9 million tons of copper in 1991, an estimated 990 million tons of ore were mined, creating further havoc to many local ecosystems, pp. 20–22.

29. John E. Young, *Worldwatch Report 109: Mining the Earth*, p. 12. Glass fiber is supplanting copper in communications uses and substitution of polyvinyl chloride pipes for copper ones effectively reduced yearly U.S. copper consumption by 13 percent in 1988.

30. John E. Young, *Worldwatch Report 109: Mining the Earth*, p. 11, Table 2, "U.S. Metal Consumption and Recycling," and p. 42 cites the OTA's *Technical Options for Conservation of Metals* (1979).

31. Investments in energy efficiency, conservation, and solar technology have proven twice as successful in employment-creation as those in new fossil fuel resources. At the local level, the money spent on energy efficiency can create four times as many jobs as the same amount invested in a new power plant. For the amount of energy produced, the solar industries (including wind, photovoltaic, and hydrogen solar) produce greater employment opportunities already than fossil fuel (including coal mining) and nuclear power. Christopher Flavin and Nicholas Lenssen, "Designing a Sustainable Energy System," in Worldwatch Institute, *State of the World 1991* (New York: W. W. Norton), p. 33.

32. Sandra Postel and John C. Ryan, "Reforming Forestry," in Worldwatch Institute, *State of the World 1991*, p. 82, 87.

PART V

A Solidarity Success Story

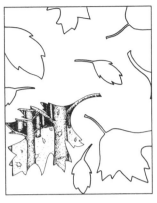

9

BINAKWI GISISS
(Moon of the Falling Leaves)

Healing, Not Winning
The Fourth Year of Spearing and Witnessing, 1991

Rick Whaley

IT IS SAID THAT THE MIGRATING loons leave their southern winter homes and fly north in spring, arriving at their chosen Wisconsin lake on the day the ice has all melted. Ice-out is the sign the waters have warmed enough for spawning and signals the advent of spearing. On most nights, 1991 was the year that spearers and witnesses could hear the loons, see the sunsets, and catch the scent of pine trees and fresh, cold waters. It was a year where the evidence of hope and healing began to crowd out the foreboding shadows, a season to take a look back with some of our former opponents at our common history here.

The weight of threatening violence still hung in the air from the first of the year through the first week of Lac du Flambeau spearing. Fears of mob violence motivated by racism, America's oldest ugliness, proved true on one night of witnessing at Sand Lake. Our early planning was occupied by fears that the sentiments around the Persian Gulf War could be whipped into more hysteria at the boat landings. "How will increased militarism and anti-Arab sentiment affect Indian people?" asked the Midwest Treaty Network. "Will anti-Indian bigots be more 'fired up' at boat landings, if next Wisconsin spearing season takes place in the middle of a war? Will Indians and Arabs be put in the same category as 'inferiors' who block access to 'our' resources?" Our boat landing witness stance for 1991 included not engaging in dialogue or demonstration on the war in order to keep the focus on the nonviolence and Native issue at hand.

The federal courts continued to make critical rulings, pro and con, that dramatically affected the tone for the spearing season. And the grassroots one-to-one breakthroughs combined with the culmination of behind-the-scenes legal work helped define a season in which the protest movement finally broke apart. The political fields were plowed for the seeds of honorable reconciliation.

At a pipe ceremony at Lac du Flambeau when I arrive for witnessing, I am reminded of a prayer from my mother's funeral, "Lord, make me an instrument of your peace. Where there is hatred, let me sow love; Where there is injury, pardon; Where there is doubt, faith; Where there is despair, hope . . ." (from the Prayer of St. Francis of Assisi for Peace). The prayer also measures the vision and hopes of the Witness. As we remember those who have gone before— the reservation and inner-city young who die too early; Walt's aunt, Victoria Gokee, who paved the way for the Madeline Island struggles and the now-annual Madeline Island ceremonies; those who struggled and died in other eras—I feel a presence so strong it may as well be ghosts.

What would this season bring? Would the legal efforts to end the violence against spearers succeed before the start of spearing? Could the year-long efforts to bring communities together in northern Wisconsin pay off or were we in store for acts of desperation by protesters? Were spearers' hearts and Witness efforts big enough to take the last of the protests and still believe in reconciliation? ("For it is in pardoning that we are pardoned," the prayer of St. Francis says.)

The Loon

One of the favorite props of Stop Treaty Abuse–Wisconsin is a human-sized loon caught in a tennis net, supposedly representing the loons killed when the Chippewa gill-net for whitefish. While gill-netting poses no proven threat to water-diving birds, the loon is honored by the Chippewa in their clan system. The loon also represents a bird loved by cottage owner and tourist, sportsman and environmentalist.

The loon is a small, powerful, dark bird, with red eyes, white vertical stripes on its neck and a black and deep green head. It bobs on the water, resting or looking for food. But it can disappear below the water for long minutes before popping up on another part of the lake. The loon is an extraordinary diver. Propelled by its big feet, it can dive up to two hundred feet below the surface, and swim faster than most fish. It consumes its capture of small fish before it returns to the surface. The loon can laugh or squeal or let out a cry in the night that sounds like panic, or a wolf's long howl or a ghostly call from another world. Some Native cultures believed it was the cry of a warrior forbidden entry into heaven or a foreboding omen of death.[1]

Loons nest one or two families to a medium-sized lake. What kills loons is lake shore development and the motorized waterski-jets that tear up nesting shoreline. Lakefront owners who put in beaches and docks, gasoline-powered boats that choke a lake with spill and exhaust, and acid rain that unleashes mercury—all these, not Chippewa spearfishing, are destroying the habitat of the loon and walleye.

When asked why he speaks more often publicly than his Feathergate cohort, Esther Nahgahnub, Walt Bresette replied, "It's not the patriarchy of *Ojibwe* women deferring to the men. Esther often gives me tobacco and asks me to speak for her. It's my clan, the speaker/leader, the loon."

Women Are the Strength

At the Witness office, women witnesses are given ribbons with colors from the Three Fires Society (a recently revived *Anishinabe* spiritual organization): gold for courage, green for the earth, the women's color, red, for water and life, and the men's color, blue, for highest thought or hope. Spiritual leader and cultural activist Eddie Benton-Banai had a vision that women would be the strength of this spearing season. He also raised the caution that a woman might be seriously harmed this year. Some women stayed away from the landings this season (Sarah Backus went to only two quiet lakes, Karen Harvey and Merle Wolford visited and stayed on the reservation), but Anita Koser chose again to face the attacks at the landings, and women spearers returned with the LdF men.

From rural northern Wisconsin and Midwest urban centers (Minneapolis-St. Paul, Milwaukee, Chicago) and from as far away as Germany, women witnesses came in the largest overall Witness effort yet, to face what spring 1991 would offer. Like the progressive urban European-American women who joined with their rural sisters in the late 1800s to fight for peace, temperance, women's rights, and an end to poverty, these women of the late 1900s would fight for peace, Native rights, and cultural respect and renewal in our time.

Healing

Yolanda St. Germaine, veteran witness and veteran spearer, had a much better year spearing in 1991 than the previous spring. But, as she told a reporter, the harassment at her place of work was worse than on the lakes last year.[2] Yolanda works as a groundskeeper at the University of Wisconsin in Madison on a crew of forty men (many of them hunters and fishermen) and three women. "I'm the only minority," she says. "One guy threatened to break both my arms so I couldn't spearfish." As the liberal university slowly moved to respond to this on-the-job racial harassment, Yolanda refused to give names for fear they would fire the men as an example. She chose healing instead with her one demand: that the university sponsor cultural awareness and racial tolerance classes for the groundskeeping employees.

Since our beginning, the Witness had sought the good in even the harshest opponent, believing that change in others was possible. We tried to find the paths of reconciliation and to establish with protesters and those adverse to treaty rights the common ground beyond the flap over fishing. Psychotherapist/medicine woman Merle Wolford, in a meditation at a Witness trainers training, pointed out that many protesters were responding from a good place: They hear the pain of the earth. They know something is wrong with the water and fish and pollution in the air. But these genuine concerns are distorted by protest leaders who blame the Chippewa for fish depletion and destroying the tourism economy of northern Wisconsin. It was imperative that we build on the genuine and point out the broader environmental benefits of keeping treaties.

Could it also be that men are called to fish in spring and hunt in autumn, to protect their ways of gathering, of providing? Didn't women and men of all cultures once gather to harvest every spring in their particular bioregion? Did this ancient calling motivate the hundreds of misinformed protesters of previous years, a calling similar to that of the spearers going to the spring lakes for a millennium?

One key to reconciliation has always been to define it clearly. As the Witness pointed out in its many trainings, reconciliation could never be the protesters' violent version of peace, where Indians go back to their place on the reservation and end all of their off-reservation property rights. Nor could reconciliation be the state of Wisconsin's version, where Indians sell out their rights in order to quell racist backlash. How could any healing take place if one group were required to give up its legal rights and the basic right to safety?

Here is the statement on reconciliation we use in the Witness Training:

Reconciliation proceeds from the understanding that all people have basic civil and legal rights and rights to be protected from violence and harassment and indignities. Reconciliation *then* means building from the common ground we have with people caught up in the misinformation and hysteria of STA–W [leaders], but who have genuine fears and concerns about northern Wisconsin's economy and the resources of the northwoods and their families' future. We need to affirm the hurts and fears these people feel in their own lives, without forgetting that the hurts for Native Americans run deeper and their fears are far more immediate at the boat landings (because of the protests). . . .

Those church and business people [who support treaty rights and oppose the protests], in addition to the European-Americans who support treaties up north, can, like us, win politically if laws are upheld and spearing safety is guaranteed. But in winning, we need to extend our hand to those who have been against the treaties, especially protesting. If we rub salt in the wounds of protesters (whose cause is waning in many circles), it will only increase the chance that anger and frustration will be hurled back at us—rocks, pipe bombs, or some crazy with an assault rifle.

Healing must spread emotionally and politically so anger and hatred are finally isolated and most of it dissipated.[3]

The ongoing common issues identified by environmentalists and the Witness for northern Wisconsin are: the mercury-poisoned fish in over 150 lakes, the threats of mining in the Wisconsin headwaters region (ceded territory), air and sludge pond pollution from Wisconsin's many paper mills, clear-cutting forestry practices, preservation and extension of Wisconsin's "outstanding resource waters (ORW)" designation, and economic development for the mom and pop businesses in the northwoods.

If we knew our history together, how could we let feelings of anger, superiority, and revenge govern our relations today? Even the names of our towns, cities, and lakes reflect the common heritage and history of Native Americans and European-Americans. Minocqua is the *Ojibwe* word meaning "mid-journey" or "pleasant place to be," signifying that this beautiful area was once one of the portage points in a journey from the upper reaches of the Wisconsin River down to Tomahawk Lake and then up to Lac du Flambeau.[4] (Minocquip was also the name of an *Ojibwe* leader who appears in early histories.) Cities throughout Wisconsin are named for Native Americans— Black Hawk (in southwest Wisconsin, named for the Sauk and Fox leader) and Oshkosh (in southeast Wisconsin, for the Menominee leader), and named for European-American lumber entrepreneurs (Woodruff, Winchester, and Mercer) and railroad owners (Rhinelander) and railroad junctions (Boulder Junction). Towns like Eagle River, Arbor Vitae, and Park Falls are named for the bird, tree, or setting loved by settler and original people alike. Sayner is named for Orrin Wesley Sayner, first European-American to settle there, who with his family could not have survived their first winter there without the help of the Chippewa. St. Germain is named for the French-Indian families that built this community. A statue in St. Germain honors the many Chippewa who have this family name (usually spelled with *e* on the end).

Pine Forests

Don Rasmussen is a witness and European-American elder who grew up in northern Wisconsin and worked on the farm and in lumber camps and eventually taught at Milwaukee Area Technical College. At a 1988 public meeting, he recalled the story his grandfather heard in the lumber camps of the 1870s about the days when a squirrel could travel from Minnesota across northern Wisconsin all the way to Lake Michigan without ever touching the ground. That's how great the white pine forest of Wisconsin once was.

The *Anishinabe* saw the wealth of the forest differently than did the timber barons who were to decimate it. The Chippewa forest culture included: the harvest of fish and game, wild rice, berries, and maple syrup; birch-bark canoes (with cedar ribs and pine gum as sealer on the birch seams), toboggans and snowshoes (with ashwood frames), torches (of rolled birch bark and pitch or butternut wood mashed to fibers at one end and dipped in tallow) for travel; maple, ironwood, or tamarack saplings for wigwams, lodges, and even for fence traps for the autumn deer drives; fish nets made of wood-fiber cords; bedding of cedar boughs and rush mats; and hardwood ash lyes for washing and root dyes for coloring.

On February 22, 1991, a week before U.S. troops entered Kuwait, Judge Barbara Crabb issued her timber rights ruling (*LCO IX*). Judge Crabb reversed her previous position (and the implication of the higher appeals court ruling) that timbering was an advanced form of tree cutting and therefore an off-reservation harvesting right. She ruled instead that because the Chippewa were not engaging in commercial timbering at the time of the treaties, this could not be one of the reserved off-reservation harvestable resources. If the Chippewa did not know at the time of the 1837 and 1842 treaties that they were giving up their white and red pine stands to the United States, she said, they did know this by the 1854 treaty. Crabb rejected arguments by tribal lawyers that the Chippewa were entitled to the non-pine harvest (the many hardwoods that originally grew under the great pine umbrella) or to the second growth of pine (sprouted or reseeded after the old growth forest was take down by the European-American timber companies). "Miscellaneous forest products" (bark, lodge poles, maple syrup, firewood) could be harvested as a reserved treaty right, but the state of Wisconsin was entitled to regulate this in the same way as they regulated Chippewa hunting and fishing.

Klauser, the WDNR, and the Wisconsin Counties Association (WCA) welcomed the decision. Governor Thompson thought it would ease tensions up north for the spearing season. Dean Crist welcomed the decision as a chance to escalate further in hopes the previous pro-Chippewa court rulings could be undone. Tribes had until mid-May 1991 to decide whether to appeal this and Crabb's other clarifying decisions on Chippewa rights and back damages.

Interestingly, following the 1854 treaty, the drive to get the great pine forests from the Chippewa included the pine still remaining on reservation land. The 1854 treaty promised eighty acres of land on reservations to Chippewa "mixed bloods." In 1863, the commissioner of Indian affairs ruled that applicants for this land need not have lived in the ceded territory at the time of the treaty. A timber rush of fraudulent claims by nontribal Chippewa and whites pretending to be Indians forced the federal government to intervene to protect reservation resources. By the 1880s, timber company logging contracts with the reservations provided significant income to the tribes.[5] Wisconsin's old-growth pine forests melted away as homes, barns, and fences sprouted throughout the Great Plains states after the Civil War and into the twentieth century.

Wisconsin Legacies

1860s "Is the [human] community lightly to be dismembered?" (the Civil War).

1866 Last native Wisconsin elk killed.

1867 State Horicultural Society offers prizes for forest plantations.

1870s "The March of Empire" and "Wisconsin's carousal in wheat" which leaves the soil here exhausted by decade's end.

1870 "A market gunner boasted in *American Sportsman* of killing 6000 ducks in one season."

1871 The Great Peshtigo Fire (caused by poor logging practices of leaving the slash behind and only taking the big logs) cleared two Wisconsin counties of trees and soil.

1872 The last wild Wisconsin turkey was killed.

1877 "Two brothers, shooting Muskego Lake, bagged 210 blue-winged teal in one day."

1883 or 1884 Eighty acres of white pine near what is now Crane City (Polk Co.) were clear-cut by Wm. McCarthy and Peter Hueber, sawed and shipped west to pineries. Native Americans used to gather here every spring for dancing and a great feast of young crane, squab, and dove. Wortley Prentice tells of the great sorrow it caused among the Indians to see the crane's nesting trees destroyed (Gard and Soren, p. 157).

1889 Arbor Day established in Wisconsin.

1890 "The largest pine rafts in history slipped down the Wisconsin River . . . to build an empire of red barns."

1899 Wisconsin leads the nation by harvesting 3.4 billion board feet of timber (Danziger, p. 101). "The last passenger pigeon collided with a charge of shot near Babcock."

1906 "The first state forester takes office and fires burned 17,000 acres in these sand counties."

1908 "A dry year when the forests burned fiercely and Wisconsin parted with its last cougar."

1910–1920s "The decade of the drainage dream, when steam shovels sucked dry the marshes of central Wisconsin to make farms, and made ash-heaps instead."

1910 "A great university president publishes a book on conservation, a great sawfly epidemic killed millions of tamaracks, a great drouth burned the pineries, and a great dredge drained Horicon Marsh."

1915 "When the Supreme Court abolished the state forests and Governor Phillip pontificated that 'state forestry is not a good business proposition.'"

"Legislature's several protestations of love for trees: a national forest and a forest-crop law in 1927, a great refuge on the Upper Mississippi bottomlands in 1924, and a new forest policy in 1921 . . . the demise of the state's last marten in 1925."

1930s The Great Depression (except for the barons of beer, fur, and mining.)

1940s The depression for farmers continues. The biocide (as Rachel Carson called it) DDT is introduced into Wisconsin agriculture. Wisconsin counties replant county land and old farms in red pine plantations.

Unless otherwise noted, all quotes and chronology to the 1930s are from Aldo Leopold's "Good Oak" in Sand County Almanac *(New York: Oxford University Press, 1949), pp. 9–15. Used by permission.*

At stake in the modern timber struggle is 400,000-plus acres of state forest land and 1.8 million acres of county-owned land that the Chippewa might have had a right to harvest timber on. Wisconsin counties earned about $3.5 million a year in timber revenues and complained mightily that this timber was paid for by Wisconsin taxpayers and didn't belong to the Chippewa. Instead of organizing people to throw rocks at the landings, the anti-Indian leadership in WCA built a war chest, rumored to be over $100,000 in county government donations, and hired lawyers. They entered into the timber phase of the treaty litigation as a friend of the court, alongside the WDNR against the Chippewa. European-American contract loggers (who might pay $15 a cord for red pine today) also feared treaty timbering (where no stumpage fee was paid) because it might undercut their sale price to paper mills or set up a dual pricing system for treaty timber and theirs.

The forces allied against Chippewa timbering were formidable. During the interim between Crabb's 1988 ruling (she declined a state motion to throw out timber rights from the treaty litigation) and her 1991 reversal, the Mole Lake reservation began off-reservation timber harvesting on state forest land.[6] They said the harvest would be sold to off-reservation mills but eventually they planned to start their own. Then-Attorney General Hanaway closed down this operation when he heard European-Americans were also being employed alongside tribal members. He argued, in effect, that if you're going to have your special Indian rights, you better not hire any whites.

Along with Green supporters, the tribes would have welcomed timbering as a sustainable economic enterprise for the reservations. European-American workers (and contract loggers) could have benefited job-wise, along with tribal members, from breaking the stranglehold of the major forestry companies, mills, and county governments in northern Wisconsin. Our great Paul Bunyan myth to the contrary, the only reason Wisconsin taxpayers had to pay to replant the forests in the first place was because the timber barons indiscriminately logged the ancient forest so honored by the *Anishinabe*.

The "Ism" That Won't Wash Out

If timber rights were not the arena to affirm forest-use traditions or to creatively engender new economic enterprises, then, at least, basic civil and safety rights would remain the line protesters could never cross with Judge Crabb. The work of the *Wa-Swa-Gon* legal team, led by Brian Pierson, culminated in a hearing before Judge Crabb on March 7, 1991. The LdF spearers, joined by the LdF tribal council, requested a preliminary injunction against STA–W and three sheriffs. A week later, Crabb issued her ruling.

Crabb threw out the request for an injunction against the sheriffs and essentially supported the state-counties law enforcement plan, including mixing protesters with Chippewa families and supporters and not providing protection to spearers' vehicles parked at or near landings.[7] However, she was crystal clear in her positions on STA–W disruption:

> Despite the presence of large number of law enforcement officials, members of defendants STA–W have subjected plaintiffs, other tribal spearers and the families of spearers to stone throwing, threats of harm, racial and sexual insults, minor batteries, and damage to vehicles. . . . STA–W members have endangered the lives of spearers by intentionally creating wakes to make it more difficult for spearers to fish.

Judge Crabb ripped apart STA–W arguments that their protests were not racially motivated or about property rights. She cited precedents from the case of the *Vietnamese Fishermen's Association v. the Knights of Ku Klux Klan* in Texas where the court enjoined defendants from engaging in acts of violence, intimidation, or harassment against Vietnamese fishermen. Saying that "although the private defendants have the right to voice opposition to plaintiffs' exercise of treaty rights, the First Amendment does not provide them with a right to threaten, assault, or commit battery on plaintiffs," Crabb granted the injunction and specifically forbade STA–W and "all those acting in concert or at the direction of these defendants" from:

a) Assaulting or battering any member of the Lac du Flambeau band or any member of the family of a [LdF] band member at any landing or on any lake within the ceded territory;
b) Intentionally creating wakes on any waterway to interfere with any spearer;
c) Planting decoys in any waterway;
d) Intentionally blocking spearing boats from moving from the boat landings out into the spawning beds;
e) Shining lights into the eyes of any spearer or spearing boat operator while on the water;
f) Playing "leapfrog" with any spearing boat, or otherwise impeding the progress of any spearing boat; and
g) Taking any other action that is intended to or may reasonably be expected to interfere with plaintiff's exercise of their spearing rights.

At the hearing on the injunction, Dean Crist and the other defendants never took the stand in their own defense. In fact, STA–W lawyers asked to be excused from the court before closing arguments. Failing to seize his day in court, Crist still had access to the front pages of the state's newspapers. It was no longer opportune for anyone to threaten Native Americans publicly. So as spearing approached, Crist warned Wisconsin DNR wardens. "The DNR better get Kelvar helmets from the National Guard when they come back because I

"THere, THere, Dear! LOOK ON THe BRIGHT SIDe—YOU CAN STILL GO OUT AND YeLL RACIST INSULTS!"

think the lakes are extremely dangerous now," said Crist. He predicted the spearing lakes would be a "free-fire zone" come spawning.[8]

The Witness renewed trainings in our established cities and extended the support work within ceded territory (e.g., in Wausau, which means "far away place" in *Ojibwe*) and regionally (e.g., in Iowa and Illinois, also Native American names). Because spearing nights had gone well in 1990, Red Cliff, Bad River, and St. Croix did not formally invite witnesses from outside their areas back again in 1991. They asked the Witness to be ready in case we were needed. LCO and Mole Lake did not request the Witness presence. PARR had put aside strategic differences with STA–W and promised to join them at the landings this spring, so *Wa-Swa-Gon* issued a call for as many witnesses as possible to come north for LdF spearing. The racial unity being built around this call was similar to the voices of support from Wisconsin and its legislature in asking the president to rescind the Chippewa removal order in 1850 and echoed the days our state was a stop on the Underground Railroad.[9]

However, we could not forget that Wisconsin was also the state that gave the nation the 1950s hysteria of Senator Joe McCarthy and the territory that gave the Sauk and Fox nations the 1832 Bad Axe Massacre. The first week of spearing protests tried to relight the fire of previous years' anti-spearing protests. At Lac du Flambeau's opening night at Big Eau Pleine near Wausau, fifty witnesses saw about two hundred angry but orderly protesters (mostly PARR) shout slogans and carrying signs like "Walleye Allies Return (WAR)" and wearing hats with a gun barrel depicted: "Spear this, fucker." Marathon

County police entered the protest crowd and made sure no angry words escalated to confrontations.

The next night at Lake Nokomis ("Nokomis" is *Ojibwe* for "grandmother") near Tomahawk an angrier PARR and STA–W crowd pushed tensions higher. There was intense whistle-blowing at Chippewa and witnesses who were well supplied with ear plugs from Kenosha factory allies. Tom Maulson intervened in one incident, when protesters tried to push through Chippewa families and supporters, stopping any escalation. Dean Crist continued to whip up the crowd with chants and jokes: "What do you get from raping a resource? Indian AIDS." Crist told Anita Koser, "You're enough to scare the fly off a gut bucket. . . . It would take a Mack truck to get rid of you."

The first week of witnessing taught us the importance of arriving at the landings before the protesters, and of recognizing when calm, festive situations could quickly turn into a dangerous scene—protesters suddenly at the landing, the drum unprotected, witness cameras not ready. The police response continued to be variable; sometimes preventative, sometimes provocative as when Vilas County police requested a state law enforcement official confiscate sage that the Chippewa were burning in one of their ceremonies at the landing. Boat landings were usually lit, but many of the big National Guard floodlights used in years previous were still in Saudi Arabia although the Gulf War had officially ended.

Like so many others in preceding springs, this week also taught the importance of personal and spiritual centeredness. Anita Koser said Crist's verbal attack hit her vulnerable spots:

> It really hurt me, his personal attack on me. He went for my flaws. I'm over-weight. I'm not that attractive. It was nothing but a nasty personal attack on a human being [that] had nothing to do with spearfishing. [But] what I go through is nothing compared to what my ancestors went through. They died to protect the land. . . . A few years ago, I had an ulcer. I gave my power to them and became sick. I decided to take my power back. Once you can accept that they might kill you, once you're at peace with that, you can face the landings.

The nastiness of week one of protests were the buildup for STA–W's major rally Saturday, April 20, in Minocqua. Crist had said he would take a vote then to see if people wanted to call off the protests or continue. Some in treaty support circles were concerned that STA–W would publicly call off the protests to avoid legal liability for what might happen at the landings. However, as former STA–W ally Kurt Krueger noted in a *Vilas County News Review* editorial, STA–W spent thousands of dollars to get anti-treaty protesters from far and wide, including many from urban southeast Wisconsin, to come to the rally. Crist thought even "treehuggers" might come and vote, but the show yielded predictable results—the protests would continue. That evening, Crist's last stand of intimidation was psychologically more terrifying than many could have imagined.

Sand Lake: The Protestor's Last Stand

Sand Lake is a gorgeous, medium-sized lake in Oneida county. A wooded hillside overlooks the landing and a bridge nearby crosses over the joining of Sand with Dam Lake. Most Saturday night witnesses first went to Turtle-Flambeau Flowage, because there had been no lights at the previous night's small protest there. (A strange phone call to police had told them spearing was cancelled there.) However, seven witnesses headed to Sand Lake, partly because of misinformation that Sarah Backus had headed there alone, and partly because the Witness knew some Chippewa families would be there. Arriving witnesses walked into the belly of the beast.

Witness Kathleen Hart reports:

At the bottom of the hill there were three family members of the spearfishers and we were watching them. When a group of about ten protesters went over to the family members and started to harass them, two witnesses went down to be with them. More of the crowd ran toward the family members. The urgency of the situation necessitated that the rest of us start down the hill to join the families and witnesses.

When the protesters saw us with the one Black witness [James Mincey], the entire mob shifted toward him and stampeded over to us. We were shoved against the fence on the edge of the blacktop where the police were. It seemed that all of the hate they ever felt in their lives for anyone was focused on one man. He was the catalyst they used to vent their anger and loathing. They kept shoving and pushing us all against the fence shouting "nigger, nigger, fuckin' nigger . . ." Whistles were blown in our ears and I was shoved along with James. He was hanging over the fence trying to get the police on the other side of the fence to do something because he feared for our safety. The police reply was that if they would see a violation they would respond.

I tried to stay between James and the crowd thinking I could block them from James but that was fruitless. It was like a scene from a surrealistic movie except that the fear I felt for James was overwhelming. The fact that they inflicted their total hatred on one fellow human being was beyond comprehension. I have never felt such intense hate [from a situation]. I feared for his life. The police were of little significance as protection.

As James was being forced over the fence, I yelled to the police asking if they weren't going to do something to disperse the crowd. They weren't doing their job. Some county police just laughed and they all stood motionless. Somehow we got an opening and we got to the bottom of the hill. The entire hill was filled with protesters and the shouting and screaming continued. I counted at least five

In one of the most fearful incidents of boat landing protests, James Mincey, an African-American Witness coordinator from Madison, Wisconsin, is surrounded, pushed, and harangued for over an hour at Sand Lake, Saturday, April 20, 1991. "Homeboy," "Roast his black ass good," and "We have red niggers, black niggers, and a few white niggers, too," are insults heard, as Vilas County police fail to intervene. 1960s civil rights veteran and 1990s witness, Kathleen Hart, to lower right from Mincey in photo (see text for her account), thought James was going to be killed that night.

The *Lakeland Times* (Minocqua) reported the next week that Dean Crist planned to give all African-American witnesses a watermelon wrapped in a ribbon to show them what it felt like to be called racists. *Milwaukee Sentinel* photo by Sherman Gessert.

hundred males and females from teens to seniors. We were verbally harassed without letup for another horrible hour. . . .

This verbal abuse continued . . . "Go back to Africa," "Alabama porch monkey," . . . "Why don't you go back to New York and shoot somebody for their shoes?" . . . "They should put a bullet right in your head" . . . "You can't be a white boy on the north side of Milwaukee—now you know how it feels." . . . The leaders of the protest groups and the police did nothing to stop the disgusting verbal abuse, threats and the physical shoving. Nothing!

After 10 P.M. we heard the drum coming down the road from the west. At that time the announcement was made over the bullhorn to the protesters to link arms at the tops of the hill to keep the drum and witnesses from getting to us. We heard shouts of "incoming scum, incoming scum" by the protesters. The crowd moved to the top of the hill and away from us. There was lot of pushing and shoving by the protesters trying to hold the witnesses back. The police did help to make a path for them to come down the hill. We all cheered and I cried with tears of relief.[10]

What the police did, instead of escorting witnesses through the crowd or around the snow fence to the bottom of the hill, was to create a gauntlet with protesters on one side, witnesses and supporters in the middle, and *police on the other side.* After walking this gauntlet of pushing and screaming, the witness contingent of two hundred from Turtle-Flambeau made it to the families, and Mincey and the other witnesses. PARR leader Larry Peterson dumped flammable materials on an Indian banner and burned it. No matter how hard they tried to deny or disguise it, the smell of racism just never could be washed out of the clothes of the anti-treaty movement. Al Shanks, director of Emergency Government and overall coordinator of the season's law enforcement, arrived late (to our minds), in about the middle of the evening's trauma. He called the events at Sand Lake a near-riot by both sides.[11]

Racism is the hatred of cultural differences, the misdirected fear of economic or psychological loss, the hidden ugliness of one's personal anger or cultural history. The fear of what we are ourselves, often but wrongly called the "dark side" by European-Americans, is projected onto darker peoples. Nick Hockings said once that the protesters are afraid that the Chippewa will do to the fish what they (European-Americans) have done to resources. Consider: overfishing, extinct species, raped pine forests, the resource terrorism of toxins, radioactivity, rivers burning with oil. "Indian-giver," that keystone concept of cultural racism in the Americas, is the kind of giving that whites in power did in every land grab and broken treaty, not what indigenous people did. Some try to drive the denial of that history deeper by doing more of the same today. Dean Crist himself says he is part Indian. When he first moved to Minocqua he tried to start a hotel/gambling business at Lac du Flambeau. After being shut out of this, he led the assault on every "special Indian right" he could find. One of the great gifts given to the Witness was that for every protester who tried to crush out the Indian in themselves by attacking treaty rights, we found twenty supporters who would accept the Indian heritage in their family histories and risk themselves for the rights and culture of tribal members.

Bill Braden of Chicago Heights, Illinois wrote a letter to the *Lakeland Times* (May 7, 1991) in Minocqua that said, in part:

I came up here to protest spearing because I care about protecting these beautiful lakes. I am leaving with a sick feeling. . . . The sexual slurs about Indian women are everywhere and sickening. The talk about running Indians off the road, spearing Indians, how to do physical harm to them and not get caught or get off in court is common conversation [in restaurants and taverns]. The night that PARR and STA–W. protesters pinned a black man against a snow fence, heaping racial obscenities against him while police refused to help, was the last straw for me. You people dare to wear an American flag and yell "equal rights" while you blatantly and violently ignore a citizen's basic right to be free from threat and fear of physical violence. . . . I will not bring my family back here— which means a good $3000 of my money is no longer in your economy each year. . . . I'll fight racism in my home in Chicago and I'll go to northern Minnesota where there is still big old forests and quiet lakes.

By this time, Crist had alienated most of his supporters except the hard core of fifty to sixty that marched with him the second week of spearing. STA–W had played out its mob tactics and practically ensured that the federal injunction would be made permanent. James Mincey returned the week after Sand Lake and was invited out with spearers to observe the fishing. Later that summer, he was honored at a LdF thank-you feast for supporters. While he welcomed the support of African-Americans in Milwaukee (Alderman Marvin Pratt and UW–M Black Student Association), he said, "Sand Lake was just as terrifying for the Chippewa families that were there. I don't want the focus to just be on me. This is a civil rights *and* treaty rights issue."

Fish Stories

Senator Inouye's much heralded federal fish study was released to the press and public on April 3, 1991, a few weeks before the start of 1991 spearfishing. It represented the consensus by biologists of the U.S. Fish and Wildlife Commission, the Great Lakes Indian Fish and Wildlife Commission, and the state of Wisconsin DNR, and by officials of Bureau of Indian Affairs, Chippewa tribal governments, the WDNR Secretary, and Senator Inouye (known as Senator "In-our-way" to the protesters). The study addressed two main questions: "Has Chippewa spearfishing harmed the resource?" and "Is the fish population in the ceded territory healthy?" The report concluded that "NO!— Chippewa spearing has not harmed the resource; and YES!—the fish population in the ceded territory is healthy." The report also stressed the validity of Chippewa treaty rights in both constitutional law and federal court precedent. If the United States didn't live up to its end of the treaty contract, Inouye said at the press conference, then the land and resources should revert back 100 percent to the Chippewa. The Inouye report, "Casting Light Upon the Waters," buried the anti-treaty movement's argument of fish depletion.

Much less heralded that April was the WDNR's fish consumption advisory that warned pregnant women and children under age fifteen against eating mercury-contaminated fish from over 150 lakes in ceded territory. Included in the advisory were the Willow and the Turtle-Flambeau Flowages, Tomahawk Lake, Lake Nokomis, Sand and Dam Lakes, North Twin Lake, and Trout Lake. Mercury is stored in the fillet or muscle of the fish not the fat, making removal difficult (whereas PCBs are stored in fish fat and easier to cut out). Mercury harms the central nervous system and may affect movement and the senses of touch, taste, and sight. The fishery in northern Wisconsin may be healthy, numberwise, but the fish themselves are not healthy, nor are those who eat them.

During the second week of spearing, as in the first week, a lack of on-lake harassment kept nights calm for spearfishers. Protesters feared federal court fines or, curse of all curses, loss of their speedboats, if they engaged in the on-the-water harassment of previous years. LdF spearer Robert Martin felt it was safe enough this year to take his son out spearing for the first time. Even police commanders grew tired of the fuss over fish. When one officer complained that a speared walleye was pretty close to the size limit, the supervisor's voice came back over the walkie-talkie, "If you're so concerned, measure the damn thing yourself." In stark contrast to the welcome quiet around them, police were overdressed gathering in full riot gear to watch the fish being measured and sexed.

On shore, the second week saw Crist show up with the STA–W hard-core of sixty and try uneventfully to get things riled up. Protester signs equating off-reservation harvesting with Saddam Hussein's invasion of Kuwait looked silly. When protesters chanted "Equal rights, equal rights," teenage Chippewa women chanted back, "Eat wild rice, eat wild rice." One night on Lake Tomahawk, witnesses set up picnic tables and had a feast. Although STA–W didn't break bread with us, the tone of the evening was more festive than tense. On other nights, witnesses built campfires and, while some eyes were peeled on the woods and landing, told stories. The storytelling worked at easing tensions and buoying spirits and helped set a conversational tone to the nights we equaled or outnumbered protesters.

The best fish story, directly from the news of the day, was the true saga of the Sheboygan fisherman.[12] Casting his net out into Lake Michigan, the fisher pulls in a seven-foot, Sidewinder air-to-air missile with a live warhead. He didn't, of course, then know that it was live (three-foot dummy missiles are not an uncommon catch around these parts). He hauls this thing out of the water and throws it in his boat. He takes a hammer or something and starts beatin' on it, as if it were some giant muskie of unknown origin, to see what it's made of. He hauls it back into shore and throws it up on the dock. A week later the U.S. Army comes to get it off the Sheboygan boardwalk and finds out it's a *very* live one he has caught. To top it off, the fisherman says, well, I was going to take it home and put it in the yard for the kids to play with, but I couldn't fit it in my truck. (To this day, no branch of the military has claimed responsibility for firing live missiles into Lake Michigan.)

Back on spearing waters, Brian Crist, Dean's brother, fishing guide and protest leader, offered Tom Maulson a ride in his boat on two nights, one at Big St. Germain Lake and the other at North Twin. Maulson accepted. Tom recalled that they joked a bit and Tom expressed hopes that this, not what Crist's navy had done in the past, would be the wave of the future at spearing lakes. "Old enemies take ride on calm waters" rang the *Milwaukee Sentinel* headlines. At season end, an offer by Lac du Flambeau to restock speared lakes

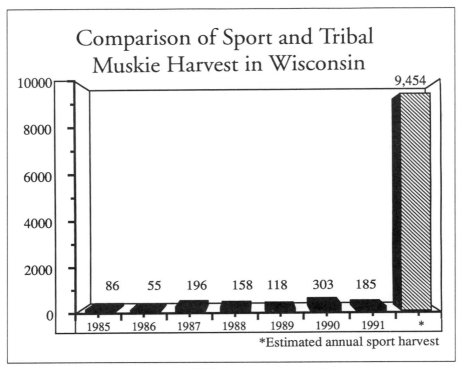

Comparison of Sport and Tribal Muskie Harvest in Wisconsin

| | | | | | | | | 9,454 |

(Bar chart with y-axis: 0, 2000, 4000, 6000, 8000, 10000)

Values by year:
- 1985: 86
- 1986: 55
- 1987: 196
- 1988: 158
- 1989: 118
- 1990: 303
- 1991: 185
- *: 9,454

*Estimated annual sport harvest

Source: Great Lakes Indian Fish and Wildlife Commission (GLIFWC).

was welcomed this time by media and state government as a sign of how much things had improved.

The Creature from Peace Lagoon:
Despite Weaknesses, the Witness Presence is Valued

From the worst night of Sand Lake to the quiet nights near season's end, it was still important for witnesses to be with Chippewa families and to document what was happening. "Witnesses give courage and strength," said Yolanda St. Germaine, "I need to know they're standing with my family." On other occasions, a handful of protesters would show up and, seeing the crowd of witness/supporters, leave. Along with state Department of Criminal Investigation agents and federal marshals, some witnesses went undercover in the protest crowd to find out the identities of those still mumbling murder and violence under their breaths at the landings. Charlotte Hockings spent many nights in long and calm dialogues with some STA–W members. Many of the witnesses proved willing to return north in the summer to witness against mining and many others work now on Native American education and lobbying issues.

There were weaknesses within our success this year. The Witness was not able to secure, as we had hoped, ministers and counselors to take a week off and work on the "res" to debrief after spearing/witnessing and or handle the post-shock from the worst nights. The drama of the spearing season also attracted many untrained supporters, a few of whom tried to stare down protesters or went off to dialogue with them for their own needs of adventure or validation, outside of the Witness discipline and requests of spearers. Some trained witnesses almost went to landings where we weren't invited. On occasion at the LdF spearing, witnesses would leave to go to another landing where Dean Crist and the action was. Despite our goal of peace, the trainings for worst-case scenarios had all but promised people high drama. The night before the adrenalin junkies (as one Native woman put it) headed off on their own, a Witness car, instead of following a spearer's vehicle back to LdF, mistakenly followed a WDNR boat back to Eagle River. Worried WDNR wardens were gracious enough to give directions back to Lac du Flambeau. At our worst, it was as if we'd created a giant amoeba we no longer had control over.

Overall, the Witness was valued again by LdF spearers and we, like most of the state, welcomed Dean Crist's remark that spring that the protests were probably and finally finished. The euphoria of a successful season and many more likely peaceful ones was sobered by Charlotte Hockings's assessment of the effects of the season on reservation children and families:

When the children are at school, I teach kindergarten, it's a two to three week tenseness that was explosive. . . . Kids are ill, angry. They don't do their home-work. They lose sleep. Some sleep in school. [There's] tension from unknown things—afraid for their parents, if they might be killed or hurt. . . . There aren't too many happy sides. . . . I had to work double hard. I had to work at school, then go out to the landings until two or three in the morning [where] I experienced a lot of emotional abuse. I didn't need that. . . . Some mornings I'd get up at 6 A.M. to listen to the radio reports and call them up and say, "You didn't get it right." . . .

It's brought a lot of tenseness into my family situation with Nick [over housework, communication]. . . . [Before] my husband quit his job, we had a wonderful thing going. He worked in the same building I did. He worked across the hall. We could kind of smile at each other during the day. We could just be home together and work on things together. It was really nice. Then all of a sudden, the tribe paid his salary and he was speaking against the tribe to get the rest of the members to vote no and not sell out our treaty rights for $50 million, and so they [tribal government] were telling people who came to our home, they were going to lose their jobs, even if people just showed up at our house!

So Nick quit his job and went on the road for the [last] three years, most every week in the winter. Sometimes nineteen to twenty days in a row so that he can give correct information to school groups, churches, organizations, and do the PR work our governor isn't doing. [Nick's] not condemning anybody . . . he's provoking critical thinking. He's doing it so well, I give of him freely, but for myself, I feel deprived of having my husband close by and doing the things we used to do.[13]

Concerns remained for future spearing years based on what we saw from law enforcement this year. The biggest improvement (besides on-lake, which Judge Crabb deserved primary law enforcement credit for) was that state and county police did regular checks, and far more arrests, for drunk driving. This cooled down many landings. Still the inconsistency of law enforcement work at the landings was a serious problem. At Lake Laura, Monday, April 22, police were slow to leave the police pen when teenagers went down the shoreline to harass spearers even though there was a death threat that night against Nick Hockings and a protester car with no license was sitting in the driveway to the landing. (But when a report came in of a wounded walleye offshore, police charged out from behind their lines, net and hip boots in hand, to recover the "Chippewa-wasted" fish.) That night of the death threat, Vilas County Police reassured GLIFWC wardens that a WDNR boat was out with Nick Hockings when he was being harassed from shore. In fact WDNR boats had put in at another landing but were nowhere near Nick. What if the combination of lack of lights, slipshod investigation, misinformation, lack of preventative action, and another hit squad possibility all happened on the same evening? Whether future boat landings have crowds big and bad or small and celebratory, great need for consistent, preventative law enforcement on and around spearing lakes still exists.

The Farmer and the End of Spearing Season

On the last Saturday of spearing (Saturday nights had been the big protest closers in previous years), Lac du Flambeau speared on North Twin Lake and Trout Lake, both in Vilas County. Rumors had abounded all week of a major showdown at North Twin near Conover, but that night only a handful of protesters showed up at the landing and two hundred witnesses had an impromptu concert there led by folk singer Mitch Walking Elk. The main body of seventy-five protesters led by STA–W and PARR went to Trout Lake where they marched into a landing where another two hundred-plus witnesses were spread out along the police fence, hill, and shoreline. Charlotte Hockings talked to her STA–W acquaintance for more than an hour while the protesters whooped it up for the media. One STA–W heavy, video camera in hand, followed a Vilas County cop around, calling him a Nazi and trying to film him.

A protester asked a farmer, with the Witness for his second year, if he would honor the flag and say the "Pledge of Allegiance" with protesters before they started their racial harangue. "Fuck your damn flag," said our rural friend, and a Witness coordinator pulled him out of the scene. Talking to him later, he reassured coordinators he would not have let things get out of control. Asking about his life, he tells us:

> I got involved because a woman friend of mine from LCO described how she and her son had been treated at the boat landings in 1989. Indians have rights and shouldn't be beaten up [because of them]. . . . I was in the Marine Corps. . . . I reject all that's been done in the name of the flag.

His wife had left him a few years ago and moved west with the kids. "I like to be around people doing something with their lives. There are a lot of smart people here [the LdF Witness]. This is my education." He can't run the farm because of a serious back injury and because of milk prices—"You know how much milk those California farms can put out." How did you get into farming? "I bought the land and farmed it with my folks." Did you ever read Wendell Berry, he's the Kentucky farmer who's a wonderful writer? "He's a writer. I couldn't make it just as a farmer." How do you make ends meet? "Disability payments are not enough. . . . It's painful to have to live off your mother's [financial] help."

At the end of the season, this witness had taken bundles of the Midwest Treaty Network treaty pamphlet to schools throughout his Rusk County area, and smoothed the way with some farm families for the anti-mining sit-in at Kennecott's Ladysmith mine. He wonders now whether the European tradition of farming is worth continuing, considering what our cattle and soy bean growing have done to the land cared for by Native people.

A Political Truce is Called

The Feathergate persecution climaxed on April 9, 1991, in Judge Paul Magnuson's U.S. District Court in Minneapolis. Walter Bresette and Esther Nahgahnub were charged with selling dreamcatchers containing migratory bird feathers—owl, goose, and redtail hawk obtained from molting birds or road kill. In his fact-finding, Judge Magnuson noted that dreams had great spiritual significance to the Chippewa and so did bird feathers. Rejecting the "government's parsimonious reading of the treaty rights," Magnuson ruled that the Chippewa had a treaty right to sell bird feathers as part of the guaranteed harvestable resource and practice from the time of the treaties.

The judge rejected the government prosecutor's argument that the Migratory Bird Act abrogated these treaty feather-gathering rights, or that Congress had intended this when they passed the act. He also ruled that this kind of arrest and prosecution was not a "permissible, nondiscriminatory conservation measure." Said Magnuson: "Here the migratory birds of northern Minnesota and Wisconsin are not faced with extinction due to the likes of Walter Bresette or Esther Nahgahnub." He dismissed the charges and left tribal governments in the three states of ceded territory wondering what to make of this remarkable precedent and its implication that gathering rights crossed state lines.[14]

Cultural and spearing rights activists hoped that tribal governments would seize the Feathergate precedent and original timber rulings, and appeal the recent Crabb decisions. For different reasons, of course, the anti-treaty movement's last political hope lay also with an appeal of the early *Voigt* decisions by Judges Doyle and Crabb. On Monday, May 22, the state of Wisconsin and tribal officials agreed that neither side would appeal the decisions made in the last seventeen years of Chippewa treaty rights litigation. The state's newspaper editorials welcomed the decision as an end to the troubles, saying each side had gained and lost something.

Tribal governments might have also been fearful of appealing anything to the conservative Court of Appeals or Supreme Court of the Reagan-Bush era. The state of Wisconsin had promised to appeal all of *Voigt* including fishing rights if the tribes appealed timber or back damages, so the perception of risk was high. In Walt Bresette's analysis, the tribes had cut a deal with Wisconsin Attorney General Doyle—an end to the state's attack on Chippewa gambling rights in exchange for no tribal appeals of Crabb. The substantial and quicker revenues from gambling looked brighter than the difficult road of appeals or the lengthy but healthier five- to ten-year journey to sustainable logging and mill operations or national marketing of *Ojibwe* walleye.[15]

Some Native American activists and traditionalists oppose gambling as a personal choice or as the best form of economic development, but they do not publicly oppose it because of the significant jobs and revenue impact it has for the reservations. Lac du Flambeau estimates twenty-nine jobs and half its annual income derive from its bingo operation. The high-stakes bingo in Milwaukee's industrial valley, run under trust status with the Forest County Potawatomi, provides income to Milwaukee's Indian Community School. Many activists and tribal leaders also point out that the opposition to Native gambling rights is but another rearguard attack (and search for new legal precedent) against Native sovereignty rights as a whole.

Borders

On the way home from the witness season, I stop and rest near a great pine tree. When I awake, the sun is behind the tree, its light broken apart by the branches, so that I think at first I'm looking at a Christmas tree all lit up. I think back to my walk along the wooded hilltop behind Treehaven: the edge of this hill is a border between designed spaces and forest wilderness. I walk other borders in my life: between white and Black culture, between Native and immigrant (four generations back) American culture, between urban and rural. These are borders that are more like different but interacting ecological communities than they are like political boundaries that can't be crossed except with great risk. I am grateful that what I learned from being on cultural borders has helped a little in northern Wisconsin. I pray that what we learned at boat landings might be of help with the daily violence and rising despair in the city. . . . A soft wind blows across my face and reminds me it is time to go home.

European-Americans cannot be healed, cannot be whole, without dealing with racism. This means dealing with the hidden wounds racism makes in ourselves. These internal wounds include: 1) fear of (cultural) strangers and fear that we might learn from others things we need or are missing; 2) inability to love the place we live in (and therefore learn how to care for it and survive) because we cannot see or face the history of that place; 3) the pain of giving up our own cultural identities and turning this into the expectation that others assimilate too; and 4) the inability to face real economic and political problems that could be solved by uniting with our neighbors who have similar visions and values but different historical/cultural backgrounds.

There is a great migratory highway that connects northern Wisconsin with southeast Wisconsin. It can bring the tourist or the witness north, or it can carry the dislocated farmer or mill worker south to compete for jobs in cities that can't employ half their young African-Americans. It can carry the message of cooperation and neighborliness—a tradition that goes back to the white settler days when Betsy Thunder, a Winnebago medicine woman, taught and doctored immigrant families. Or the highway can carry hit teams from Chicago.

Urban-rural solidarity can heal the division we feel from the land and our history if we understand that the loss of rural culture is as grave as the crisis in our urban cores. The cities' food, water, and electricity comes from rural or "wild" areas. The land rights of Native Americans and small-scale farmers are pith to the same system that our urban energy and economic development come from, and the sustainable technological transitions we will have to make. The cities can not go on surviving at the expense of the countryside/wilderness. The countryside/wilderness cannot thrive without cities becoming ecologically sustainable.

The urban-rural border can melt away into a healthy interdependence that is political as well as economic and ecological. Like the treaty rights and anti-mining movements, Green politics in Wisconsin started in rural areas and is kept in balance by having small-town leadership right from the beginning. The urban-rural success of European-American solidarity and support programs with Native Americans can show the way to antiracist and neighborhood ecology alliances with African-Americans. While groups like the Midwest Treaty Network and the Greens have memberships and political clout that is small but growing, our credibility and lessons learned on issues that combine environmentalism and antiracism carry more value for the future than the fumblings of most political leaders today.

The political barrier that often seems to exist between urban and rural politics is really a place where progressivism intersects with meaningful conservatism—one that conserves the earth and traditions of cultural value. Some of the Greens were given Menominee squash seeds from an ancient line that have flourished even in Wisconsin's drought years. Our ability as humans to survive and flourish in this place depends on learning to love and care for our ecological and cultural communities. Who can teach us more about politics as well as ecology than those who have lived here the longest?

Shifting Sands

When a spearer spots a walleye in the lake shoals, he or she must aim, because of the refraction of light, at a spot different than where the walleye appears. Similarly, the focus of the treaty rights movement has shifted to other, related ground in Wisconsin. The day after the July 5, 1991 thank-you feast in Lac du Flambeau, *Wa-Swa-Gon* members and witnesses traveled to Ladysmith, Wisconsin, to join the anti-Kennecott Take Back the Site rally, the kickoff event to the Flambeau Summer of resistance to the mine.

Tom Maulson spoke and challenged PARR and STA–W to get involved in this real resource fight. Zoltán Grossman of Midwest Treaty Network announced that money raised through the treaty rights benefit concert (with John Trudell and Floyd Westerman) would go to help fight the Ladysmith mine and to fund a GLIFWC study of mining's impact in ceded territory. Speaking on behalf of LCO tribal chair Gaiashkibos, Gene Begay lent LCO support to the effort to stop Kennecott and said LCO would hire an expert to look at the WDNR's inadequate protection of endangered species in the Flambeau River. Purple warty-back and bullhead clams had been recently discovered by the WDNR after the EPA required a look in the river in order to relicense a dam. Where was this kind of firsthand impact study when the mining permitting was being done?

In response to grassroots opposition to mining, in July 1991 the state assembly passed a bill that would overturn the local agreement section of the 1988 mining law, prohibit mining on wetlands and shore areas, extend the liability for mining pollution to the parent company, and place a two-year moratorium on any further mining in the state. This return to tough but environmentally reasonable mining laws was expected to be vetoed by Governor Thompson. Meanwhile, *Wa-Swa-Gon* and towns around the LdF reservation began to take a closer look at Noranda's exploratory drilling for zinc near the town of Lynne in Oneida county.

A provision requiring education in the public schools (twice in elementary school and once in high school) about the history, culture, and sovereignty of Wisconsin Native nations passed with the 1990 budget bill. PARR and STA–W adamantly opposed this kind of "Indian propaganda in the schools" as their next issue, rather than moving on to the real resource issues of mining and nuclear dumps. Jeff Peterson, an elementary school teacher in Balsam Lake, a witness and Green spokesperson, said, in a widely read editorial:

> Because the public schools have until now chosen to ignore Indian issues, much of the adult population is not only ignorant, but ignorant of its ignorance. Much of what they think they know about Indians is learned in the bars or on the boat landings. . . . The sooner these [PARR] people are exposed as the bigots they really are, the sooner the rest of us can get on with the task of building

understanding between Indians and non-Indians in northern Wisconsin. It's time to let the healing begin.[16]

Future springs would bring those witnesses needed north again along with the migrating birds and warm weather. They would find that the common concerns of many about the land and waters of Wisconsin have overtaken the bitterness of a few about different rights and cultural traditions.

Notes

1. This paragraph is based on John McPhee, *The Survival of the Bark Canoe* (New York: Farrar, Straus, and Giroux, 1975), pp. 29–31. Paul Strong of Loon Watch (Wisconsin) has said that loons face no imminent or widespread danger from the (relatively small) Chippewa gillnet harvest. Gillnets, placed in deeper water, have a floatline along the top and weights along the bottom. While smaller fish swim through the nets, bigger fish are caught by their gills or fins.

2. George Stanley, "Spearer reports harassment at UW job," *Milwaukee Sentinel,* April 27, 1991.

3. From the *Witness Training Manual* (1990) essay "Cultural Sensitivity to European-Americans in northern Wisconsin" p. 50.

4. The Chippewa say Tomahawk Lake got its name in the aftermath of a battle between them and the Sioux, when a tomahawk was buried on the shores to commemorate a peace agreement. All place name sources in this and the following paragraph come from Robert E. Gard and L. G. Sorden, *Romance of Wisconsin Place Names* (New York: October House Press, 1968).

5. "Indian logging reached a high point in 1888, when . . . 190,206,080 board feet . . . sold for $4.75 to $7.00 per 1,000 feet." E. Danziger, Jr., *The Chippewa of Lake Superior*, p. 102.

6. Mole Lake applied and was granted the right to begin harvesting on public lands. The WDNR, mandated by the federal courts to permit this, opened up the state's Northern Highland Forest where the Chippewa could harvest some of the best hardwood in Wisconsin. Forester (and witness) Bob Simeone speculated that this was done so the big timber interests, independent loggers, and county governments would be aroused against the prospect of what Chippewa timbering would mean. They were.

7. Al Shanks, coordinator of the state's Division of Emergency Government, testified at this 1991 injunction hearing. In 1989, as part of Governor Thompson's effort to call off spearing *because* of the violent protests, Shanks testified before Judge Crabb that things were very dangerous and out of control at the landings. This time around he said everything was under control, the state plan was working and sheriffs were doing their part, and it wasn't a good idea to separate protesters from Chippewa families and witnesses. To spearers and families, the difference wasn't so noticeable.

8. John Sherer, "Crist says wardens will be in danger," *Milwaukee Sentinel*, April 3, 1991.

9. International support for Chippewa treaty rights was built again in 1991. Solidarity groups in Austria, Canada, Britain, and Czechoslovakia demonstrated at U.S. embassies and consulates in April 1991. In September 1991, Governor Thompson was picketed at a Vienna hotel by the Associated for Endangered Peoples while on a European trade mission.

10. From Kathleen Hart's written report of the events of that night. Two other items of note: 1) some protesters had just come from the funeral of a St. Germaine soldier killed in the Gulf War. They referred to this throughout the evening: e.g., "He died for [our] flag!"; and 2) an anonymous source quoted police as saying that if a riot had broken out, Mincey would have been arrested for inciting it (*1991 Witness Report*, p. 83).

11. James B. Nelson, "Spearing protest called near-riot by both sides," *Milwaukee Sentinel*, April 22, 1991.

12. "Missile find no surprise to fisherman: But finding out it was a live Sidewinder was a little more of a shock," *Milwaukee Journal*, April 25, 1991. Public radio also carried the story and an interview with the Sheboygan fisherman, retold at the boat landings by Brent Harring.

13. Rick Whaley interview with Charlotte Hockings at LdF, July 13, 1991.

14. U.S. attorneys in Minneapolis had initially indicated they would appeal Judge Magnuson's Feathergate ruling, apparently finding the persecution of Native cultural and artistic freedoms an important aspect of the attack on Chippewa sovereignty. By end of summer 1991, they had decided to not pursue their appeal.

15. Tribes are allowed to run any game of chance legal in a particular state, but without state regulation (because of sovereignty, tribes can regulate their own such games). This has allowed, in Wisconsin, Native groups to run the state's only high stakes bingo operations for the last few decades. Native American casino gambling had become a possibility in Wisconsin when Governor Thompson legalized lotteries in 1987. The federal government ordered all states to negotiate compacts with Native American tribes over reservation gaming in 1989. In February 1990, following the October 1989 Lac du Flambeau buyout rejection, then-Attorney General Hanaway reversed his position on Indian casino gambling, ruling it illegal in Wisconsin (thus overthrowing his previous position) and shutting down LdF and Mole Lake gaming operations.

Governor Thompson, who led the way to lotteries and dog racing in Wisconsin, has steadfastly opposed any Indian casino games and promised to appeal Judge Crabb's June 1991 ruling that the state must indeed negotiate a gambling compact with LdF and Mole Lake. Thompson has urged the state legislature to ban all casino gambling in the state, including river boat gambling, as a way to also stop Native gambling. Attorney General Doyle didn't believe that this would stop Native rights to Las Vegas-style gaming, but he has signed on with Thompson to the appeal of Judge Crabb's ruling. By late 1992, Indian gaming had become more controversial than spearfishing. The state proposed a referendum on gambling, and tribes defended their sovereign right to decide such matters and to continue the alleviation of poverty and the development of other economic ventures, both of which gambling money allowed.

16. Jeff Peterson, "Required Indian courses in public schools long overdue," *Milwaukee Journal*, April 29, 1991.

GASHKADINO GISISS
(The Freezing Moon)

Maybe these are the Oski-Biimaadizig
*we heard about in the Seventh Fire
Prophecy . . . the New People that come
together from all races to save the Earth.*
—Nick Hockings
Treehaven, April 22,1989

"The New People"
Lessons and Projections

Rick Whaley and Walt Bresette

The Witness and Its
Nonviolence Philosophy Proved a Success

The Witness program, overall, had the respect and appreciation of spearers from the reservations that requested a Witness presence under the leadership of spearing coordinators. Jerry Maulson, Tom's brother and a longtime spearfisher himself, said the Witness made a big difference: someone might have gotten killed without that support at the landings. Trust and lasting friendships have marked the *Anishinabe*-Witness efforts over the last five years.

Despite the Witness's lack of political influence or connections to affect the major power players in the state—federal courts, the governor and state law enforcement, northern Wisconsin district attorneys and sheriffs, and the mining and energy companies—we were able to facilitate some major breakthroughs. The Witness helped provide the opening for lawyers to get involved and secure the federal injunction against harassment of spearers. This ACLU-Wisconsin court initiative and Judge Crabb's favorable ruling successfully shut

229

down the harassing protests. We educated the public on treaty rights, empowered hundreds to become directly involved in stopping or diffusing violence,
lobbied for adequate law enforcement, aided in gaining a significant measure
of public acceptance of treaties, and helped to end the boat landing violence.

For My People: Spearfishing a Success for the Chippewa

Both the continuance of off-reservation spearing rights and the success of the
Witness effort depended upon the Chippewa spearfishers' courageous stance of
nonretaliation to the harassment and violence from anti-treaty protesters. The
spearers' principled call for allies led to the development of the boat landing
Witness strategy and all the accompanying educational/lobbying/empower-
ment work that reached so many communities in the Midwest. The dramatic
threat of violence to Native peoples brought many supporters forward. The
boat landing Witness became a risky yet effective way to stand up for non-
violence and a just solution for Native people. The Witness complemented the
growing coalition of church and mainstream political support for the
Chippewa cause. Experienced activists from other movements—Wounded
Knee, Black Hills, southern civil rights, anti-Vietnam war, women's, and
environmental movements—found that their issues and political identities tied
in well with the treaty support efforts. They witnessed at landings or raised
money, had food drives for the reservations during spearing season, and
lobbied for *Anishinabe* rights.

Critically, a new generation of Native and non-Native people became active
in the struggle. Milwaukee's Dave Denomie, of Polish and Bad River
Chippewa descent, joined the Witness in 1989 and became the Milwaukee
Witness spokesperson for 1990–1991. He said,

> Witnessing at the boat landings [in] spring and being active with the Midwest
> Treaty Network is part of my journey back home. This is preparing me for the
> day my wife, Mary, and I can move to Bad River where my grandfather lived.
> We will bring back there our experiences and skills and our many friendships for
> the benefit of my people.

Another key to success was that many of the leadership roles in the treaty
rights/witness movement were divided up, spreading both the work and the
risk around. Walt Bresette was the orator and instigator who spread the word,
heightened the politics of the cause, and opened the door to new allies,
including funding sources. The Witness and Midwest Treaty Network found
willing and successful grant writers as well as many Witness trainers and public
speakers throughout the state, the Twin Cities, and Chicago. Tom Maulson
and the other reservations' spearing coordinators were the frontline tacticians

Logo used by Citizens for Treaty Rights and the Witness for Non-Violence. Illustration by Katy Ralph Moore.

in the on-lake and boat landing engagements with volatile protesters, curious media, and wavering law enforcement. Maulson was the commander in the nonviolent army of Lac du Flambeau spearers and witnesses. While many spearers from all the reservations speared lakes on their own, without protesters or witnesses present, the fact that *Wa-Swa-Gon* and Witnesses played out the political drama at LdF-chosen landings each night allowed a certain safety and anonymity to those not officially working along with *Wa-Swa-Gon*'s leadership.

While the movement was grounded in solid antiracist politics, with many good organizers, the people involved recognized that something more than good politics was needed. "If I'm going to die, I want it to be out exercising my rights," contended spearer Nick Hockings. Yet, he acknowledged, "There are three things that center me: AA [Alcoholics Anonymous], my faith [Baha'i], and my culture." The pipe ceremonies that preceded some spearing nights, the early season sweat lodges, and the drums at the landings provided grounding for many spearers, families, and supporters. Merle Wolford spent time on LdF reservation during the 1990 and 1991 spearing seasons doing counseling and visualizations with those women enduring the stress of landing protests and fears for their people.

There is a power to metaphor. Imagining celebration instead of confrontation at the landings, along with years of taking insults and anger and diffusing it with listening love and patience, finally paid off. On the last Saturday night of 1991 spearing, which could have brought the worst protests, Mitch Walking Elk and others sang at the quiet North Twin landing. Over at the Trout Lake landing, where PARR and STA–W had concentrated their forces, strangers walked up to me [RW] and said, "Do you remember me? I was at the that big training you did in 1990. We're here with a large contingent . . ." Protesters' anger was desperate but diffused. Their tactics looked silly. Good, well organized, can defeat evil.

Leading the Parade:
A New Generation of *Anishinabe* Leadership

With his brother Mike, Fred Tribble began what Milwaukee's WITI-TV called "Wisconsin's million dollar headache." In a 1990 TV interview by TV 6 reporter Roseann St. Aubin, Tribble said he had only meant to engage the WDNR and never imagined things would develop as they did. Fred, who assiduously avoided the press throughout the years of controversy, regretted that Lac du Flambeau had turned down the 1989 settlement offer and hoped that Governor Thompson would offer a new proposal that might provide jobs and housing for all the Chippewa reservations.

The next wave of treaty testers picked up the spearing torch and carried it the distance of its political possibilities in the 1980s. Many who speared off-reservation in this last decade did so because it was a tradition going back centuries, because it's what you do in spring, and because it feeds your family. "Because of treaty rights, we've uncovered a new air," Tom Maulson asserted, "the pipe, the drum, *Ojibwe* culture is at the forefront." *Anishinabe* youngsters now go out and learn spearing with their parents.

Words do have power to summon up courage in order to risk abuse and injury each night of spearing. Words can unlock spiritual sources that can temper or dissipate fear—words like "honor," prayers "to those who have gone before," "Witnessing" for the Earth knowing what the Earth bears witness to when the spearing night is over or when the mining company has left. The power of the past can be felt in the present. Through the words of elders at the Mediwiwin *naming ceremony, the names/spirits of the past are renewed. So also the legacies of the past—the struggles, the lessons, the sacrifice, the old friends, the descendants—band together to create the new movement.*

A new generation of *Anishinabe* leaders, some official, some grassroots, came into their own as a result of the momentous changes in the 1980s. The renewal was spiritual and political, the personal changes significant. "I was a hellraiser in my day . . . no different than any other Indian having a good time," acknowledged Tom Maulson. "Now, I'm a hellraiser in a different way." Like Bresette, Maulson speaks to audiences nationwide now, as well as stumping the anti-mining community circuit in northern Wisconsin. Tom ran against Mike Allen for LdF tribal chair in September 1990 and lost, but won a seat on the LdF tribal council in 1991.

"[The] struggle we're involved with in northern Wisconsin," Walt recounted to the national Greens conference in 1990,

it's the same story you have heard at Big Mountain. It's the same story that is going on now at Oka [Quebec]. It's the same story that's going on all over this globe. It just happens to be our story, that's all . . . We are one speech away from imprisonment. We're one payment away from homelessness. We are all Mohawks. You must believe me on that. And some day the troops will be here, knocking at your door, saying, "You can't say that. You can't do that. We're going to put a golf course on your cemetery." And it'll be your turn to say, "Okay, sir . . ." or "No."

At the Lac du Flambeau thank-you pow-wow in 1991, Native elder Bea Swanson from the Twin Cities related a story. "When I was young," she reminisced, "I always wanted to win the beauty pageant and ride in the parade waving to the crowd. I didn't realize then that Indian girls couldn't win [those contests]. But when I was asked to lead the *Wa-Swa-Gon* group in the Minocqua Fourth of July parade, it didn't matter all the harassment we got there. I was so proud. I finally got to lead the parade."

Lessons, Contradictions, Next Issues

The Witness struggled with a number of critical questions, not all of them resolved smoothly. Should we have gone north to witness in those first years without tribal government invitations? While the spearing groups wanted us and eventually three tribal governments approved it, we never overcame the disdain of the LdF tribal council. Because of our disciplined presence backed by the authority of spearers, the Witness exerted influence over supporters at the landings, but we could not always control the behavior or attitudes of untrained supporters, especially those wishing to convey hostility to the protesters. Some supporters' attitudes were not appreciated by our *Anishinabe* hosts. Some European-Americans took on Native spirituality and represented it as their own. Some witness and supporters came looking "for an Indian to marry" or to party down with spearers after the evening harvest. These criticisms became part of the education work the Witness took on.

How do you know which Native people to take direction from, someone asked Sauk and Fox/Quapaw activist Dennis Jennings (then with the International Indian Treaty Council) at the North American Bioregional Congress in Vancouver, 1988. Look to the traditional people, he said, those closest to the land, usually the poorest, but with the strongest sense of culture and history, and listen to them. By answering the call from spearing activists, the Witness found those traditional people who speared for religious and cultural reasons as well as for subsistence food.

Non-Native supporters who want to be Indian, are they cultural interlopers, lost souls, non-blood Indians, allies, or enemies? For Walt Bresette, they are not enemies. They are not throwing rocks and threatening to kill Indians like some treaty protesters. Even these bad neighbors who have harassed spearers for five years are not the real enemies. The Klausers, the mining companies, the paper mill polluters, and the Monsantos with their BGH for dairy cows, these are the real enemies, trying to force their brand of economics on northern Wisconsin to the detriment of all but a few. If supporters are willing to work on the racism of the state and the white backlash movement, Dennis Jennings noted, that's the first step. The next step is looking at patterns of racism within solidarity work and learning what respecting Native culture means. The Midwest Treaty Network, especially through the work of the Madison Treaty Rights Support Group, is carrying this work forward.

The label of outsiders was one the protesters and often the press stuck on the Witness, even though at least half of the witnesses came from northern Wisconsin and Minnesota (i.e., from ceded territory). Milwaukee African-American mediator and Witness trainer Ron Ballew declared, "You don't have to be from South Africa to work against apartheid. These justice issues affect everyone." However, those who didn't live in the immediate vicinity of spearing lakes pledged not to do anything to make life worse for those who had to live there all year and face the consequences of whatever happened during the spearing season.

Good organizing moves beyond the original issue into related and broader issues. The trainings on background issues and cultural sensitivity became the means to get witnesses to the boat landings. In turn, the boat landing experience became the way to get people involved in the "background" economic and cultural issues such as the anti-mining efforts in northern Wisconsin, stopping nuclear waste storage at the Mdewakantan Sioux (Dakota) Prairie Island reservation in Minnesota, and funding mining impact research. Led by Wisconsin tribes, allies like HONOR, and teaching activists, the mandated Indian education in the public schools has begun. AIM, the Native press, HONOR, and the Midwest Treaty Network have raised challenges against sport team logos that demean Native Americans. And we all turned our attention in 1992 to the possible meaning of the last five hundred years on this continent: for European-Americans and all other immigrant groups, for African-Americans and Asian-Americans, and for all the indigenous and descendent peoples of the Americas.

The Good and the Difficult of Tribal Government

The Witness for Non-Violence story is one worth celebrating, but the struggle is far from over. The *Anishinabe,* Walt Bresette points out, lost more in court than we gained in the Doyle-Crabb rulings since 1983. More than that, the policing mechanism over traditional gatherers/hunters is more firmly in place, on- and off-reservation, *under the auspices of tribal governments themselves.* The unwillingness of tribal governments to press the Feathergate ruling (that implied harvesting rights across state lines), or to appeal the no timber rights/no back damages rulings, left Walt and other Native activists despairing.

The willingness to extend treaties to environmental protection of all communities within the province of the treaties is a potentially powerful strategy to forward-looking earth politics. In the Wisconsin struggle the use of this approach varied dramatically from the strong role of Gaiashkibos at LCO in challenging Kennecott, to the LdF government's lack of leadership in challenging the attempted buyout of treaty rights.

In Walt Bresette's view, it is important to consider the relationship of on-reservation activists and traditionalists to tribal governments throughout the treaty rights struggle. In Bresette's analysis, the elders' pro-treaty advice, along with the grassroots activists nipping at the heals of tribal governments: 1) stopped the buyout of treaty rights; 2) widened the arena of debate—from the 1979 La Pointe meeting about reunification of all the Chippewa bands, to the use of treaties to protect northern Wisconsin from mining; and 3) proved peripherally that the tribes had power in the treaty negotiations and interpretations because of the countless *individual* Chippewa acts of sovereignty. When *Wa-Swa-Gon* invited other reservations to spear with them, when artists Nahgahnub and Bresette sold dreamcatchers, when Mole Lake harvested timber, when Gaiashkibos threw the weight of LCO behind Rusk County Citizens Action, each of these actions widened the options of tribal governments and also strengthened treaty rights.

As Walt sees it, tribal governments are in a bind. They are the main policing agency, on behalf of state and federal policymakers, against hunters and spearers. Because their existence is especially beholden to federal aid, they can rarely be a strong advocate for their rights or act as the cutting edge of new or traditional interpretations of the treaties that could develop into healthy economic enterprises. Though whatever their failings, Bresette adds, "Tribal governments did enough to prove their bravery. They stood up to the 1989 congressional blackmail letter. The Lac du Flambeau tribal government joined *Wa-Swa-Gon* in the lawsuit against STA–W harassment. LCO took on Kennecott and the Wisconsin DNR." In Walt's diagram of Indian politics, tribal governments and militants/traditionalists each have a role to play: they need each other.

Chippewa spearfishers and tribal governments had secured the sovereignty, treaty right to off-reservation harvesting, and, in doing so, had reestablished the right to what was really an ancient cultural and religious practice—the intertwining and honoring of spring's bounty and our survival.

Contributories: *Groups That Helped Our Success*

[The Black struggle for freedom is a river] sometimes powerful, tumultuous, and roiling with life; at other times meandering and turgid, covered with ice and snow of seemingly endless winters, all too often streaked and running with blood . . . The dynamics and justice of its movement have continually gathered others to itself, have persistently filled other men and women with the force of its vision, its indomitable hope.[1]

St. Croix (the river), the city (St. Croix Falls), and the reservation, are all named for the French words meaning Holy Cross. The early missionaries canoeing the St. Croix were reminded of the cross as the river, running red with the color of tamarack roots, met the Mississippi at nearly a right angle. One story said that French explorers saw a cross in relief on the rocks on the Wisconsin side of the river.[2]

How much did the modern religious community do to prevent bloodshed of Chippewa lives and protect rights in northern Wisconsin? Some spearers, Native activists, and witnesses were critical of clergy for not coming to the landings in greater numbers. It certainly involved less risk and suffering, in most communities, to pass resolutions against violence and for treaties, but not go to the frontlines. Yet resolutions from the Wisconsin Conference of Churches and other ecumenical gatherings (like the 1984 Ad Hoc Commission on Racism) carried far more weight politically than Witness pronouncements or evidence and reached a significant audience in many denominations, and so were an important contribution.[3] Mainstream denominations in northern Wisconsin set in motion many healing discussions behind the scenes in their communities. This process was slower than the solidarity movement's responses to boat landing troubles or to protest organizations' press conferences, but the change thus begun was effective in bringing a broader constituency to a position of tolerance and acceptance of treaty rights and support for towns dialoguing with the reservation in their area.

Those ministers who did come to the landings played an invaluable role for both the religious community and for the public in giving treaties and the Witness credibility. Reverend Tim Kehl of Madison was a strong advocate of nonviolence and honoring treaties from the beginning years of witnessing. Minister Bryan Catlett-Serchio of Citizens for Treaty Rights was one of the first witnesses at 1988 boat landings. United Church of Christ Reverend Jeff Wartgow's Good Friday appeal and Lutheran Reverend Dick Inglett's (of Conover, near North Twin Lake) sermon on the sinfulness of the protests shrunk support for protesters' tactics at the landings. The Milwaukee Jewish Council condemned the overt racism and violence of the anti-treaty movement in 1989. And significantly, members of the Bethel Hillel Congregation of Champaign-Urbana, Illinois, took Witness training together and witnessed at Lac du Flambeau in 1991.

The religious community listened to and helped legitimize the experiences of spearfishers. Many denominations including the Milwaukee Catholic Archdiocese moved away from supporting a "negotiated settlement" to support for off-reservation harvesting rights after the 1989 LdF buyout defeat. Along with tribal activists, religious allies like HONOR challenged grassroots witnesses to look at the full range of Native sovereignty issues under attack. Bearing truthful witness for one's neighbors took many forms, at and away from the landings, during these years.[4]

The movement became a river of allies joining the cause for justice and reconciliation. The treaty rights movement in Wisconsin gathered to it allies from the peace and women's movements, from college campuses and law schools, from churches and synagogues, from the state legislature (Reps. Marcia Coggs, Gwen Moore, Frank Boyle, and David Clarenbach), and from labor, civil rights, and especially environmental constituencies. The involvement of Lew Gurwitz and then the ACLU brought, by the end of 1991, all but three of the protest defendants to an out-of-court settlement in the federal injunction against harassment of spearers.[5]

In the face of the life and death issue of the boat landings, progressive groups in Wisconsin put aside ideological differences among and within themselves.[6] Treaty supporters as a whole have been able to work publicly on other specifically environmental issues without avoiding the question of racism towards Native Americans. The treaty rights and anti-mining cause gave Midwest Treaty Network and Wisconsin Greens issues to define a statewide identity and direct action/lobbying/local outreach work. Along with stopping racial violence and honoring America's treaties, green politics, broadly inclusive, resonated with traditional Native economics and spirituality— Native cultures more practiced in rituals that respect and reciprocate what is taken from nature. In a programmatic, political way, Native rights supporters have taken on issues and organization building in the hope of influencing and then shaping sustainable economic development policy and just relations among communities in Wisconsin.

Upstream to the Source: *A Look at the Media's Role*

Early on in our work, one inquiring media phone call to the Witness began, "You're white and you're for peace. That's a new angle." Witnesses and other allies worked angles, openings, and differences over media coverage to get television and the press to pay attention to what was happening in northern Wisconsin.

During 1989, media coverage both in the press and on television began to reflect the reality of what was said and done at the boat landings. Editors began to loosen restrictions on reporters and the real story of the protests was finally printed. For example, Walt Bresette was excitedly told by an Associated Press reporter in 1989, "I finally got permission to print 'timber nigger' [as an example of what protesters were saying]." Like the Witness, the responsible media held up a mirror to what was happening and said: is this acceptable? Incorrect references to Chippewa rights being "given" in exchange for land began to disappear and be replaced by accurate legal and cultural history. Significantly, it was the shift in media coverage that helped break the power of the protests and split Crist off from his former mentors, Thompson and Klauser.[7] Many politicians who once feared the backlash voting constituency became fed up with the protests, not to mention the $2 million annual cost of policing the protests in its heaviest years.

Papers like the conservative *Milwaukee Sentinel* that kept steady, quality reporters (James Nelson, Quincey Dadisman, Terry Koper) on the treaty story did better than papers like the *Milwaukee Journal* that bounced assignments around or like the *Duluth News Tribune* that removed Susan Stannich for writing too well on an issue editors differed with her on. By 1990, many newspapers, including the *Milwaukee Journal,* the *Wisconsin State Journal* in an award-winning series, and the *Wausau Record Herald,* as well as television stations, were doing in-depth stories saying sportsmen and tourist livelihoods were not threatened by Chippewa spearing.[8] Minocqua radio reporter and *Milwaukee Sentinel* stringer John Sherer said, "The media goes through a learning process too."

Diligent reporters followed the story upstream past the fear and prejudice to the economic and political sources of the conflict. Ron Seely of the *Wisconsin State Journal* and Mary Jo Kewley of the *Wausau Record Herald* took extensive looks at the mining issue in northern Wisconsin in 1991. The *Milwaukee Journal* changed its editorial stance to favor treaty rights and regularly blasted

Crist/STA–W and PARR for their tactics. The *Journal* covered the 1990 Lady-smith mining hearings, including hearing examiner David Schwartz's critical remarks about LCO's opposition, but the paper discontinued the services of the stringer who broke the story.[9]

The main shortcomings of the press overall continued to be: 1) Not digging deeper into James Klauser's connections to the anti-treaty work of the Wisconsin Counties Association and all those corporations—timber, paper mill and mining—that benefit so clearly from the limiting of Chippewa treaty rights; 2) the way the press covered the *1990 Witness Report* that documented extensive harassment, interference, and racism on the lakes and landings during LdF spearing was incomplete. The *Milwaukee Journal* gave Al Shanks, coordinator of state law enforcement, headlines the next day calling the 135-page *Witness Report* (and videotaped evidence) "rubbish."[10] Why wouldn't the media investigate whether it was the *Witness Report* or Shank's remarks that were "rubbish?"; 3) another problem was that they did not uncover the source of Crist's/STA–W's financial support. The hundreds of thousand dollars needed to launch Treaty Beer and, even now, to continue fighting the injunction "all the way to the Supreme Court" could not possibly come from a small town pizza business or even regional STA–W memberships.

The Chippewa found allies in the media and, along with their other allies, changed the nature and terrain of the debate. What was radical five years ago is now mainstream: fish, number-wise, are in good shape. Tourism is not threatened by Chippewa spearing. Neighboring communities have far more to gain by working together with tribes than by confronting them. The state inflamed the situation at landings (Strickland Report, 1990). Treaties have something to do with mining. By May 1991, a *Wisconsin State Journal* poll reported that 59 percent of southern Wisconsinites and 42 percent of northern Wisconsinites supported treaty rights.

The Weaver's Tale: *Creating a Sustainable Economic Future*

Why are Native American subsistence rights and rural culture even important in this information age, in this global marketplace? Defending treaty and rural rights is more than a question of stopping racial violence and keeping northern Wisconsin safe for tourism. Rural and urban destinies are interwoven. Borne on the winds from factories in Milwaukee and Chicago is the acid rain that poisons northern Wisconsin lakes and replaces the crayfish in rivers there with "elephant snot" algae. Back through the cities come the rivers with farm manure runoff and the toxins from the mines. The foreclosures of small farms and the boom and bust economy of mining drives more rural Americans to the cities and exacerbates rural anger towards the urban crime-welfare tax drain. City people (upper-middle and working class, and some poor) leave the big cities for the safety, slower pace, and less expensive lifestyle of the countryside. Neither migration is likely to find a booming economy, freedom from racial strife, or less toxic environments.

Instead of creating jobs from the urban recycling stream, we try to ship our garbage to reservations or to rural landfills, or we incinerate it and send out the toxins air-direct.[11] We tear up Rusk county farms and ruin the Flambeau River because sending Rio Tinto Zinc $4 million a month out of state is "better" economically.[12] Is solar technology really less sensible than tearing up the Arctic Reserve, drilling in Bayfield county, or going to war over Middle East oil? On whose sacrifice is the future being built?

Talking about subsistence living for cities, now so dependent on far-away places for food, energy, and "economic development," may seem farfetched until your water becomes rationed because of drought or toxins in well water. The already homeless in urban centers live at less than subsistence, with no recourse to local hunting, fishing, or real-food gathering. In the United States, 37 million people have no health insurance and therefore little access to medical care. They have also lost access to and knowledge about plants traditionally used in healing. To live a simpler life with clean air, drinkable water, and foods, medicines, and building materials you can harvest yourself, and energy sources you can tap yourself for part of your home/work energy needs—this is not "going back in time." It is an argument for preserving indigenous cultures, and wilderness as well, and the best and healthiest of rural culture where it still exists. A simpler, *better quality* of life is the only choice for the future of cities and urban-dominated regions.

Regionally based economics would not exclude a global exchange of information, skills, and appropriate design and technology innovations. Regionally based production and marketing could put rural and urban America back to work as well as preserve precious resources now wasted on transportation and overproduction of nonnecessities. The entrepreneural and job opportunities of a government-supported solar economy could offer a far different future than work in prisons, toxin waste sites, and casino halls. Sustainable timber practices, together with support for Wisconsin's family farmers and tourism that is in-scale and respective of the place and culture where one is a guest, are what will heal the communities where we'll live together and give northern Wisconsin a viable economic future.

One example of a long-term, regionally based, sustainable enterprise is the Menominee Reservation timber operation. In 1865, the reservation had an inventory of 2.5 billion board feet. They have averaged a cut of 25 million board feet a year since and today have an estimated 2.6 billion board feet of standing timber. They have not lost any species (except the American elm, dying everywhere from Dutch elm disease), and have increased their inventory of veneer and hardwood trees. Northern Wisconsin forester Bob Simeone, who spends part of every year working and advising in South America's rain forest, said the Menominee succeed because of their long-term vision and land ethic. This land ethic involves managing for quality, and selective cutting, which employs more people in the woods, more pay because stumpage is worth more than fiber, and spin-off industries that create better paying and more sustainable jobs compared to clear-cutting aspen for pulp paper mills.[13]

To develop Wisconsin's timber in a ecological and job sustaining way, going beyond the Menominee model, forester and boat landing witness Simeone recommends: a) adopting the 1988 Kotan system Forest Habitat Classification System, used for converting aspen stands back into hardwoods; b) giving U.S. foresters lifetime tenures to manage only 10–20,000 acres each; c) using only designated skid roads so no new logging roads are built; and d) using the Forest Stewardship Charter that certifies forest products as sustainably harvested.[14]

The best imagined solutions lie in real-life political action and responsible cultural interaction. Witnessing against boat landing violence was a journey into hope and fear, a test of personhood, a direction, at least for some, and for others, a spiritual or political redemption. Urban neighborhoods can similarly support rural farm communities by: 1) direct farmer-to-city markets for responsibly raised produce; 2) witnessing against family farm foreclosures the way Wisconsin's Labor-Farm Party did in the early 1980s; and 3) stopping the legalization of the bovine growth hormone, so healthy food and methods of production are defined by farmer and consumer, not by agrichemical corporations and state politicians.[15] The political weave of stopping the violence while developing sustainable economics defines the priority work for rural *and* urban America.

Former dairy farmer, Tom Quinn, now works with The League of Rural Voters and is president of the Wisconsin Farmland Conservancy. He says that the survival of sustainable and small family farming depends on making public policy that guarantees the marketplace is equitable, so farmers can get prices for their products that cover their average productions costs.[16] "In the long term," he argued, "our ability to survive will depend on affecting federal farm policy . . . in 1994, they'll rewrite the Farm Bill. We need to build a real coalition of farmers and consumers to affect national farm and food policy." Land tax needs to be governed by long-range policy principles that define farmland and tax it at a different rate than development land.[17] Quinn also promotes the Farmland Conservancy model where retiring farmers help new farmers get going on land that is held in permanent trust as farmland. The survival of rural culture, indigenous and transplanted, is interlaced with a non-exploitive, sustainable land ethnic. Such a land ethic would return fertility to the soil and forests, restore health to rivers and to cities, and provide the best hope for continuing jobs and honest livelihoods—surely a better hope than racial scapegoating for healing white frustrations and fears.

Like the leaflets dropped on reservations in the 1950s promising jobs and excitement in the cities,[18] the hype of the global marketplace promises the economic boom, jobs, and "where the action is" of the corporate world today. What it really brings is national insecurity through dependence on foreign resources, an out-of-control military budget, overuse of the world's precious resources, and international conflicts.

On the way north to Bayfield and the Madeline Island Memorial Day ceremonies, Walt and I stop at Ursula's farm. A woman in her 60s, she runs the farm alone, proudly tending her vegetables, raising sheep, and spinning the yarn from her animals. Inside her farmhouse, the one orderly, spacious room displays a huge loom where she weaves her art pieces. On the wall of the living room is a weaving depicting her favorite cove, Little Girls Inlet along Saxon's Harbor on Lake Superior. "I had a bad winter," she says. "The war in the Middle East reminded me of World War II. The allies then too dumped gasoline out of the sky and ignited it. I was in Dresden after those bombings. The Nazis made us clean up the bodies. When you kill people that way they pop open like burnt hot dogs. I almost didn't make it through this last winter. I'm still not doing well."

In Closing: The Club and the Drum

Blackhawk's War Club: A Healing by Walt Bresette

When the U.S. bombs started falling on January 16, 1991, we were sitting down to supper; me, my wife and our three children. ABC Nightly News interrupted its regular newscast to report that the war against Iraq had begun; reporters live on phones in Baghdad entered our living room and began describing the incoming missiles and aircraft, and the anti-aircraft fire underway. I was riveted to the scene as I had been since August 1, 1990, when Iraqi troops had entered Kuwait.

Tears and rage welled up inside because of not wanting to accept what was happening; I sat quietly. "What's wrong with Daddy, mom?" our six-year old asked. We attempted to explain to our children what we ourselves could not understand. We are bombing other people.

My cousin Andy Gokee's daughter asks him, "Are they going to bomb us, Daddy?"

"No, don't worry; but tonight there are little children who look very much like you who are under the bombs." These words from Andy Gokee, the tribal judge at Red Cliff, the leader of the spearers who only last year was shot at while on the lakes of northern Wisconsin.

As the reports that first evening of the bombing continued, my wife said she couldn't stand to listen any more; with tears in her eyes she said good night. I tried to divert my attention from the war to my children and eventually they too went to bed. I stayed up most of the night, watching and listening to reports. Early the next morning my wife got up, tears still in her eyes and said that we must do something. I agreed, but was lost at what to do.

"I think we need to build a fire, but I don't how so you'll have to do it." I said I would and began planning inside where and how the fire would begin.

The last time we had a fire was when my father died. Elders have said that it takes four days for the spirit of those who die to find their way home and we who are left must provide for this journey with a fire and food and tobacco and other medicines. So as the bombs crushed the bodies of those unfortunates underneath, across the world, in a small town in northern Wisconsin, we built a sacred fire to help them find their way home. We cut a cedar tree—this one with two branches going straight up—on it we hung tobacco ties and feathers from our personal bundles.

Once the fire is lit, it must burn continuously for four days. Knowing that my wife and I would not be able to keep the fire ourselves, we announced through WOJB Radio and the local network that the fire would be lit and that volunteers would be needed to help tend it. We also threw together a "cease-fire" peace concert to help us survive with some sanity these next days. Some came to the fire lighting ceremonies and many others came to the benefit; volunteers to keep the fire came from around the region.

Our little store next to the post office in Bayfield became a halfway house, open twenty-four hours a day; the fire was a sanctuary for personal thought and prayer. Out front at the post office the anti-war protest continued but we were quickly outnumbered by pro-war supporters. For me and for others who found the fire, we once more found some grounding; in a tragic, ironic way, something positive to do during these cold days of January. When I would take my turn at the fire I would bring with me items from my personal bundle.

On one visit to the fire I brought with me the Black Hawk war club. I felt strange doing so, yet it seemed that the club should also witness the sacredness and purpose of the fire. I had carried this club for many years, sometimes bringing it out at small gatherings. When I received it (see chapter 4), I was told it was like getting a sacred pipe and that I should use it likewise. However, since the club had come to me it had felt more like a burden; something I neither wanted nor understood. With the club came instructions and even though they were vague and mysterious, in my mind I did try to follow them.

As bombs threatened I spoke with many people around the country, asking what could be done. I don't remember how or in what order, but when the bombs started falling and the fire needed tending, the conversations all became one. From this difficult time came the long-sought answer—not of the war, but of the club. And, it was simple. "The club must be buried," said the voice, without doubt, without wavering. I took out the club and immediately went to the fire and indeed it was confirmed, without doubt. Of course, I said, it must be buried. It was something, once said, which made absolute sense; it was a knowing within—no need for any further explanations.

While at the fire, as the bombs were falling in Iraq, I looked deeply inside and the meaning of the club came clearer. While I didn't question the what, I continued to wonder why. Was it me because I was once a soldier; me because I was a man; me because I had traveled in such diverse circles? I concluded that yes—these circumstances, difficult as they were, brought the clarity of the why. The club, representing the most traditional of our people, had outlived its purpose. While it once provided security for self and family and community, it now did just the opposite. The club, representing the instruments of war, threatened the young, the old, family, and community.

The old ways have lost meaning, value, purpose: the men's way, the fighter's way represented by the club, was itself ending its life. It needed to be buried like all instruments of war, just as the soldier way needed to also be put to rest. At the fire at the end of this part of the journey in the midst of a massive bombing campaign I came to accept what I had once mouthed. Oh, we talked of nonviolence and post-patriarchy in the Green circles but deep down it had no meaning in the heart. I had merely become another member of the debate club, able to argue either side of the issue at the drop of the hat. Although I certainly favored certain positions over others, much of the passion of belief was missing. This witnessing of the war through the club changed all that radically for me.

Finally, at the fire I see a mound—a new Indian mound. In it is placed a war club. It's at a park or public setting or land where Vietnam vets now go for healing. And when the club is entombed something new is allowed to be, to surface. And the old way, like the club, is buried and it becomes the collective responsibility of those who know this story to oversee this mound. It becomes a collective responsibility to keep this story alive, and as long as the story lives the mound and its instrument of war remains buried. And when the story is forgotten and the mound left unattended, some future group, out of curiosity or ignorance, will dig up the mound, expose the club once more to the earth and the cycle of violence will return.

The Drum Call by Rick Whaley

Modern European-American men can choose many selves. Among the progressive ones are: nurturer (father, friend, lover), provider, protector (e.g., organizing neighborhood safety patrols or preparing day-care staff to deal with parents who abuse), organizer, and warrior. While there may be many other roles or selves for men to choose from, the only fundamental choice is between dominating or healing.

When we obscure the choices made in the past, we end up glorifying cardboard heroes like Christopher Columbus. As the person who came to represent the (supposed) first encounter, he was a brutal man, killing the Taino people in sets of thirteen, to honor the Lord and twelve apostles, because they did not secure gold for him fast enough. Behind the historical legend, Columbus is an empty man—almost nothing is known about his cultural background, his homeland, his real name, where he thought he was going when he set out from Spain. Yet mainstream America fills him today with all the pride of false accomplishments and their missing history of principled women and men.

We obscure these choices that our forebears made because we don't want to see or face similar choices today. Do we turn away from the violence others face or will we witness against violence toward women, against violence to the Earth, against the urban violence wrought by drugs, poverty, and anger, against the rise of the David Dukes and Dean Crists in our midst? Do we support wars against other nations to protect (or gain) "our" resources or do we create true national security through self-sufficient renewable energy production and sustainable economics?

For me, the image of a shack full of weapons was replaced by the pine bough arbor at Lac Courte Oreilles. Under that arbor in 1991, on Labor Day weekend, sat a circle of men—Lakota riders from the December Wounded Knee commemorations, witnesses gathering to celebrate and share stories, men talking about the pain of relationships, spearer Mike Chosa publicly thanking witnesses, and (in the larger circle of men at the gathering) a young Native man just out of prison and two elders (and Marine veterans), one Menominee and one European-American, who now fight the WCA and Exxon.

Frances Densmore, the supporter and ethnographer of *Anishinabe* culture, had said, "I heard the Indian drum when I was very, very young. Others heard the same drum and the sound was soon forgotten, but I have followed it all these years. . . . Always the Indian drum calling me." In the late 1980s and early 1990s, many heard the *Anishinabe* drum call for justice in northern Wisconsin and responded.

When in Danger, Move to the Light

Into the keen and mourning night,
I see the dead who have gone before me.

Into the mean and moaning night,
I see fisted faces who could have been me.

Into the lean and glowing light,
I see the children who wait for me.

Into the clean and honing light,
I see a land of no enemies.

—Rick Whaley, 1991

Notes

1. Vincent Harding, *There Is A River: The Black Struggle for Freedom in America* (New York: Vintage, 1983), p. xix.

2. Robert E. Gard and L. G. Sorden, *Romance of Wisconsin Place Names* (New York: October House, 1968), p. 112.

3. Three Episcopal bishops, including the outspoken treaty advocate Bishop William Wantland, signed a letter sent to Wisconsin Senator Bob Kasten and Congressman James Sensenbrenner in August, 1987, criticizing the former's forced negotiation position (on the buyout of treaty rights) and the latter's treaty abrogation efforts in Congress.

4. Sharon Metz, director of HONOR, received a threatening letter after an 1989 speech in Milwaukee, and she and Senator Inouye were given PARR's "Enemy of the Constitution" award in 1990.

5. All but Dean Crist, Tommy Handrick, and STA–W itself agreed to abide by the federal injunction and pay some of the lawyers' fees for the spearers' legal team. Crist promised to pursue in court the argument that today spearers were mixed-bloods, and therefore not entitled to rights covered in the treaties. *Wa-Swa-Gon* lead lawyer, Brian Pierson, said the argument had little chance given the federal courts' consistent rulings in favor of tribes defining their own members. Then, on January 6, 1992, Judge Crabb issued a summary judgment against these final three defendants, making permanent the injunction against any and all harassment of Chippewa spearers and families.

6. For example, Greens in Wisconsin avoided rancorous debates over deep vs. social ecology, Left vs. New Age, party vs. movement, so divisive elsewhere in U.S. Green politics. The Witness helped build the Greens—from Walt Bresette and Frank Koehn's work with Lake Superior Greens, to St. Croix tribal member Gloria Merrill joining the St. Croix Valley Greens, to Green campus groups from Northland College in Ashland and UW–Madison witnessing at landings in 1990 and 1991, to the first meeting of Milwaukee Area Greens initiated by six members of the Witness in summer 1988. In turn, the Greens helped build the Witness.

7. Madison's WISC-TV reporter Joel Despain featured a 1989 report comparing the harassment of spearers to that Dr. King and the civil rights movement faced. This signaled the public shift in understanding the nature of the anti-treaty protests. By 1990, many reporters found Crist so out of control and unreliable that they stopped quoting him.

8. Tax receipts to the town of Minocqua treasurer's office showed the revenue from the municipal room tax had doubled since 1986. "This figures indicate spending at hotels, motels and resorts could exceed $3.5 million dollars this year compared to $1.7 million four years ago," reflecting a growth rate better than two other major tourist centers in the state, Wisconsin Dells and Lake Geneva. "Tourism survives fishing friction in Minocqua," *News from Indian Country*, January 1991, p. 5, quoting an undated article from the *Milwaukee Sentinel*.

9. Freelance correspondent Scott Kerr was asked by the *Milwaukee Journal* for the story and they ran it that summer of 1990. Kerr quoted hearing examiner David

Schwartz's opinion that the Lac Courte Oreilles' position lacked substance, an unusual public statement for a government official to make before all the testimony was in and before he made his final decision. Kerr was permanently dropped as a correspondent after this story ran because of an alleged lack of objectivity and questions about representing himself as a *Journal* reporter.

10. Mark Lisheron, "Group criticizes state effort to protect spearfishers," *Milwaukee Journal,* November 13, 1990; and Mark Lisheron, "Official says spearers were well protected," *Milwaukee Journal,* November 14, 1990.

11. For example, the proposed 6,000-acre trash dump on the Lakota Rosebud Reservation.

12. The projected Kennecott Ladysmith mine revenues would be between $269 million and $627.6 million. $4 million/month times 12 months times 9 years would equal $432 million, not quite the middle of the estimate. Again, the state expects to get overall from the mine, $10 million, and Rusk Company $18 million.

13. These spinoff industries include sawmills, veneer mills, furniture component and flooring manufacturing, cabinet making, and carpentry. Off-reservation forestry in Wisconsin is dominated by private timber interests producing for the paper pulp market. Here, the bard owl is an indicator species for the health of our forests and is in decline because of the clear-cutting practices, especially of the pulp industry.

14. According to Simeone, this plan also parallels economic trends in the industry. Fewer plants are being built for virgin aspen pulp. Underutilized research has created a glut in recycled newspapers that could and will be used to create future newspapers. Recycling will continue to undermine aspen growing and clear-cut logging.

15. Bovine growth hormone (BGH) would also drive more dairy farms under because the increased milk production would again lower milk prices, a price that is now often already below production costs. The Wisconsin state legislature passed a ban on BGH in 1991 but Governor Thompson vetoed the ban. Thompson asserted that calls to his office were running two to one against the ban on BGH. In reality, his office received 346 calls and 382 pieces of mail in favor of the ban, and 22 letters and one call against banning BGH (Bill Lueders, "Dishonorable mentions," *Isthmus,* December 27, 1991).

16. For example, dairy farmers now get about $12.50 per hundred pounds of whole milk. Their average cost for producing 100 pounds of whole milk is $14.50.

17. A graduated land tax would tax the larger acre and corporate farms more, instead of making the small farmer and taxpayer pick up the breaks given the largest farms.

18. This corresponded to the era of the 1950s housing boom when Native timber was a prime resource for America's new prairie—the great suburban expansion.

MANIDOO GISISSONS
(The Little Spirit Moon)

Epilogue
Recent Developments in Wisconsin Politics, 1992

Rick Whaley

IN JANUARY, 1992, JUDGE BARBARA Crabb issued a summary judgment against Dean Crist, Tommy Handrick, and STA–W, thus making permanent the injunction against the remaining protest defendants. Judge Crabb held, in effect, that all the extensive plans and actions to stop Chippewa spearing that Crist admitted to in his depositions were strong enough evidence to make the injunction final without a formal court hearing.

Shortly thereafter, state of Wisconsin officials announced that they would curtail their security efforts at the landings in 1992—no state coordination of law enforcement, no floodlights, no snow fences. Not covered by the injunction, PARR promised to take STA–W's place at the boat landings in the spring. (An Associated Press story in the *Milwaukee Journal* said officials would monitor the landings but not prepare *"for possible riots between spearers* and those who oppose the Chippewa's exercise of treaty rights" (emphasis added)). Continuing their annual political ritual of blaming the Chippewa, the WDNR lowered the angler bag limits on spearing lakes from five a day to three a day on 107 lakes and to two a day on 115 lakes. Showing their bias, newspapers around the state worried in headlines that a late thaw would mean Chippewa spearing would run into the opening of angler season (rather than vice versa).

Tom Maulson, autumn 1992 at an anti-mining gathering at Treehaven Conference Center. Tom was not "traditional" when the treaty struggle began. He was a hunting and fishing guy who stood up for his people and grew politically and spiritually as the struggle intensified.

In early autumn 1992 Tom was elected chair of LdF Reservation defeating long time opponent Mike Allen. Tom is also on the Vilas County Board of Supervisors.

Photo by Ellen Smith.

Once again, preventative deterrence was left to the Witness treaty support network. Members of the Midwest Treaty Network (MTN) met with state officials in March about the need for continued security to monitor possible rock throwing at spearers and hit-and-run sniping from the shoreline. At the meeting, Ralph Christensen of the WDNR sounded the annual law enforcement trumpet, "We're not there to deter violence, only to respond to it."

Because of the state's pullback and the other unknowns (what would PARR do? what would local sheriffs do if state coordinators weren't around? were there individual terrorists bent on revenge now that the anti-treaty sentiment was waning in the public eye and STA–W was defeated in the courts?), *Wa-Swa-Gon* again asked witnesses to come to Lac du Flambeau spearing. *Wa-Swa-Gon* and MTN emphasized the need for documentation, especially video cameras, lanterns and flashlights to light the landings and boats to get witnesses on the lakes (where WDNR wardens were also pulling back their presence).

STA–W leaders stayed away from the landings in 1992. PARR organized one major protest to Lac du Flambeau's opening at Big Eau Pleine near Wausau. Three hundred protesters showed up to yell at spearers. Witnesses documented death threats, and two protest boats tried to muddy the shallows and create wakes. Harassers of St. Croix spearers forced them off Lipsett Lake in Burnett County and rocks were reported thrown at LdF spearers at Lake Mohawksin. Almost all other evenings were quiet and successful for Chippewa spearfishers. I was with James Mincey and Kathleen Hart when they returned to Sand Lake for a calm and starry night of witnessing in early April.

Ice-out was late this year and the last week and a half of spearing overlapped with the anglers' fishing season. Besides occasional grumblings or "drive-by starings," no trouble occurred as spearers and anglers shared the spring harvest from the lakes. Chippewa spearers took approximately 21,000 walleyes in 1992 spearing (compared to about 23,000 in 1991). As reasons for the lower harvest, spearers and political observers noted the late thaw, the fact that some former spearers were too busy with work in the reservation casinos, and the lack of protest opposition.

On April 15, the WDNR issued its Supplemental Study on Kennecott's Ladysmith mine, saying that wastewater discharge from the mine would not adversely affect the purple warty-back clam and other endangered species in the Flambeau River ecosystem. In their special Earth Day issue of the *Flambeau News*, mining propagandists echoed the WDNR proclamation that only safe mining would be allowed in Wisconsin. Opponents of the mine held early May rallies in Ladysmith and in London (England). Later that month on the day Kennecott officially started up again, Flambeau Summer activists, including Walt Bresette, crossed over the Kennecott fence line and were arrested for trespassing and theft. A U.S. flag was taken down, folded neatly, and (briefly) kept hostage until such time as it could be reclaimed by Americans wishing to reclaim their country.

The Sierra Club and Lac Courte Oreilles went back to court to contest the supplemental environmental impact study and process for Kennecott's Ladysmith mine, in part because no public hearings were allowed. Meanwhile, Environmentally Concerned Citizens of the Lakeland Areas (ECCOLA), whose membership includes former protesters and former witnesses, formed to fight the Noranda mining project at the Willow River near Lynne, Wisconsin, and not far from Lac du Flambeau, Minocqua, and Tomahawk.

On May 5, HONOR and the Mille Lacs Chippewa sponsored a Peace Roundtable in Hinckley, Minnesota, to head off the rising anti-Indian, anti-spearing sentiments in Minnesota. Representatives from Minnesota's legislature, the attorney general's office, WDNR, as well as law enforcement and media heard about the experiences of Wisconsin and Washington state and learned how cooperation could save money and acrimony if responsible people in mainstream society and government stepped forward to set policy with Native communities.

In July, the Peace and Dignity Run came through Wisconsin on its way from Alaska to Mexico City to meet runners from the southern continent for the October 12 gathering to celebrate 500 years of indigenous survival. In a mutual show of solidarity, the runners made stops at seven reservations—St. Croix, Lac Courte Oreilles, Lac du Flambeau, Mole Lake, Potawatomi, Menominee, and Oneida—as well as stops in various off-reservation small towns, urban areas, and at the ancient Indian grounds at Aztalan State Park. Later that autumn, in tribal elections, on October 6, 1992, walleye warrior Tom Maulson defeated Mike Allen to become chair of the Lac du Flambeau Chippewa.

Bibliography

Armstrong, Benjamin, *Early Life Among the Indians: Reminiscences from the Life of Benj. Armstrong, Treaties of 1835, 1837, 1842, and 1854: Habits and Customs of the Red Man of the Forest: Incidents, Biographical Sketches, Battles &c.* Dictated to and written by Thomas Wentworth. Ashland, WI: Press of A. W. Bowron, 1892.

Benton-Banai, Edward, *The Mishomis Book: The Voice of the Ojibway*, St. Paul: The Little Red School House, 1988.

Berry, Wendell, *The Gift of Good Land: Further Essays Cultural and Agricultural*, San Francisco: North Point Press, 1981.

Berry, Wendell, *The Hidden Wound*, San Francisco: North Point Press, 1989.

Berry Wendell, *The Unsettling of America: Culture and Agriculture*, San Francisco: Sierra Club Books, 1977.

Branch, Taylor, *Parting of the Waters: America in the King Years 1954–63*, New York: Simon and Schuster, 1988.

Brown, Lester, et al., *State of the World 1991*, New York: W.W. Norton, 1991.

Brown, Victoria, *Uncommon Lives of Common Women: The Missing Half of Wisconsin History*, Madison: Wisconsin Feminist Project, 1975.

Center for Democratic Renewal, *When Hate Groups Come to Town: A Handbook of Effective Community Responses*, Atlanta: Center for Democratic Renewal (PO Box 50469, Atlanta, GA 30302), 1992.

Cohen, Felix S., "Americanizing the White Man," *The American Scholar*, vol. 21, (1952).

Cohen, Felix S., *The Handbook of Federal Indian Law*, Albuquerque: University of New Mexico Press, 1942, 1971.

Crabb, Barbara

  Lac Courte Oreilles (LCO) et al. v. State of Wisconsin et al., 1987 (*LCO IV*—clarifying "modest standard of living," and extent of state regulation of harvests);

  LCO et al. v. State of Wisconsin et al., 1988 (*LCO V*—tightening limits of "modest standard of living");

  LCO et al. v. State of Wisconsin et al., 1989 (*LCO VI*—clarifying walleye and muskellunge off-reservation harvest under GLIFWC plan);

  LCO et al. v. State of Wisconsin et al., May 9, 1990 (*LCO VII*—Chippewa entitled to 50% of off-reservation harvest of deer and fish);

  LCO et al. v. State of Wisconsin et al., October 22, 1990 (*LCO VIII*—no back damages to Chippewa for state's decades of denial of harvesting rights);

  LCO et al. v. State of Wisconsin et al., February 21, 1991 (*LCO IX*—Chippewa not entitled to off-reservation timber rights);

  Lac du Flambeau Band and Wa-Swa-Gon Treaty Association v. Stop Treaty Abuse Wisconsin et al., March 15, 1991 (preliminary injunction against protester harassment and interference with spearfishing);

  LCO et al. v. State of Wisconsin et al., March 19, 1991 (Crabb's final judgement summarizing all the rulings on *LCO et al. v. State of Wisconsin et al.*);

  Lac du Flambeau Band and Wa-Swa-Gon Treaty Association v. Stop Treaty Abuse Wisconsin et al., January 6, 1992 (permanent injunction against protester harassment and interference with spearfishing).

Danziger, Edmund Jefferson, Jr., *The Chippewas of Lake Superior*, Norman: University of Oklahoma Press, 1978.

Deloria, Jr., Vine, and Clifford M. Lytle, *American Indians, American Justice*, Austin: University of Texas Press, 1983.

Deloria, Jr., Vine, and Clifford M. Lytle, *The Nations Within: The Past and Future of American Indian Sovereignty*, New York: Pantheon Books, 1984.

Densmore, Frances, *Chippewa Customs*, St. Paul: Minnesota Historical Society Press, 1979 (Smithsonian Institution Bureau of American Ethnology, Bulletin 86, 1929).

Donato, Marla, *Spearfishing Treaty Rights*, Earth Network video (#36–37; Jan. 1991). Earth Network, Box 831, Highland Park, IL 60035.

Doyle, James, Sr., *Lac Courte Oreilles (LCO) v. Voigt*, Wisconsin DNR (Doyle rules against Chippewa off-reservation harvesting rights), 1978; *LCO [and other Wisconsin Chippewa bands] v. State of Wisconsin et al.*, 1987 (*LCO III*—following directive of 7th Circuit Court of Appeals rulings in *LCO I* and *LCO II*, Doyle affirms Chippewa off-reservation harvesting rights, their right to make a modest living from this harvest, and the right to use traditional and modern methods in the harvest).

Evans, Sara, *Personal Politics: The Roots of Women's Liberation in the Civil Rights Movement and the New Left*, New York: Knopf, 1979.

Gard, Robert E., and L. G. Sorden, *The Romance of Wisconsin Place Names*, New York: October House Press, 1968.

Gedicks, Al, Jane Clokey, Robert Kennedy, and Michael Soref, *Land Grab: The Corporate Theft of Wisconsin's Mineral Resources*, Madison: Center for Alternative Mining Development Policy, 1982.

Gedicks, Al, "Multinational Corporations and Internal Colonialism in the Advanced Capitalist Countries: The New Resource Wars," *Political Power and Social Theory: A Research Annual,* Vol. 5 (1985): 169–204.

Gedicks, Al, "Exxon Minerals in Wisconsin; New Patterns of Rural Environmental Conflict," *Wisconsin Sociologist,* 25–2/3 (Spring–Summer 1988): 88–103.

Gedicks, Al, *The New Resource Wars: Native and Environmental Struggles Against Multinational Corporations,* Boston: South End Press, 1993.

Gedicks, Al, *The New Resource Wars,* video, Wisconsin Resource Protection Council (210 Avon St., #9, La Crosse, WI 54603), 1990.

Gedicks, Al, "Racism and Resource Colonization in the Ceded Territory of the Wisconsin Chippewa," paper presented at "Earth Day Conference," June 2, 1991, Eau Claire, WI.

Great Lakes Indian Fish and Wildlife Commission (GLIFWC, PO Box 9, Odanah WI, 54861):

"The Anishinabe," 1987;

"1989 Chippewa Spearing Season—Separating Myth From Fact," 1989;

Masinaigon (newspaper), 1989 spring spearing edition;

"Moving Beyond Argument: Racism and Treaty Rights," 1989;

"1990 Chippewa Spearing Season—Conflict and Cooperation The Two States of Wisconsin," 1990;

Masinaigon (newspaper), "The 1990 spearfishing season in review," Spring 1990, pp. 13–20;

"Chippewa Treaty Harvest of Natural Resources—Wisconsin, 1983–90," 1990;

"Guide to Understanding Chippewa Treaty Rights," 2d edition, 1991;

"1991 Chippewa Spearing Season: Building Cooperation and Bridging Conflicts," 1991

Grossman, Zoltán, "Wisconsin Treaty Conflict: No End in Sight," *Z Magazine,* August 1990.

Harding, Vincent, *There Is A River: The Black Struggle for Freedom in America,* New York: Vintage, 1983.

Harvey, Karen, "Notable Mining Laws and Regulations (1991)," "Wisconsin's Radioactive Status and Future (1991)," and "Bush Has Domestic Economic Policy— Title X of the NES (1991)," unpublished.

Honor Our Neighbors Origins and Rights, "Native American Treaties: The Religious Communities Speak," Milwaukee, WI: HONOR (PO Box 09685, Milwaukee, WI 53209), 1990.

Jackson, Donald, ed., *Black Hawk: An Autobiography,* Urbana, Chicago: University of Illinois Press, 1964, 1990.

Johansen, Bruce E., *Forgotten Founders: How the American Indians Helped Shape Democracy,* Boston: Harvard Common Press, 1987.

Johansen, Bruce E., and Roberto Maestras, *Wasi'Chu: The Continuing Indian Wars,* New York: Monthly Review Press, 1979.

Johnson, C. Montgomery, and Ann Quantock, *First Our Land, Now Our Treaties: The Story of Washington State's Initiative 456 and Sponsors' Plans to Export It Across*

America, Hadlock, WA: C. Montgomery Johnson Associates (PO Box 300, Hadlock WA, 98339), 1985.

Johnston, Basil H., *Ojibway Heritage,* New York: Columbia University Press, 1976, and Lincoln: University of Nebraska Press, 1990.

Johnston, Basil H., *Ojibway Ceremonies,* Lincoln: University of Nebraska Press, 1990.

Leopold, Aldo, *A Sand County Almanac and Sketches Here and There,* New York: Oxford University Press, 1949.

LeSueur, Meridel, *Ripenings: Selected Work, 1927–1980,* Old Westbury, NY: Feminist Press, 1982.

Lurie, Nancy O., *Wisconsin Indians,* Madison: State Historical Society of Wisconsin, 1987.

Matthiessen, Peter, *In the Spirit of Crazy Horse,* New York: Viking Press, 1983, 1991.

McPhee, John, *The Survival of the Bark Canoe,* New York: Farrar, Straus, and Giroux, 1975.

Midwest Treaty Network (731 State St., Madison, WI, 53703):
Chippewa Spearfishing Witness Report: 1988 [Witness for Non-Violence], 1988;
Chippewa Treaty Rights Issue, presentation to Wisconsin Equal Rights Commission, September 15, 1989 [Madison Treaty Rights Support Group, Indian Treaty Rights Committee, *Wa-Swa-Gon* Treaty Association, and Witness for Non-Violence];
1990 Witness Report: Chippewa Spearfishing Season [Madison Treaty Rights Support Group], 1990;
1990 Witness Report: Chippewa Spearfishing Season [Madison Treaty Rights Support Group], 1991;
"Wisconsin Treaties: What's the Problem?" 1991.

Minneapolis Bureau of Indian Affairs, U.S. Department of Interior, *Casting Light upon the Waters: A Joint Fishery Assessment of Wisconsin Ceded Territory* (Senator Inouye, U.S. Fish and Wildlife Commission, W-DNR, and GLIFWC), Minneapolis: Minneapolis BIA, 1991.

Moody, Roger, *The Indigenous Voice: Visions and Politics,* London: Zed Books, Ltd., 1988.

Moody, Roger, *Plunder!,* Chippenham, United Kingdom: PARTiZANS, 1991.

"New Mining Era Comes to Wisconsin," *Wisconsin Academy Review,* vol. 28, no. 1 (Dec. 1981): 16–31. (Articles by geologist Meredith Ostrom, lobbyist James Derouin, journalist Don Behm, public intervenor Peter Peshek, the WDNR's Gordon Reinke, and others.)

Olson, Sigurd F., *Reflections from the North Country,* New York: Alfred Knopf, 1976.

Olson, Sigurd F., *Wilderness Days,* New York: Alfred Knopf, 1972.

Paull, Rachel, and Richard Paull, *Geology of Wisconsin and Upper Michigan,* Dubuque: Kendall/Hunt Publ., 1977.

Peck, M. Scott, *People of the Lie: The Hope for Healing Human Evil,* New York: Simon and Schuster, 1983.

Ryser, Rudolph C., "Anti-Indian Movement on the Tribal Frontier" (Occasional Paper 16 on the New Right and Far Right in the Modern Anti-Treaty movement),

Kenmore, WA: Center for World Indigenous Studies, (Kenmore: WA: PO Box 82038, Kenmore, WA, 98028, $8.50), 1991.

Sale, Kirkpatrick, *The Conquest of Paradise: Christopher Columbus and the Columbian Legacy,* New York: Alfred A. Knopf, 1990.

Satz, Ronald N., *Chippewa Treaty Rights: The Reserved Rights of Wisconsin's Chippewa Indians in Historical Perspective,* Madison: Wisconsin Academy of Sciences, Arts and Letters, 1991.

Satz, Ronald N., Anthony G. Gulig, Richard St. Germaine, *Classroom Activities on Chippewa Treaty Rights,* Madison: WI: Wisconsin Department of Public Instruction, 1991 ($16).

Schaaf, Gregory, *Wampum Belts and Peace Trees: George Morgan, Native Americans and Revolutionary Diplomacy,* Golden, Colorado: Fulcrum Publ., 1990.

Stark, William, *Along the Black Hawk Trail,* Sheboygan, WI: Zimmerman Press, 1984.

Stephens, Jim, *The Journey Home: The Literature of Wisconsin through Four Centuries,* vols. 1–3, Madison: North Country Press, 1989.

Strickland, Rennard, Stephen J. Herzberg, and Steven R. Owens, "Keeping Our Word: Indian Treaty Rights and Public Responsibilities—A Report on a Recommended Federal Role Following Wisconsin's Request for Federal Assistance" (The Strickland Report), submitted to the U.S. Select Committee on Indian Affairs on April 16, 1990. Unpublished manuscript, University of Wisconsin School of Law, 1990. (Available from GLIFWC or the News and Information Service of the University of Wisconsin–Madison.)

Strickland, Rennard, *Handbook of Federal Indian Law,* rev. ed., Charlottesville, VA: Michie/Bobbs-Merrill, 1982.

Stop Treaty Abuse–Wisconsin, "Wisconsin's Treaty Problems: What are the Issues?" Woodruff, WI: STA–W, n.d. (c. 1989).

Taylor, Richard K., Phyllis B. Taylor, and Sojourners, *Practice of Peace: A Manual and Video for Non-Violence Training,* Washington, D.C.: Sojourners (PO Box 29272, Washington, D.C. 20017; manual, $12.50; with video, $24.50), 1987.

Thayer, Crawford B., *The Battle of Wisconsin Heights* (from the Sesquicentennial First Edition series of books published in commemoration of the 150th anniversary of the Black Hawk War), 1983.

U.S. Seventh Circuit Court of Appeals
   Lac Courte Oreilles (LCO) I, January 25, 1983. Ruling on LCO's appeal of Doyle's 1978 *Voigt* decision. 7th Circuit reverses Doyle and affirms off-reservation harvesting rights as reserved treaty rights.
   LCO II, 1985. Three-judge panel of 7th Circuit Court rules off-reservation harvesting rights apply to public and private lands in ceded territory.

Wachtel, Paul L., *The Poverty of Affluence: A Psychological Portrait of the American Way of Life,* Philadelphia: New Society Publishers and New York: MacMillan, 1989.

Warren, William W., *History of the Ojibway People,* St. Paul: Minnesota Historical Society Press, 1885, reprint ed., 1984.

Whaley, Rick, editor, *Witness for Non-Violence Training Manual,* Milwaukee: Witness for Non-Violence (Madison: Wisconsin State Historical Society), 1990.

Wrone, David, "Economic Impact of the 1837 and 1842 Chippewa Treaties," unpublished paper, History Department, University of Wisconsin–Stevens Point, 1989.

Yellowbank, James, with Walt Bresette, "Regional Resource Co-Management: Saving the Land for the Next Seven Generations," *Indian Treaty Rights Newsletter*, vol. 2, no. 1 (Winter 1991): 1–2.

Appendix
The Work of 500 Years of Resistance and Dignity Continues—Resources for the 1990s and Beyond
(an abbreviated listing)

Rick Whaley

Organizations

Artic to Amazonia Alliance, PO Box 73, Stafford, VT 05072

Alliance for Cultural Democracy, PO Box 7591, Minneapolis, MN 55407

America Discovers America, c/o Indian Treaty Rights Committee, 59 E. Van Buren, Ste. 2418, Chicago, IL 60605

American Indian Institute, PO Box 1388, Bozeman, MT 59715.

Anishinabe Akeeng, PO Box 356, White Earth, MN 56591.

Canadian Alliance in Solidarity with Native Peoples (CASNP), PO Box 574, Sta. P, Toronto, Ontario M58 2T1, Canada.

Center for Alternative Mining Development Policy, 210 Avon St. #9, La Crosse, WI 54603.

Center for World Indigenous Studies, PO Box 82038, Kenmore, WA 98028.

Clergy and Laity Concerned, 340 Mead Road, Decatur, GA 30030.

Friends Committee on National Legislation, 245 Second St., N.E., Washington, DC 20002.

Good Land Coalition, PO Box 393, Rosebud, SD 57570.

Greens/Green Party U.S.A., PO Box 30208, Kansas City, MO 64112.

Honor Our Neighbors Origins and Rights (HONOR), 2647 N. Stowell, Milwaukee, WI 53211.

Indian Law Resource Center, 601 E St., SE, Washington, DC, 20003.

Indigenous Women's Network, PO Box 174, Lake Elmo, MN 55042.

Indigenous Environmental Network, PO Box 369, Southwold, Ontario, WOL 260, Canada; U.S. Midwest Regional Office, PO Box 485, Bemidji, MN 56601.

Lake Superior Greens, Box 1350, Bayfield, WI 54814.

Mexico–Quito Conference follow-up: Yolanda Hernández Esteban, Consejo Central de Hidalgo, la Cerrada de Independencia #3, Barrio de Jesús, Ixmiquilpan, Hidalgo, CP 42300, Mexico.

Midwest Treaty Network, 731 State St., Milwaukee, WI 53703.

Milwaukee Greens, PO Box 16471, Milwaukee, WI 53216.

Morning Star Foundation, 403 10th St., SE, Washington, DC, 20003.

National Coalition on Racism in Sports and the Media, c/o AIM, 2300 Cedar Ave. S., Minneapolis, MN 55404.

1992 Alliance, c/o Richard Hill, PO Box 20007, Sante Fe, NM 87504.

PARTiZANS (People Against Rio Tinto Zinc and its Subsidiaries), 218 Liverpool Road, London N1 1LE, United Kingdom.

South and Meso American Indian Information Center, PO Box 28703, Oakland, CA 94604.

Sovereignty Network, HCO1, PO Box 6051-H, Palmer, AK 99645.

Turtle Island Bioregional Congress, c/o The Learning Alliance, 494 Broadway, New York, NY 10012.

Wa-Swa-Gon Treaty Association, PO Box 217, Lac du Flambeau, WI 54538.

Witness for Non-Violence, 1759-A N, Marshall, Milwaukee, WI 53202.

Women of All Red Nations (WARN), American Indian Center, 1630 W. Wilson, Chicago, IL 60640.

Publications

Akwesasne Notes, Mohawk Nation, via Rooseveltown, NY 13683.

Beedaudjimowin, 263 Roncesvalles Ave., Toronto, Ontario M6R 2L9, Canada.

The Circle, 1530 E. Franklin Ave., Minneapolis, MN 55404.

FNCL newsletter, $15 yr. Once a year their newsletter is the FNCL Indian Report.

HONOR Digest, PO Box 09685, Milwaukee, WI 53209.

Huracán, Alliance for Cultural Democracy, PO Box 7591, Minneapolis, MN 55407.

Indigenous Women, Indigenous Women's Network, PO Box 174, Lake Elmo, MN 55042.

Lakota Times, PO Box 2180, 1920 Lombardy Dr., Rapid City, SD 57709.

Masinaigan, Great Lakes Indian Fish and Wildlife Commission, PO Box 9, Odanah, WI 54861.

Native Nations, 175 5th Ave., Ste. 2245, New York, NY 10010.

News from Indian Country, Rt. 2, Box 2900A, Hayward, WI 54853.

Northeast Indian Quarterly, 300 Caldwell Hall, Cornell University, Ithaca, NY 14853.

Red Nations Movement, Alliance of Native Americans, PO Box 30392, Los Angeles, CA 90032.

Rethinking Schools, 1001 E. Keefe Ave., Milwaukee, WI 53212.

Treaty Council News, International Indian Treaty Council, 710 Clayton St. #1, San Francisco, CA 94117.

Index